Jack C. Ellis
Northwestern University

THE DOCUMENTARY IDEA
A Critical History
of English-Language
Documentary Film and Video

PRENTICE HALL, Englewood Cliffs, New Jersey 07632

Library of Congress Cataloging-in-Publication Data

ELLIS, JACK C., [date]
    The documentary idea.

    Bibliography: p.
    Includes index.
    1. Documentary films—History and criticism.
I. Title.
PN1995.9.D6E45   1989   791.43'53   88–17801
ISBN 0-13-217142-2

Editorial/production supervision: Andrea Lohneiss
Cover design: *Photo Plus Art*
Cover Photos: National Film Archive/Stills Library and Museum of Modern Art/Film
    Stills Archive
Manufacturing buyer: Ed O'Dougherty

For Shirley, David, and Cameron

 © 1989 by Jack C. Ellis

Printed in the United States of America

10 9 8 7 6 5 4 3 2 1

ISBN 0-13-217142-2

Prentice-Hall International (UK) Limited, *London*
Prentice-Hall of Australia Pty. Limited, *Sydney*
Prentice-Hall Canada Inc., *Toronto*
Prentice-Hall Hispanoamericana, S.A., *Mexico*
Prentice-Hall of India Private Limited, *New Delhi*
Prentice-Hall of Japan, Inc., *Tokyo*
Simon & Schuster Asia Pte. Ltd., *Singapore*
Editora Prentice-Hall do Brasil, Ltda., *Rio de Janeiro*

CONTENTS

PREFACE

The title of this book is intended as an oblique homage, a small obeisance, to John Grierson, British documentary film pioneer and leader. His name will appear prominently in the pages following. It was Grierson who first used the word *documentary* in relation to film. He came to prefer that the word stand for a concept, a purpose, an *idea*, rather than for a film mode. As an idea, documentary allowed for the use of many means of communication to contribute to social betterment, Grierson's ultimate goal. When he started his work in the 1920s, he decided that, given his intentions, the motion picture would be the most effective medium for him to use.

Film could record the world around us, "the living scene," as Grierson put it, more fully and accurately than any of the other arts or media of communication. This is what his friend Robert Flaherty had attempted in *Nanook of the North* (1922) and in *Moana* (1926). The latter film was the first to which Grierson applied the term "documentary." Where Grierson departed from Flaherty was in bringing this observation of actuality back from the distant lands and vanishing cultures of the Eskimos and the Polynesians to the here and now of modern, urbanized, industrialized societies. Rather than merely recording actuality, Grierson used film to try to motivate those societies to action and to guide the courses of their action. His metaphor for the contrast between Flaherty's way and his own was that Flaherty used film as a mirror while he was more interested in using it as a hammer—presumably to knock down the old and construct the new.

The documentary idea, in the theory and practice of Grierson and others, rests on artistic forms used to articulate and advance social purposes. Though the subtitle of this book promises a critical history, before commencing that history I will discuss further what documentary means. The descriptions and defintions that begin this book include assumptions and observations about why and how documentary is made, and about the intellectual contexts and historical precedents of its development. The bulk of the book concerns the evolution of documentary functions and forms.

Documentary originated in the 1920s in North America, the Soviet Union, France, Germany, and Holland. These sources were drawn upon by Grierson at the end of the twenties in his formation of the British documentary movement. British documentary of the 1930s then became a model for documentary development elsewhere. This chronicle follows the coherent main line of the English-language documentary in Great Britain, the United States, and Canada, up to the present.

Along the way a look is taken at contemporary French documentary, which provides a cross-cultural comparison (contrast really) with the dominant Anglo-Saxon line. Also surveyed are some recent developments out of aesthetic and political modernism beginning in Europe in which filmmakers have attempted to create new forms by mixing documentary actuality with narrative fiction and avant-garde experimentation.

The final chapter returns to the English-language tradition and North America. Mainly it concerns the large-scale political documentaries that have given distinction to the most recent past and the new possibilities opened up by portapack video and public access cable television.

Listed at the end of Chapter One are books relating to the general history of documentary and to documentary theory. Each subsequent chapter concludes with a list of documentary films that seem to me most valuable or interesting in the national period under consideration and a listing of additional books that deal with it.

Thank you to George C. Stoney, New York University, for his assistance in reviewing the manuscript.

Permission to use quoted material has been granted by the following institutions and persons: The Regents of the University of California, for John Grierson, "Postwar Patterns," *Hollywood Quarterly,* 1, no. 2 (January 1946), pp. 73–74, and for Alan Rosenthal, *The Documentary Conscience: A Casebook in Film Making,* pp. 283–84; The British Film Institute, for Cesare Zavattini, "Some Ideas on the Cinema," *Sight and Sound,* 23 (October–December 1953), p. 160, and for Gavin Lambert, "Free Cinema," *Sight and Sound,* 25 (Spring 1956), pp. 208–209; Michelle Citron, for interview conducted by Mimi White, "Exploring *What We Take for Granted*," *Afterimage* (December 1984), pp. 265–66; and George C. Stoney, for Appendix, p. 302. "Buffalo Bill's" is reprinted from *Tulips & Chimneys* by E. E. Cummings, edited by George James Firmage, by permission of Liveright Publishing Corporation; Copyright © 1923, 1925, and renewed 1951, 1953 by E. E. Cummings; Copyright © 1973, 1976 by the Trustees for the E. E. Cummings Trust; Copyright © 1973, 1976 by George James Firmage. And to General Publishing Co. for R. Blumer and S. Schouten, "Donald Brittain: Green Stripe and Common Sense," in *Canadian Film Reader,* ed. by S. Feldman and J. Nelson, p. 281.

ONE
WHAT IS DOCUMENTARY?

Documentary is one of three basic creative modes in film, the other two being narrative fiction and experimental avant-garde. Narrative fiction we know as the feature-length entertainment films we see in theaters on a Friday night or on our TV screens; they grow out of literary and theatrical traditions. Experimental or avant-garde films are usually shorts, shown in nontheatrical film societies or series on campuses and in museums; usually they are the work of individual filmmakers and grow out of the traditions of the visual arts.

One approach to the theory, technique, and history of the documentary film might be to describe what the films generally called documentary have in common, and the ways in which they differ from other types of film. Another possible approach would be to consider how documentary filmmakers define the kinds of films they make. Both approaches will be followed in this chapter.

DESCRIPTION

Characteristics documentaries have in common that are distinct from other film types (especially from the fiction film) can be thought of in terms of: 1) subjects; 2) purposes, points of view, or approaches; 3) forms; 4) production methods and techniques; and 5) the sorts of experiences they offer audiences.

As for *subjects*—what they're about—documentaries focus on something other than the general human condition involving individual human actions and relationships, the province of narrative fiction and drama. For example, *The Fourth Estate* (1940), a British documentary made by Paul Rotha, is about a newspaper, the London *Times,* whereas Orson Welles' *Citizen Kane* (1941) is more concerned with a character modeled on William Randolph Hearst, the powerful newspaper publisher, than the process of publishing newspapers. *City of Gold* (1959), made at the National Film Board of Canada by Wolf Koenig and Colin Low, comprises still photographs taken in Dawson City in 1898 set within a live-action frame of the actualities of present-day Dawson City. In terms of library catalogue headings, *City of Gold* would be listed under "Canada. History. Nineteenth century," "Gold mines and mining. Yukon," "Klondike gold fields," and the like. On the other hand, if *The Gold Rush* (1925), by Charles Chaplin, were a book in the library, it would be shelved under the general heading "Fiction." Though its recreation of the file of prospectors climbing over Chilkoot Pass is remarkably painstaking, *The Gold Rush* is not really about the Klondike Gold Rush of 1898 as much as it is about loneliness and longing, pluck and luck, poverty and wealth, friendship and love. Generally, documentaries are about something specific and factual and concern public matters rather than private ones. The people, places, and events in them are actual, and usually contemporary.

The second aspect—*purpose/point of view/approach*—is what the filmmakers are trying to say about the subjects of their films. They record social and cultural phenomena they consider significant in order to inform us about these people, events, places, institutions, and problems. In so doing, documentary filmmakers intend to increase our understanding of, our interest in, and perhaps our sympathy for their subjects. They may hope that through this means of informal education they will enable us to live our lives a little more fully and intelligently. At any rate, the purpose or approach of the makers of most documentary films is to record and interpret the actuality in front of the camera and microphone in order to inform and/or persuade us to hold some attitude or take some action in relation to their subjects.

Third, the *form* of a film is the formative process, including the filmmakers' original conception, the sights and sounds selected for use, and the structures into which they are fitted. Documentaries, whether scripted in advance or confined to recorded spontaneous action, are derived from and limited to actuality. Documentary filmmakers confine themselves to extracting and arranging from what already exists rather than making up content. They may recreate what they have observed but they do not create totally out of imagination as creators of stories can do. Though documentarians may follow a chronological line and include people in their films, they do not employ plot or character development as standard means of organization as do fiction filmmakers. The form of a documentary is mainly determined by subject, purpose, and approach. Usually there is no conventional dramaturgical progression from exposition to complication to discovery to climax to denouement. Documentary forms tend to be functional, varied, and looser than those of short stories, novels, or plays. They are more like non–narrative literary forms, such as essays, advertisements, editorials, or poems.

Fourth, *production method and technique* refer to the ways images are shot, the sounds recorded, and the two edited together. One basic requirement of documentary is the use of nonactors ("real people" who "play themselves") rather than actors (who are cast, costumed, and made up to play "roles"). The other basic requirement is shooting on location (rather than on sound stages or studio back lots). In documentaries no sets are constructed. Lighting is usually what exists at the location, supplemented only when necessary to achieve adequate exposure, not for atmosphere or mood. Exceptions to these generalizations occur, of course; but, in general, any manipulation of images or sounds is largely confined to what is required to make the recording of them possible, or to make the result seem closer to the actual than inadequate technique might.

Finally, the *audience experience* documentary filmmakers seek to provide is generally twofold: an aesthetic experience of some sort, on the one hand, and an effect on attitudes, possibly leading to action, on the other. Though much beauty exists in documentary films, it tends to be more functional, sparse, and austere than the beauties offered in fictional films. Also, documentary filmmaking offers more that could be described as professional *skill* than as personal *style;* communication rather than expression is what the filmmaker is usually after. Consequently, the audience is responding not so much to the artist (who keeps under cover) as to the subject matter of the film (and the artist's more or less covert statements about it). Generally the best way to understand and appreciate the intentions of documentarists is to accept the criterion of the Roman poet Horace that art should both please and instruct. John Grierson stated that in documentary, art is the by-product of a job of work done.

DEFINITION

The English-language documentary could be said to start with American Robert Flaherty's *Nanook of the North,* shot in Canada and released in the United States in 1922. In making his first film, Flaherty's intention was not unlike that of today's home moviemakers: He wanted to show the Eskimos, whom he had gotten to know in his travels, to the folks back home. To accomplish this purpose, he fashioned a new form of filmmaking. The success of *Nanook* drew Flaherty out of exploring, which had been his profession, and into filmmaking. His second film, *Moana* (1926), prompted John Grierson—a young Scot visiting the United States, exploring in his own way—to devise a new use for the word *documentary*. It was introduced casually, as an adjective, in the first sentence of the second paragraph of Grierson's review of *Moana* for *The New York Sun:* "Of course, *Moana* being a visual account of events in the daily life of a Polynesian youth and his family, has documentary value."[1]

Documentary has as its root word *document*, which comes from the Latin *docere,* to teach. As late as 1800, according to the *Oxford English Dictionary,* documentary meant "a lesson; an admonition, a warning." When Grierson wrote that *Moana* has "documentary value," he would have been thinking of the modern meaning of document—a record which is factual and authentic. For scholars, documents are "primary sources" of information; for lawyers "documentary evidence" is opposed to hearsay or opinion. Perhaps Grierson was also thinking of the French term *documentaire,* used to distinguish serious travelogues from other sorts of films including mere scenic views. Grierson would move the term from his initial use of it back to the earlier one of teaching and propagating, using the "documents" of modern life as materials to spread the faith of social democracy. Flaherty, for his part, continued to document the subjects of his films as he saw them and, to some extent, as they wanted to present themselves to the world and to posterity.

Grierson carried the word and his developing aesthetic theory and sense of social purpose back to Great Britain. Beginning with his own first film, *Drifters,* in 1929, British documentary advanced to full status. Most of the characteristics we associate with the word documentary and see evident in the films to which it is applied were present by the mid-thirties.

Documentary, then, as an artistic form, is a technique and style that originated in motion pictures. There are still photographic precursors and analogues, to be sure: the Civil War photographs of Mathew Brady, the remarkable photographic documentation of turn-of-the-century New York City by Jacob Riis, and the photographs made during the Depression for the United States Farm Security Administration by Walker Evans, Dorothea Lange, Ben Shahn, and others. Documentary radio appeared in the early thirties in pioneering broadcasts of the British Broadcasting Corporation and in the American "March of Time" weekly series; documentary television (which usually means documentary films made for television) is prevalent. In literature the concept of documentary has established itself as the nonfiction novel (Truman Capote's *In Cold Blood* and Norman Mailer's *The Prisoner's Song*) and in newspaper reporting in the late 1960s and early 1970s as the "new journalism" (Tom Wolfe's *The Electric Kool-Aid Acid Test,* Hunter Thompson's *Hell's Angels,* or Norman Mailer's *The Armies of the Night*). The documentary idea is by now pervasive. But *Webster's New Collegiate Dictionary* offers as the primary meaning of documentary: "*n.* A documentary film."

Rather than documentary, however, Frances Flaherty chose to call what she had helped her husband create "the film of discovery and revelation." This seems appropriate for the work of a man who had begun his filmmaking while exploring the Hudson Bay region looking for iron ore. Notice the observational bias of her phrase, its implied emphasis on seeing. Flaherty was primarily concerned with what the camera could discover and reveal. "All art is a kind of exploring," Mrs. Flaherty quoted her husband as saying. "To discover and reveal is the way every artist sets about his business."[2]

Flaherty's films were created more in the camera than on the cutting bench. To him, editing was not the central creative act of filmmaking that it is for many filmmakers. In his silent films Flaherty cut together long–running takes to give continuous view of the essential action. He never really understood sound editing and had to rely on others to help edit his sound films.

Grierson's definition of documentary was "the creative treatment of actuality."[3] Flaherty would certainly have accepted *creative* and *actuality*, but *treatment of* suggests one way in which his and Grierson's filmmaking methods differed. Grierson's bias was analytical; his emphasis was on editing.

Documentary has always allowed for a distinction between shooters and cutters, Flahertyites and Griersonites. If Flaherty and Grierson agreed that actuality was the base or subject of documentary, they differed in their techniques of recording and presenting it. Grierson's way permitted footage shot by others to be made into a Griersonian documentary; Flaherty shot, or at least completely controlled the shooting of, his major films.

Instead of filmmaking methods, other documentarians have centered their definitions around the purposes, functions, and effects of documentary. Paul Rotha, for example, one of the early documentary filmmakers alongside Grierson and historian of the British movement, offered what may at first appear merely a verbose and less catchy rephrasing of Grierson's "creative treatment of actuality." But Rotha's "The use of the film medium to interpret creatively and in social terms the life of the people as it exists in reality"[4] seems to allow for nonactuality. Indeed, Rotha did not exclude the use of actors and studios from documentary as long as the filmmaker's purpose was to help a society function better, to contribute to more satisfying lives for its people.

Basil Wright, one of the earliest and most loyal of Grierson's lieutenants, offered a frank definition that may have nettled Grierson. Wright wrote that documentary is "a method of approach to public information;" its function "to be in the forefront of policy."[5] This characterizes very well what British documentarians of the 1930s were actually doing. What Grierson might not have liked was the public acknowledgment that it was the documentarians who chose the topics and problems about which documentaries would be made, and who suggested ways in which these topics might be considered or these problems solved. In other words, British documentary filmmakers were directing public attention to what they considered important, promoting their view of it, and suggesting what they thought ought to be done about it. A member of Parliament might well have asked (and some did), "By whose consent are documentary filmmakers in the forefront of policy? Who gave them this right?"

Willard Van Dyke, an American documentarian whose work also began in the thirties (his most famous film is *The City,* 1939, which he co-directed with Ralph Steiner), once observed in informal conversation that he thought defining documentary a simple matter. In his view documentary is film intended to bring about change in the audience—change in their understanding, their attitudes, and possibly their actions. To the objection that Flaherty's films didn't seem designed to bring about social change, Van Dyke replied that Flaherty's consistent subject selection of people living in simpler, earlier ways of life implied a belief. Flaherty was in fact arguing, Van Dyke felt, that we need to become more like those people; that we must adhere to the age-old verities reflected in nature, in family, and in the work necessary for survival.

Among the various definitions of documentary, one offered by Raymond Spottiswoode in *A Grammar of the Film,* first published in 1935, seems to me among the most adequate; certainly it applies quite satisfactorily to documentaries of the 1930s. For Spottiswoode "The documentary film is in subject and approach a dramatized presentation of man's relation to his institutional life, whether industrial, social or political; and in technique a subordination of form to content."[6] This definition contains some of the same terms as my five-part formula (presented in the "Description" section)—subject, approach, technique, and form. Spottiswoode does not acknowledge as part of documentary the filmmakers' social purposes or their concern with the effects of their films on audiences. He wrote his book as an Oxford University student. He was subsequently hired by Grierson at the General Post Office Film Unit as a "tea boy"—a general assistant, what we could call a gopher ("go for" this and that). According to a popular anecdote, when Grierson read *A Grammar of the Film* he decided that Spottiswoode had better remain in that humble position a while longer. Grierson regarded the purposes and effects of films of ultimate importance.

In my own attempts to arrive at a working definition of documentary, I have tended to give more weight to the actuality of the material than to the purposes for which that material is used or its possible effects on audiences. It seems to me that documentary filmmakers have in common their desire to record actuality. They select and shape representations of that actuality in order to (1) communicate insights, achieve beauty, and offer understanding (Flaherty), or (2) improve social, political, or economic conditions (Grierson). To elaborate a bit, a catechism of documentary could go something like this:

Q. What is documentary for?
A. To record actuality.
Q. Why would one want to do that?
A. To inform people about it.
Q. Inform to what ends?
A. *Either* to affect our understanding—to change, increase, reinforce it—which may (but is not necessarily designed to) lead to action, may make better persons of us, and which may in turn make the world a better place to live in (Flaherty); *or* to make better citizens of us and to move us to collective action in order to make a better society (Grierson).

In addition to, or instead of, describing and defining documentary, as I've been attempting to do, it is possible to understand it simply as all of those films that have been called documentary. A historical survey of the total corpus of (the mostly English-language) documentary comprises the remaining chapters of this book. The final two sections of this chapter outline intellectual contexts out of which documentary came and discuss those films made before the 1920s which contain documentary-like aspects.

INTELLECTUAL CONTEXTS

Though various forms of nonfiction film preceded and existed alongside the story film, the latter early became the main line of both film art and film industry. In aesthetic terms, the fictional motion picture is an extension of nineteenth-century artistic forms: literature, theater, and photography. The documentary mode appeared, was invented in a sense, to meet new artistic and communication needs arising in the twentieth century. Documentary is purposive; it is intended to achieve something in addition to entertaining audiences and making money. This purposiveness is reflected in the four traditions Paul Rotha identified in his seminal book of theory and history, *Documentary Film* (1935), as feeding into documentary: naturalist (romantic), newsreel, propagandist, realist (continental).[7]

The beginning of the naturalist (romantic) tradition, exemplified by the films of Robert Flaherty, roughly paralleled the development of anthropology as a social science. Sir James Frazer, a Scot who lived from 1854 to 1941, was the pioneer. His monumental survey of the evolution of cultures, *The Golden Bow,* was published in 1890 in two volumes; the twelve-volume edition appeared between 1911 and 1915. (Flaherty began to film the Eskimos in 1913.)

Contemporary with Frazer was Franz Boas (1858–1942), a German-born American anthropologist and ethnologist. Boas maintained that the immediate task of anthropology should be to record endangered cultures that might soon vanish. He stressed the specifics of each culture and taught that only after extensive data had been collected through fieldwork could any theories be put forward. Fieldwork has been a foundation of anthropology ever since. (Though Flaherty had no training as an anthropologist, he approximated fieldwork more closely than any filmmaker preceding him, living with and observing the Inuit of the Hudson Bay region many years before filming them.)[8]

Boas' work was followed by that of Polish-born Bronislaw Malinowski, who lived from 1884 to 1942. (Flaherty lived from 1884 to 1951.) Malinowski's *Argonauts of the Western Pacific* was published in 1922 (the year *Nanook of the North* was released). It was about the people of the Trobriand Islands, located off the coast of New Guinea. Margaret Mead (1901–1978), published her *Coming of Age In Samoa* in 1928. (Flaherty's *Moana*, dealing with the Samoans, was released in 1926.) In the next chapter, the history of documentary proper will begin with the naturalist tradition.

The newsreel tradition came out of the phenomenal expansion of journalism in the twentieth century. Mass circulation newspapers (and a practicable theory for radio transmission) appeared about the same time as the movies—1896.[9] The popular press, with its dramatization of the news, functioned not only as dispenser of information but as informal educator for millions of avid readers. Newsreels appeared in movie theaters in regular weekly form from 1910 on. They were simply an extension into motion pictures of equivalents to the rotogravure sections of the tabloids. They are touched upon in Chapter Three.

The concept and term *propaganda,* Rotha's third tradition, goes back at least to the *Congregatio de propaganda fide* (Congregation for propagating the faith), a committee of Cardinals established by Pope Gregory XV in 1622. A subsequent use of propaganda grew out of the revolutionary theory set forth by German political philosopher and socialist Karl Marx (1818–1883). Propaganda became a key concern of Russian communist leader Vladimir Ilyich Lenin (1870–1924). Following the October revolution of 1917, the new government in Russia—Union of Soviet Socialist Republics—was the first to make sustained, extensive, and coordinated peacetime use of film propaganda. Modern interest in propaganda is related to the intellectual disciplines of sociology, social psychology, and political science.

Rotha's final tradition, realist (continental), emerged as part of the European avant-garde of the 1920s, headquartered in Paris. One of its preoccupations was finding artistic means for dealing with the interrelatedness of time and space. This modern understanding, originating in the physical sciences, was enunciated by Max Planck in his quantum mechanics, by Albert Einstein in his theory of relativity, and by others beginning about the turn of the century. Another preoccupation of the avant-garde was with expressing the understanding of the unconscious human mind offered by Sigmund Freud, Carl Jung, and others in the new psychological science at about the same time. The contributions of the avant-garde to documentary will be the subject of Chapter Four.

PRE-DOCUMENTARY ORIGINS

Depending on how one defines documentary, it could be said to have begun with the birth of film itself. The filmed recordings of actuality in the experiments of technicians at the Edison laboratory in West Orange, N.J., might qualify. For example, the sneeze of an employee named Fred Ott was filmed in 1893 and two of the workers dancing to phonograph music can be viewed during an attempt to synchronize sight with sound in 1896. Closer in content and approach to subsequent documentaries are the first films produced by Louis Lumière and projected for paying customers in Paris on December 28, 1895. They included *The Arrival of a Train at the Station, Feeding the Baby,* and *Workers Leaving the Factory.* A member of the audience at this showing is supposed to have exclaimed of the film being projected: "It is life itself!"

Workers Leaving the Factory (France, 1895, Louis Lumière). National Film Archive/ Stills Library.

In the first years of the motion picture that followed, films were mostly similar brief recordings showing everyday life, circus and variety acts, and skits. Only Georges Méliès used specially conceived narrative and fantasy to any extent in the films made before 1900, and even he began by record-ing snippets of life on the streets of Paris (*Place de L'Opéra, Boulevard des Italiens,* both 1896). Gradually, as the novelty of the moving photographic image began to pale, the actualities recorded by filmmakers were selected for extra–cinematic interest.

Foreign and exotic subjects had a strong appeal. Traveling projection-ists or cameramen of the Lumière organization roamed widely, showing "scenic views" of the Eiffel Tower and Parisian boulevards to Russians or Spaniards, for example. While in Russia, they photographed troika rides and Cossacks, and in Spain, Flamenco dancing and bull fights, to be shown to audiences in France and elsewhere. In addition to such early travelogue forms—*Moscow Clad in Snow,* 1909, is a surviving French example (produced by Pathé Frères); *The Durbar at Delhi,* 1911, a British one—were filmed re-ports of exploratory and anthropological expeditions, more serious in pur-pose and educative in effect—*With Scott in the Antartic,* 1913, is a British

Production still taken during shooting of *In the Land of the Head-Hunters* (U.S., 1914, Edward S. Curtis)—Curtis operating the camera. Courtesy of Thomas Burke Memorial Washington State Museum.

example, made by Herbert Ponting. *In the Land of the Head-Hunters*, 1914, is an American one, made by Edward S. Curtis. About the Kwakiutl Indians of the Pacific Northwest, it was the most ambitious experiment of its sort up to that time. Curtis was not only a professional photographer but a trained and experienced ethnologist. Although working quite separately from Flaherty, he was headed in a similar direction. Flaherty met Curtis and saw his film in 1915.

The newsreel tradition may be said to have begun in France with Louis Lumière's *Excursion of the French Photographic Society to Neuville*, made in 1895. Called "interest films" at first, the subjects quickly became events of greater newsworthiness. Many of them featured heads of state and ceremonial occasions. Some examples are: the crowning of a czar (*Coronation of Nicholas II*, 1896), the campaign of a presidential candidate (*William Mc Kinley at Home*, 1896), and the final rites for a queen (*The Funeral of Queen Victoria*, 1901). Warfare was another frequent subject. The Spanish-American War (*Dewey Aboard the "Olympia" at Manila, Tenth U.S. Infantry Disembarking*, both 1898), the Boxer Rebellion (*The Assassination of a British Sentry, Attack on a China Mission*, both 1900), and the Russo-Japanese War (*The Battle of the Yalu, Attack on a Japanese Convoy*, both 1904) had films made about them—though these were mostly reenactments rather than actualities. Among other examples that have lasted down to the present are *Launching of "H.M.S. Dreadnought"*

McKinley's Inaugural Address (U.S., 1896, probably the Edison Company). Museum of Modern Art/Film Stills Archives.

by King Edward VII (U.K., 1906) and *Suffragette Riots in Trafalgar Square* (U.K., 1909). The newsreel in weekly form was begun by Charles Pathé of France in 1910.

Isolated examples of what might be called propaganda films, in Rotha's sense of the term, appeared before the outbreak of World War I in 1914. In the United States, the Department of the Interior produced and distributed motion pictures as early as 1911 to entice Eastern farmers to move to the newly opened agricultural areas of the West. The Civil Service Commission used a film, *Won Through Merit,* in a recruiting campaign in 1912.[10] In the same year the city of Cleveland had a movie made as part of a campaign to alleviate slum conditions.[11]

When America entered the war in 1917, training films were produced to instruct troops in certain activities. Propaganda films were intended to inspire military personnel and civilians alike with hatred of the enemy and desire for victory. *Pershing's Crusaders, America's Answer,* and *From Forest to France* were used to boost morale and the sale of war bonds.[12] Newsreels took on propaganda dimensions and the filmic documentation of warfare was much more comprehensive and skillful (and actual) than in preceding wars. *The Battle of the Somme* (1916), made by J.B. McDowell and Geoffrey Malins, and *The Western Front* (1919), are British examples.

The continental realist tradition, as Rotha called it, was an aspect of the avant-garde movement of the 1920s. Only a few earlier films (perhaps

Newsreel of Berlin, probably 1919, following World War I. Museum of Modern Art/Film Stills Archive.

Romance of the Railway, 1907, by Charles Urban) might be related to that creative line.

Of Rotha's four traditions—naturalist, newsreel, propaganda, continental realist—it is with the naturalist tradition and the work of Robert Flaherty that the next chapter begins. Newsreel and propaganda follow in Chapter Three and continental realist is covered in Chapter Four.

NOTES

[1]John Grierson (as "The Moviegoer"), "Flaherty's Poetic *Moana*," *The New York Sun*, February 8, 1926. Reprinted in Lewis Jacobs, ed., *The Documentary Tradition* (New York: W.W. Norton & Company, Inc., 1979), pp. 25–26, and in Forsyth Hardy, ed., *Grierson on the Movies* (London: Faber and Faber Limited, 1981), pp. 23–25.

[2]Frances Flaherty, "Robert Flaherty: Explorer and Film Maker: The Film of Discovery and Revelation" (mimeographed, 15pp., c. 1958), p. 1. This is the text for a lecture-screening Mrs. Flaherty gave on a number of occasions following her husband's death.

[3]Quoted in Paul Rotha, in collaboration with Sinclair Road and Richard Griffith, *Documentary Film* (New York: Hastings House, Publishers, 1970), p. 70.

[4]*Ibid.*, p. 5.

[5]Basil Wright, "Documentary To-Day," *The Penguin Film Review*, No.2 (January 1947), 37–44.

[6]Raymond Spottiswoode, *A Grammar of the Film: An Analysis of Film Technique* (Berkeley: University of California Press, 1950), p. 289.

[7]Rotha, *Documentary Film*, p. 7.

[8]Claudia Springer, "Ethnographic Circles: A Short History of Ethnographic Film," *The Independent*, 7, No. 11 (December 1984), 13–18.

[9]Nicholas Pronay and D.W. Spring, eds., *Propaganda, Politics and Film, 1918–45* (London: The Macmillan Press Ltd., 1982), p. 13.

[10]James E. Gibson, "Federal Government," *Sixty Years of 16mm Film* (Evanston, Ill.: Film Council of America, 1954), pp. 148–60.

[11]Lewis Jacobs, *The Rise of the American Film* (New York: Harcourt, Brace and Company, 1939), p. 152.

[12]Gibson, "Federal Government," p. 149.

BOOKS ON DOCUMENTARY THEORY AND GENERAL HISTORIES OF DOCUMENTARY

Theory

BARSAM, RICHARD MERAN, ed., *Nonfiction Film Theory and Criticism*. New York: E. P. Dutton & Co., Inc., 1976. 382 pp.

BENOIT-LEVY, JEAN, *The Art of the Motion Picture*. New York: Coward-McCann, 1946. 263 pp.

GRIERSON, JOHN, *Grierson on Documentary*, ed. by Forsyth Hardy. Berkeley: University of California Press, 1966. 411 pp.

HUGHES, ROBERT, ed., *Film: Book 1: The Audience and the Filmmaker*. New York: Grove Press Inc., 1959. 184 pp.

HUGHES, ROBERT, ed., *Film: Book 2: Films of Peace and War*. New York: Grove Press Inc., 1962. 255 pp.

LEVIN, G. ROY, *Documentary Explorations: 15 Interviews with Film-Makers.* Garden City, N.Y.: Double-day & Company, Inc., 1971. 420 pp.

ROSENTHAL, ALAN, *The Documentary Conscience: A Casebook in Film Making.* Berkeley: University of California Press, 1980. 436 pp.

ROSENTHAL, ALAN, *New Challenges to Documentary.* Berkeley: University of California Press, 1987. 460 pp.

ROSENTHAL, ALAN, *The New Documentary in Action: A Casebook in Film Making.* Berkeley: University of California Press, 1972. 287 pp.

STARR, CECILE, ed., *Ideas on Film: A Handbook for the 16mm Film User.* New York: Funk & Wagnalls Company, 1951. 251 pp.

WALDRON, GLORIA, *The Information Film.* New York: Columbia University Press, 1949. 281 pp.

WRIGHT, BASIL, *The Use of the Film.* London: John Lane, 1948. 72 pp.

History

BAECHLIN, PETER and MAURICE MULLER-STRAUSS, *Newsreels Across the World.* Paris: United Nations Educational, Scientific and Cultural Organization, 1952. 100 pp.

BARNOUW, ERIK, *Documentary: A History of the Non-fiction Film.* New York: Oxford University Press, 1983. 360 pp.

BARSAM, RICHARD MERAN, ed., *Nonfiction Film Theory and Criticism.* New York: E. P. Dutton & Co., Inc., 1976. 382 pp.

BARSAM, RICHARD, guest ed., *Quarterly Review of Film Studies,* 7, 1 (Winter 1982), 108 pp. Special issue on documentary.

Film Council of America, *Sixty Years of 16mm Film, 1923–1983.* Evanston, Ill.: Film Council of America, Inc., 1954. 220 pp.

JACOBS, LEWIS, ed., *The Documentary Tradition.* New York: W. W. Norton & Company, Inc., 1979. 594 pp.

LEYDA, JAY, *Films Beget Films.* New York: Hill and Wang, 1964. 176 pp.

MANVELL, ROGER, ed., *Experiment in the Film.* London: The Grey Walls Press Ltd., 1949. 285 pp.

ROTHA, PAUL in collaboration with Sinclair Road and RICHARD GRIFFITH, *Documentary Film.* New York: Hastings House, Publishers, 1952. 412 pp.

WAUGH, THOMAS, ed., *"Show Us Life": Toward a History and Aesthetic of the Committed Documentary.* Metuchen, N.J.: The Scarecrow Press, Inc., 1984. 508 pp.

TWO
BEGINNINGS
The Americans and Popular Anthropology, 1922–1929

THE WORK OF ROBERT FLAHERTY

Between 1910 and 1915, at the time Edward Curtis (mentioned in Chapter One) was making *In the Land of the Head–Hunters* in western Canada, another American, Robert J. Flaherty, was exploring and mapping in the Hudson Bay region. Flaherty was employed to search for iron ore by Sir William Mackenzie, the great developer of the northern wilderness ("the Cecil Rhodes of Canada," Flaherty called him). Though he found some iron ore, the deposit was not rich enough to tempt anyone to try to mine and transport it. In the course of his travels Flaherty discovered the main island of the Belcher group, which was named after him. But the most important discovery of his expeditions was how to make a new kind of motion picture. Through this discovery he would reveal to the rest of the world the far north country and its friendly inhabitants, the Eskimos, on whom he depended for his very existence.

It was on his third expedition in 1913 that Flaherty, encouraged by Mackenzie, took along motion picture equipment to record what he saw. He shot some 70,000 feet (almost twelve hours) of the Eskimos, their activities, and their surroundings. After he had returned to Toronto and begun to edit, he dropped a cigarette onto a mass of film on the floor. Since it was the highly flammable cellulose nitrate stock of the time, it went up in a great flash of flame nearly taking Flaherty with it. Though the original footage was almost totally destroyed, an edited work print survived and Flaherty showed it around a bit. John Grierson, who subsequently managed to see it, reported his reaction as follows: "In the first version Flaherty was still with the old travelogue of Hale's Tours, and planning learning from the ground up, not to mention the backs and fronts of sledges."[1]

Apparently Flaherty had agreed with Grierson's assessment. Another novice might have given up filmmaking altogether following such a disastrous entry into the field; Flaherty not only persisted, he learned from the experience. In the initial version, though he had faithfully recorded aspects of Eskimo existence, his feelings for the people and their way of life had not been expressed in a form that would permit audiences to share them. As his interest in filmmaking took precedence over exploring, Flaherty obtained backing from Revillon Frères, the fur company, for a return to the north to make another film. What resulted from his shooting between 1920 and 1922 was the *Nanook of the North* we know.

When Flaherty took the completed *Nanook* around to film distributors in New York City, one by one they turned it down. "Who would want to see a movie about Eskimos, a movie without story, without stars?", they seemed to be asking. It was Pathé Exchange, a firm with French origins (like the sponsoring Revillon Frères), which eventually undertook distribution. No doubt much to the surprise of Pathé and perhaps to Flaherty, this new kind of film received an enthusiastic reception by the critics and became a sub-

Nanook of the North (U.S., 1922, Robert Flaherty). Museum of Modern Art/Film Stills Archive.

stantial box office success. Apparently a lot of people wanted to see a movie about Eskimos. In this movie ordinary people reenacted things they did in everyday life—working, eating, sleeping, traveling, playing with their children—doing for the camera what they would have done if the camera hadn't been there.

Following the success of *Nanook,* Flaherty was approached by Jesse L. Lasky of Famous Players-Lasky (which became Paramount Pictures), the first firm to have turned down distribution of *Nanook.* Lasky offered Flaherty what amounted to a blank check. He was to go anywhere in the world and bring back "another *Nanook.*"

Flaherty had become interested in the South Seas through the eloquent descriptions of a friend, Frederick O'Brien, who had written a popular book on the subject, *White Shadows in the South Seas.* O'Brien urged Flaherty to go to Samoa to record the lovely culture of its gentle people before it was further eroded by the incursions of foreigners and disappeared altogether. With his wife Frances, three small daughters, their nursemaid, and his brother David, he set sail for the southwest Pacific.

Flaherty was aware of what Hollywood expected from him—another box office success—and wondered what he would find in Samoa that could provide the drama of human survival that *Nanook* contained. (Two years after the film was released Nanook died of starvation, as many of his people had.) On the way to Samoa, Flaherty learned that a giant octopus had been sighted from another ship. Maybe enormous sea creatures threatened human life in Samoa.

Once there he found no sea monsters. On the contrary, Samoan existence seemed to provide no drama at all. Nature was munificent beyond belief; if you weren't hit on the head by a falling coconut you might live forever. For weeks a dejected Flaherty sat on the veranda drinking apple beer, gloomily contemplating what form he might give to a film about Samoans.

Through his informal investigations into the culture he had learned of a practice no longer carried out that interested him. Formerly, young Samoan men had been initiated into manhood by undergoing elaborate and intricate tatooing over much of their bodies (the knees being particularly painful) which took some weeks. Flaherty had concluded that because there were few physical threats to their existence, the Samoans had invented a test of endurance involving considerable pain. Flaherty revived this custom for the purposes of his film and organized it around the initiation of one Samoan youth named Moana. Preceding and paralleling the scenes of tatooing are scenes of the gathering of food—in the jungle, from the sea, and along the shore—the making of clothing and ornaments, the preparing and cooking of a feast, and the dancing of the Siva by Moana and his intended bride. When the tatooing was completed there was a ceremonial drinking of kava (an intoxicating beverage made from the crushed root of

Moana (U.S., 1926, Robert Flaherty). Museum of Modern Art/Film Stills Archive.

a shrubby pepper) by the chiefs and a celebratory dance by the men of the village in honor of Moana's courage.

In his first two films—*Nanook* and *Moana*—Flaherty's subjects and purposes led him (one might almost say forced him) into innovations in film form. He found a means other than the plotted story, or the simple topical organization of newsreels and travelogues, to present real people and their everyday lives on the screen. Unlike other documentary pioneers whose work will be discussed later (Dziga Vertov or John Grierson, for instance), Flaherty was no theorist. Rather, he was intuitive and pragmatic. He tended to talk about the subjects of his films—the Eskimos and Samoans—rather than the nature of the medium. Nonetheless, he made profound contributions to film aesthetic and technique and to the uses to which film could be put.

The organizing structures of Flaherty's films involve loose narratives set within natural chronology. (Subsequent documentarians would move away from narrative towards exposition and argument.) *Nanook* extends through almost a year, beginning in late spring and ending in deep winter. *Moana* covers the period of its hero's initiation rites, from preparations through festive conclusion—somewhere between a month and six weeks (the tatooing itself takes three weeks, we are told).

The separate sequences within the overall time spans describe the various kinds of work, ceremony, children's play, and other activities most characteristic and distinctive of these peoples. We see Nanook spearing fish, catching and rendering walrus, hunting seals, and building an igloo. Moana and his family are seen snaring a wild boar, collecting giant clams, gathering coconuts, smoking out a robber crab, capturing a huge tortoise, making custard, scraping breadfruit, and baking little fish. What Flaherty chooses to show are traditional skills and customs that, while different from "civilized," modern ways, are rooted in common sense we can appreciate. Nanook's kayak appears an extremely servicable craft for navigating the ice-clogged waters of the far north; the igloo he builds seems an efficient and comfortable home. In Samoa, clothing made from the bark of the mulberry tree and outriggers of carved wood and spars bound together with vines seem good use of what is easily available and well suited to tropical climate and rolling surf.

What Flaherty offers mainly is visual description of unfamiliar human activities and artifacts, of exotic flora and fauna—a purpose achievable by and perhaps sufficient for a maker of silent films. (Spoken commentary would be needed to analyze significant implications or nonmanifest aspects of these lives, but Flaherty seems to have had little interest in such analysis and interpretation.) His films are all virtually silent films. When sound became available, he used it essentially as an accompaniment to the images, filling in another sensory dimension of reality with natural sounds, adding emotional color with music. Dialogue is used sparingly in Flaherty's two major sound films—*Man of Aran* (1934) and *Louisiana Story* (1948)—espe-

Man of Aran (U.K., 1934, Robert Flaherty). Museum of Modern Art/Film Stills Archive.

cially in the former. Mainly it serves to characterize the sound and style of his subjects' speech and to suggest their attitudes, more than to convey information or reveal psychological motivation.

Those who spent long evenings in Flaherty's company remember him as a teller of tales, a consummate raconteur with a sure sense of drama. In all his films the dramatic conflict is achieved with man against or at least in relation to nature. In *Nanook* it is man against the arctic cold and desolation. In *Moana,* amidst the warm, soft abundance of a tropical paradise, it is man against invented pain. In Flaherty's later *Man of Aran* it is man against the infertile rock of a barren island off the west coast of Ireland and the towering waves of the North Atlantic. And in *Louisiana Story,* with the most complex conflict of the four major films, it is still man in ecological relationship with nature—a boy and his raccoon moving amidst the secrets and dangers of a primordial swamp, and an oil drilling crew wresting treasure from deep beneath its surface.

If Flaherty was a story teller, he was also a teacher. His pedagogy employed mystery and suspense to arouse our curiosity, to make us want to learn about the subjects that fascinated him. One of many similar instances of this method occurs early in *Moana* when Moana's younger brother, Pe'a,

Louisiana Story (U.S., 1948, Robert Flaherty). Museum of Modern Art/Film Stills Archive.

climbs a palm tree. First we see him mid-frame, on a section of the trunk. He is allowed to climb up out of frame; then the camera tilts up to re-center him. Pe'a again climbs out of frame and is again pursued by the camera. On the third climb-tilt the top of this majestic tree is revealed. By that time we are not only craving to see the top, we are prepared to accept this as the tallest palm in the world. In another scene from the same film we see Pe'a looking at something and a title tells us he has come upon "a telltale bit of evidence—an empty coconut shell." We do not learn what it is evidence of, however, and the mystery builds as Pe'a scrambles about the rocks, peers in the crevices between them, tries to move one, and starts a small fire accompanied by smoke until a creature emerges. Only then does a title say, "Ah, Mr. Robber Crab, you won't climb my father's coconut trees any more." Also, Flaherty's visual exposition is generally exemplary in its simplicity and clarity. Nanook's construction of an igloo is presented so clearly and simply we feel we could go out and build one, given enough snow. Much the same can be said for the making of soil in *Man of Aran.*

The dramatis personae of the Flaherty films are the nuclear family structured along conventional lines. He did not acknowledge the polygamy practiced in traditional Eskimo culture nor the looseness of the Samoan family arrangement described by Margaret Mead in *Coming of Age in Samoa.* A Flaherty film family usually has: a strong, mature father, gentle but heroic; a mother devoted to him, to their children, and to the concerns of the family; and a son who is learning his way into his cultural and natural surroundings. The women in Flaherty's films are subordinate and supportive to the men in the struggle for existence, assisting them in domestic and ceremonial activities. Maggie, in *Man of Aran,* is somewhat unusual in her demonstrated strength of character, independence, resourcefulness, and bravery. I take the Flaherty film family as deriving from what he thought his own to have been like as he was growing up the son of a mining engineer in northern Michigan and Canada before the turn of the century. In this view the young boys of his films are surrogates for the young Flaherty himself. Water, small boats, and fishing are prevalent in the life of his films, as they would have been in the life of the region in which he grew up.

The families were artificially created for the films, for the most part, with considerable care given to the casting. Those selected to become father, mother, son, sister, and the rest are physically representative of the culture and also attractive—not necessarily handsome or beautiful but best of type. Community life is scarcely represented in the Flaherty films. The sudden appearance of numbers of Eskimos, or Samoans, or Aran Islanders for the trek to the fur trader's, the performance of a tribal dance, or the hunt for basking sharks seems incongruous with the prevailing intimacy and isolation of the central family. Ages and stages of life are represented—early childhood through maturity—but little attention is given to old age or infancy. There are no human deaths or births in Flaherty's films.

What he seeks out among his peoples are their consistent patterns of physical behavior—activities related to obtaining food, clothing, and shelter—rather than aberrations of human psyches and antisocial actions which are the basis for Western drama from the Greeks on. Flaherty may ultimately have been most concerned with the human spirit, but what he chose to show were its basic material manifestations. He pays no attention to how his societies govern themselves. Nor is there anything in his films about the spiritual life of the people he is depicting. Religious beliefs and practices are absent—remarkable considering the importance of religion in the cultures he chose. We see neither anger or grief. While a lot of generalized affection is evident—of his subjects for each other and (implicitly) of the filmmaker for his subjects—there is no sex. (The relationship between Moana and his betrothed, Fa'angase, might be mistaken for that of brother and sister.) Personal feelings, the emotions of individuals, are not central to Flaherty's concerns. Rather, more generalized notions of what a man, a woman, and a child do are operative. What it means to survive, to exist in the culture and in the environment one is born into, are the stuff of which his films are made.

Shooting films in exotic places and the ways Flaherty shot them were unprecedented—at least in the feature filmmaking of the major studios. His methods of conception and production were especially original and unusual in two respects. One was what was characterized by his wife and coproducer Frances Flaherty as "nonpreconception." Rather than approaching a society with an idea of the film he wanted to make about it, Flaherty chose to live with and observe the people, to discover their true story, like the Eskimo sculptor who cuts into the ivory tusk until he finds the seal figure in it. The other, corollary characteristic was Flaherty's practice of shooting a tremendous amount of footage on the aspects of the people and their environment that struck him as significant, or beautiful, or interesting. That initial lack of fixed intention and seemingly random shooting were accompanied by long evenings of screening, looking for the essences of the culture in the images, seeking the particular rhythms and beauties of their life. His subjects and members of his family and crew screened the uncut footage with him and discussed it. But the final decisions about what to include were always made by Flaherty.

As innovative as his production methods were, his use of film language followed accepted practice. Flaherty's camera was always mounted on a tripod. His nonactors were directed to reenact things he had observed them do and to repeat their actions in multiple takes. They became "performers" to a degree that is no longer usual in documentary. The conventional continuity editing evidently rested on some sort of postproduction script that took form in Flaherty's head during the repeated screenings. (He seems to have never used written scripts, only scribbled notes.) Though occasional lapses and "errors" are evident, the sequences are constructed with long shot-medium shot-closeup, matching action, and consistent screen direction.

Shooting in out-of-the-way locations required certain technological improvisations and innovations. In the studio it is comparatively easy to adjust the technology to the filmmaker's needs. If movement of the Mitchell camera is limited by its size and weight, it can be put on a dolly or crane; if film emulsion is insensitive to light, more Klieg lights can be added to the set. In the field the filmmaker has to adapt to existing conditions. Many technological advances and alterations of technique have come about through filmmakers working outside the studio trying to get close to unaltered real life.

Though he tended to profess ignorance of technological matters, Flaherty seems to have been a natural and perhaps superb technician. For his first filming in the north in 1913, he used a 1912 Bell and Howell studio camera, adapting it to his needs. Later he would use the Akeley, a sophisticated gyroscopic camera employed by newsreel cameramen, and then the Newman Sinclair, which became a standard camera for documentarians. On *Nanook* Flaherty began his practice of developing and printing film in the field, necessary if he was to see what he was shooting while still on location. His Eskimo helpers cut holes in the ice to obtain water for processing, carried it in barrels to the hut, and strained out the deer hair that fell into it from their clothing. The "printer" was a rectangle of clear glass left on a window painted black. It corresponded to the 35mm film frame in size and shape. Through it the low Arctic sun shone. That such a system worked at all is amazing; that the quality of images in *Nanook* show little sign of the crudity of the "laboratory" involved is even more astounding.

For *Moana* Flaherty was the first to use the new panchromatic film. Though black and white (before color was available), panchromatic film is sensitive to all colors of the spectrum, unlike the orthochromatic film then in standard use. While orthochromatic film did not respond to red and was prone to harsh contrasts, *Moana* offers a Samoa rich in varied tones of gray. It was also on *Moana* that Flaherty first began to make extensive use of long (telephoto) lenses. Almost all of *Moana* was shot with lenses of six inches focal length and upward (two inches is standard). Their use had the obvious advantage of permitting the filming of distant and inaccessible subjects— the outrigger in the surf, for example. Also, Flaherty found that his people were less self-conscious and behaved more naturally if the camera was some distance from them. He also thought certain special photographic qualities resulted through the use of long lenses: "The figures had a roundness, a stereoscopic quality that gave to the picture a startling reality and beauty. . . . alive and real, the shadows softer, and the breadfruit trees seemed like living things rather than a flat background."[2]

For *Man of Aran,* Flaherty's first sound feature, recording sound on Inishmore would have been next to impossible with the cumbersome opti-

Robert Flaherty with a Newman Sinclair camera, England, 1930s. Museum of Modern Art/Film Stills Archive.

cal equipment then in use. (Magnetic recording was not yet available.) To solve this problem Flaherty post–recorded in a London studio a sound track made up of music and noises and fragments of speech, laying it over the images in a complex and poetic blend unlike—far in advance of aesthetically—the synchronous sound track standard on fiction films of the time. *Louisiana Story* was the first feature shot with the 35mm Arriflex camera, which had a through-the-lens viewing capability developed from the 16mm combat model used by the Germans in World War II.

THE FLAHERTY WAY

In thinking about Flaherty's overall significance, what seems most important to me is his special use of the film medium, which grew out of his creative impulse and began one main line of documentary. Stated simply, Flaherty used film to show people he loved and admired to the rest of us. He was not an anthropologist; he idealized and interpreted as an artist does, a visual poet in his case. The view he offers is his view, admittedly. In some respects his films are as much about him—his pleasures, his prejudices, his convictions—as about the people he was filming. Often he set them back in time to recapture and preserve cultures that were disappearing, and he always presented them at their finest, simplest, and noblest, gaining their cooperation to achieve this presentation. *Man of Aran* especially, in which the hunting of basking sharks was recreated from past practices and the real economic problems of Aran ignored, has been criticized for its "distortions." But Flaherty did not invent or glamorize. His films were not created from make-believe or fakery; all that he shows did happen or had happened in the lives of the people. (*Louisiana Story* is the exception; though based on actuality, it is a story, as its title announces.)

True, Flaherty usually stuck to simple peoples in far corners of the earth and dealt only with the essentials of their traditional existence. But this is not exoticism à la "Hollywood" (as in *Tabu*, 1931, which Flaherty made with F. W. Murnau in Tahiti but which became Murnau's film, replete with love story, villainy, and native superstitions). In Flaherty's films there are neither "colorful natives" nor "native color." He was attempting to show how other cultures are like our own; how understandable, rather than how different and strange. When *Nanook* ends with a closeup of Nanook's face, we may think "There's a man I've enjoyed getting to know. If I were in his situation, I hope I would be able to do things as well as he does."

Flaherty frankly liked and felt comfortable with people living close to nature; he was raised in the north woods with Indians and miners as companions. Also, his choice of "primitive" peoples and traditional cultures followed from what he wanted to say. An artist concerned with the conditions of survival—work for subsistence, family for procreation—and the timeless and universal requirements of humankind, may do better to stay away from the complex and sophisticated in order to see the essentials more clearly. Incidentally, the people Flaherty chose to make films about led a physical life and reveal themselves more fully through external action, visible work and ritual, than would city dwellers. Most of us would have a hard time explaining through images alone how we earn our livings.

To patronize Flaherty as a "romantic," as Paul Rotha and others did in the 1930s, seems to me to miss the point. One can see what Rotha is thinking of if the people and settings Flaherty chose and the way he chose to present them are linked with the noble savage of Jean-Jacques Rousseau and the idealized landscapes of early nineteenth-century painters. But Flaherty's films have little to do with the romanticism of the romantic movement, resting as it does on individual imagination and subjective emotions. On the contrary, his work might be said to be "classical," as I understand the romantic/classical dichotomy; it is spare and uninvolved with individual psychologies. Flaherty seems like a genial pagan or a prefall Adam—lacking interest in Christian notions of sin and guilt in any case.

Flaherty worked with what he understood and said what he had to say. Like many artists of substance this was essentially one thing. The French director Jean Renoir once remarked that a filmmaker spends his whole life making one film, over and over again. What Flaherty said throughout his work was that humankind has an innate dignity, and beauty dwells in its patterns of survival and existence.

Let me end this discussion of the Flaherty way with a substantial quotation from Frances Flaherty, who became an eloquent spokesperson for her husband's views after his death.

> Robert Flaherty loved primitive peoples, he loved their simplicity and their dignity, and the way they were free to be themselves. He loved the courage and generosity he found absolute in Eskimo life. But because he made his films of primitive cultures and cultures that are dying, and because he was not interested in their dying but only in them when they were most alive, he has been called a romantic and an escapist. Actually what he was deeply concerned with in these pictures of machineless people was the emergence of the machine. What he is saying in *Nanook, Moana* and *Man of Aran* is that the spirit by which these peoples came to terms with Nature is the same spirit by which we shall come to terms with our machines—that the continuity of history throughout its changes is written in the human spirit, and we lose sight of that continuity at our peril.
>
> Robert Flaherty seldom talked about his work. Yet he never, never for a moment was away from it. His dedication was more, however, than the dedication of an artist to his art; it was rather a dedication to his vision of the new power and new values that this new medium had brought into the world AS ART. All he cared about his films was that they should show this power and these values, that they should be great enough so that people would see, see the importance of an approach to this medium that gave them life and love and a deeper communion and greater awareness, so that they would see that this approach was the true greatness of the medium, its *art*.[3]

OFFSHOOTS FROM FLAHERTY

Though a school or movement never formed around him, Flaherty's example was followed in a general way by other Americans who worked along popular anthropological lines. Merian C. Cooper and Ernest B. Schoedsack were two of them. Their first film, *Grass* (1925), records the migration of 50,000 Bakhtiari tribesmen in central Persia (Iran) who cross a wide river at flood stage and a 12,000 foot mountain to reach pasture for their herds. *Chang* (1927), which followed *Grass,* is Cooper's and Schoedsack's concocted account of a family in the jungles of Siam (Thailand) struggling for survival against hostile animals—tigers, leopards, elephants.

In the 1930s the husband-wife team of Martin and Osa Johnson made a number of popular travel/expedition pictures with meretricious "educational" trappings and condescending asides about the natives: *Wonders of the Congo* (1931), *Baboona* (1935), and *Borneo* (1937), are among them. Frank Buck, in much the same vein, filmed his expeditions to capture wild animals in Africa: *Bring 'em Back Alive* (1932), *Wild Cargo* (1934), *Fang and Claw* (1935).

A much more significant offshoot from Flaherty's nonfiction form was the application by John Grierson and the British documentarians to purposes and subjects quite different from Flaherty's. The British were concerned with people in an industrialized, interdependent, and largely urban society. Their interests were social and economic (and political by implication). But Grierson, in a moving epitaph to his old friend and ideological adversary, said at the time of Flaherty's death in 1951, that perhaps, after all, he had been right in pursuing the timeless rather than the timely. Flaherty's films may have even contributed as much to social well-being as had Grierson's own, he conceded, in spite of his (Grierson's) concentration on improving the conditions of living in the here and now. Having acknowledged Flaherty's seminal importance in the history of film, Grierson ended his tribute with a quote from e e cummings, in loving acknowledgment of what Flaherty had meant to him personally:

> Buffalo Bill's
> defunct
> > who used to
> > ride a watersmooth-silver
> > > > stallion
> and break onetwothreefourfive pigeonsjustlikethat
> > > > > > Jesus
>
> he was a handsome man
> > > > and what i want to know is
> how do you like your blueeyed boy
> Mister Death

NOTES

[1]Forsyth Hardy, *John Grierson: A Documentary Biography* (London: Faber and Faber, 1979), p. 41.

[2]Robert Flaherty, "Filming Real People," *Movie Makers* (December 1934). Reprinted in Lewis Jacobs, ed., *The Documentary Tradition* (New York: W.W. Norton & Company, Inc., 1979), pp. 97–99.

[3]Frances Flaherty, "Robert Flaherty: Explorer and Film Maker: The Film of Discovery and Revelation" (mimeographed, c. 1958), pp 14–15.

[4]John Grierson, "Robert Flaherty: An Appreciation," *The New York Times* (July 29, 1951), sect. II, p. 3, col. 4.

FILMS OF THE PERIOD

1922
Nanook of the North (U.S., Robert Flaherty)

1925
Grass (U.S., Merian C. Cooper and Ernest B. Schoedsack)

1926
La Croisère noire (The Black Cruise; France,
    Léon Poirier)
Moana (U.S., Flaherty)

1927
Chang (U.S., Cooper and Schoedsack)
Voyage au Congo (Voyage to the Congo; France,
    Marc Allegret and André Gide)

BOOKS ON THE PERIOD

BARSAM, RICHARD, *The Vision of Robert Flaherty: The Artist as Myth and Filmmaker*. Bloomington:
    Indiana University Press, 1988. 144 pp.
BROWNLOW, KEVIN, *The War, The West, and the Wilderness*. New York: Knopf, 1979. 602 pp.
CALDER-MARSHALL, ARTHUR, *The Innocent Eye: The Life of Robert J. Flaherty*. London: W. H. Allen,
    1963. 304 pp.
FLAHERTY, FRANCES HUBBARD, *The Odyssey of a Film-Maker: Robert Flaherty's Story*. Urbana, Illinois:
    Beta Phi Mu, 1960. 45 pp.
GRIFFITH, RICHARD, *The World of Robert Flaherty*. New York: Duell, Sloan and Pearce, Inc., 1953,
    165 pp.
HOLM, BILL and GEORGE IRVING QUIMBY, *Edward S. Curtis in the Land of the War Canoes: A Pioneer
    Photographer in the Pacific Northwest*. Seattle: University of Washington Press, 1980. 132
    pp.
MURPHY, WILLIAM T., *Robert Flaherty: A Guide to References and Resources*. Boston: G. K. Hall &
    Co., 1978. 171 pp.
ROTHA, PAUL, *Robert J. Flaherty: A Biography*. ed. Jay Ruby. Philadelphia: University of Pennsylva-
    nia Press, 1983, 359 pp.

THREE
BEGINNINGS
The Soviets and Political
Indoctrination, 1922–1929

Paralleling the nonfiction films of Flaherty and others in the United States in the 1920s were those of Russian filmmakers. After the Revolution in 1917, one of the first acts of the new Communist government was to set up a film subsection within the State Department of Education. It was headed by Nadezhda Krupskaya, wife of Vladimir Ilyich Lenin, the principal architect of the Revolution. In 1919 the film industry was nationalized and the State Institute of Cinematography (VGIK) established in Moscow to train filmmakers. The theme of sponsorship sounded by *Nanook* and crucial to the economy of documentary was greatly amplified—from public relations for a fur company to communication by a government to its citizens.

In Russian the word *propaganda* is said to lack the pejorative connotations it has acquired in English. Soviets working in the media understand that ideological bias operates in the selection and presentation of content of all information and entertainment, and that it is naive or hypocritical to think otherwise.[1] The Soviets whose work will be considered in this chapter came to documentary and related realist forms as dedicated Marxists with a desire to help educate and indoctrinate the Russian people in ways that would be useful to this first socialist state.

Lenin had said, with remarkable foresight, given the uses of film generally up to that time and the negligible czarist film production: "Of all the arts, the cinema is the most important for us." He instructed Soviet film-makers to begin with newsreels and other nonfiction short films. This seemed advisable at the time partly because of the drain on resources that production of fiction feature films would have caused. Even more important was the urgent need to communicate the experience and spirit of the Revolution to the still largely uninformed and apathetic Russian public. Three types of Soviet nonfiction films were prominent in the 1920s: news-reel-indoctrinational series, compilations of archival footage tracing recent history, and epic-scale celebrations of contemporary Soviet achievement. They were paralleled by fiction features based closely on past or present conditions and events.

NONFICTION

Reportage

Among the most active and influential of the pioneer Soviet film-makers was a young man who called himself Dziga Vertov. Actually his name was Denis Arkadievitch Kaufman. He had two brothers who became film-makers as well: Boris, a famous cameraman who worked with such directors as Jean Vigo, Elia Kazan, and Sidney Lumet; and Mikhail, also a cameraman, for Vertov, and then a documentary maker in his own right. Dziga Vertov translates as "spinning top," which characterized well his energy. While his talent and originality are unquestionable, he seemed a whirling dervish to some, an eccentric fanatic to others. Before becoming a filmmaker Vertov had been an experimental poet and writer of fantasy and satire. In 1918 he joined the staff of "Kino-Nedelia" (Film-Weekly), the first newsreel produced in Soviet Russia.

What attracted Vertov to cinema was what he saw as a close relation-ship between the filming process and human thought. (Sergei Eisenstein, whose work will be discussed later, would develop much the same idea in his theories of montage.) Also, Vertov saw human perception as having limitations compared with the more perfectable "machine eye" of the motion picture camera. (Flaherty, too, thought of the motion picture camera as a seeing machine, like the telescope or microscope, offering "a sort of extra sight."[2]

In his delight in the scientific and mechanical bases of cinema, Vertov was consistent with the great emphasis placed on the machine in Soviet life and art. The government felt the need to bring the Soviet Union up to a level of industrial production comparable to that of other nations and to use modern technology to harness the vast natural resources of the country. The aesthetic movement of futurism, prominent in Russia in the 1920s, was

Dziga Vertov (right) with brother Mikhail Kaufman. Museum of Modern Art/Film Stills Archive.

marked especially by an effort to give formal expression to the dynamic energy and movement of mechanical processes.

As corollary, Vertov's aesthetic position demanded anti–narrative, anti-fictional forms. His iconoclasm was intended to free film from bourgeois obfuscations of story and the effete pleasures of theatrical performance in order to arrive at the truths of the actual world. Vertov eschewed the exotic subjects sought by Flaherty and chose to stay close to home and contemporary reality.

In 1920, during the continuing warfare between the counter-revolutionaries and the Communists, which threatened the very existence of the new state, Vertov worked on "agit–trains" and made *agitki*. Agit is short for agitation; sometimes the term agit-prop was used, for agitation and propaganda. *Agitki* were little political propaganda pieces. The agit-trains were variously equipped with small printing presses, actors who gave live performances, filmmaking and processing equipment, and other means of entertainment and communication. They would travel to the far-flung battlefronts to instill the troops and peasants along the way with revolutionary zeal.

In 1922 (the year *Nanook of the North* was released) Vertov began to produce "Kino Pravda." *Kino pravda* means, literally, film truth; *Pravda* was the name of the Soviet daily newspaper, central organ of the Communist Party. The film series was released irregularly for 23 issues until 1925. It was a precursor to "The March of Time" series in the United States (1935 to 51) and to the technique known as *cinéma vérité* (which began around 1960; the French term, meaning film truth, is a homage to Vertov). These two subsequent developments are dealt with in Chapters Six and Fourteen, respectively.

In "Kino Pravda" the newsreel and propaganda traditions merged. Each issue, running about twenty minutes and frequently comprising three or more reports on separate subjects, undertook to inform and indoctrinate Soviet audiences regarding the necessity for and values and progress of the Revolution. The sampling of "Kino Pravda" available in the United States begins and ends with a sequence portraying methods used for exhibiting the films. The beginning contains images of a reel of film, a projector being loaded, and a poster announcement sharing a split screen with an overhead pan of a city. The ending is of a mobile projection unit setting up a screen (with a mosque in the background), generator, and projector in a city square. This reflexivity would become increasingly characteristic of Vertov, culminating in *The Man With a Movie Camera* (1929).

The available "Kino Pravda" contains six separate reports. The first is on the renovation and operation of the Moscow trolley system, with rails being laid, electric lines installed, meters measuring power, and trolleys running. Second is the building of Khodinka Airport, with army tanks pulling graders to level the landing field. The third deals at some length with the trial of the Social Revolutionaries (members of the immediate post–czarist government under Alexander Kerensky that had been replaced by the Bolsheviks, that is, Communists, led by Lenin). Fourth is the organizing of peasants to form communes. Fifth is a sanatarium for crippled children at the town of Gelenzhik. Last is a report on starving children at the Melekes rail junction.

The subject matters of all six reports are of a practical, immediate, and materialistic nature: social, economic, and political problems being solved and things remaining to be done. Vertov's purpose in "Kino Pravda" seems to have been to inform Russians about what was going on in their country: to show various activities to the public at large; to awaken interest in what citizens are doing and gain respect for government progress; to engender pride in contemporary achievements, and occasionally to encourage action ("Save the starving children!" a title in the last report exclaims).

In the persuasion accompanying the information, Vertov contrasts the new with the old. For example, in the collectivization sequence, a shot of Czar Nicholas II, reviewing his troops, in stiff, formal military elegance is preceded by an intertitle that reads "Before we never had enough animals

"Kino Pravda" series (U.S.S.R., 1922–25, Dziga Vertov). Museum of Modern Art/Film Stills Archive.

for individual needs." The shot of the Czar is followed by the title "Now in the communes we work together with machines," and we subsequently see Lenin wearing a soft worker's cap, appearing without emphasis in a group. Or, in the sequence on the building of the airport, the (czarist) tanks are no longer being used as instruments of destruction. "Tanks on the labor front" a title announces, making a propaganda point that would not be lost on the audience.

There appears to have been no overall organizational form to the "Kino Pravda" issues. Each offered merely a collection of a few quite separate reports, vignettes, slices of life; not unlike the subsequent "March of Time" in this respect. Some of the reports in the available sample are organized in a slightly narrative way—the one on the Moscow trolley system, for example. Mostly they are descriptive. An issue of "Kino Pravda" was much less shaped than Flaherty's work—overall or even within its parts.

Initially Vertov's production method did not involve recreation or direction, as did Flaherty's. Vertov confined himself, for the most part, to capturing what he could of undirected action as it was occurring—"Life as it is" and "Life caught unawares" were his slogans. "All the people must continue to act and function in front of the camera just as they do in everyday life," he wrote. This strategy of shooting became a principle that has remained at the core of subsequent theories of documentary filmmaking. Vertov insisted that the camera "strive to shoot events 'unnoticed' and approach people in such a way that the cameraman's work does not impede the work of others"; and, conversely, the cameraman was not to hide when people reacted to the camera even if they expressed their displeasure at being photographed.[3]

To be sure, in "Kino Pravda" there are some exceptions to these generalizations. In the sequence about the trial of the Social Revolutionaries, for example, the selling of newspapers on the streets and the reading of newspapers in a moving auto and trolley have been enacted for the camera. But even if Vertov generally confined himself to recording what was happening in front of the camera without intervention, he felt free to manipulate this filmed actuality. He edited as fully as he chose in order to make clear and emphatic the meanings he wanted to communicate to his audience. Like Flaherty in not using a script, Vertov was unlike Flaherty in doing his shaping much more by editing than by directing or shooting. The brevity of the shots in "Kino Pravda" may have been necessitated by the shortage of available film in the Soviet Union at the time, which would have required the use of odds and ends of raw stock. On the other hand, the rapid cutting is consistent with the new editing theory and technique Vertov was developing. In either case, there is much more intercutting between bits of related action within a single scene in "Kino Pravda" than can be found in Flaherty's silent films (the only ones he edited). Vertov's use of editing marked the beginning of Soviet montage and would lead to the work of Esfir Shub, Sergei Eisenstein, and others to be discussed shortly.

Most people would find the aesthetic experience offered by "Kino Pravda" less satisfying than that of *Nanook* or *Moana*. Vertov's images are more restricted and didactic in intent than are Flaherty's. At the same time they seem less carefully composed, even cluttered and unlovely. The editing continuity is rougher, the action fragmented. The resultant style could be called naturalistic nitty-gritty—as opposed to naturalist (romantic), as Rotha called Flaherty's work. If "Kino Pravda" is less an artwork than are Flaherty's films, the cause was not that Vertov was incapable of achieving artistic expression—he would gravitate toward it. Rather, for the kind of filmmaking represented by "Kino Pravda" beauty would be thought of as a distraction.

Instead of aesthetic pleasure, "Kino Pravda" offered its audience close relationship with ongoing events that affected them more or less directly. One title announces: "The Trial of the Social Revolutionaries will be continued in the next issue of Kino Pravda." A final title instructs the audience: "For inquiries regarding traveling film shows/ For inquiries on all film and photo work/ Write to Kino Pravda, Moscow," and then provides the street address. Vertov clearly intended a direct and active relationship with his audience, what might be thought of as "interactive," as the term is currently used in referring to a viewer-medium relationship envisioned for cable television.

What Vertov contributed with "Kino Pravda" was a new kind of screen journalism through which he could communicate immediately and dynamically with the people. And, incidentally, through his emphasis on the visual, Vertov was able to transcend the problem of illiteracy then prevalent in his country. "Kino Pravda" conveys the drama and optimism of the time—a sense of a new society being built. The brief reports are socially purposeful; there are no beauty parades or animals at the zoo, ubiquitous in the newsreels of other nations. Also, emphasis is placed on work being done and on working people rather than on celebrities and state occasions. The reports are not all sweetness and light by any means—they include seemingly honest, hard-hitting exposés—but the tone is generally inspirational: There's a job to be done. Reporting on one geographic location or one aspect of national life to the nation at large was a mission that would be picked up by the British documentarians in the 1930s.

Vertov's film practice was accompanied by his steadily developing film theory. In a 1925 article, "The Basis of 'Film Eye' [*Kino Glaz*]," he explained his conception. Deciphering "life as it is" began with the direct recording of facts found in real life. "Film Eye" had to act not through the medium of theater or literature, since they were "surrogates of life," but on its own terms. (This bias stimulated Vertov's followers, called *kinoks,* to become extremely antagonistic to drama and fiction, as well as to "pay little attention to so-called Art.") This authentic film material ("life facts") was then reorganized into cinematic structures ("film things") to give a new unity with a particular ideological meaning. According to the Marxist view, the world could not be known through naive observation because its operation is hidden. The empirical world is the starting place (the source of raw material) for the "scientific" (that is, Marxist) analysis of the world. This reorganization was to be multileveled and perfected during the process of montage, the final step of the "Film Eye" method. The completed film would thus help the audience perceive reality as they otherwise never could. Vertov repeatedly pointed out that the "deciphering" of life through cinema "must be done according to the communist view of the world." Consequently, the "Film Eye" method combined an aesthetic concept of unstaged film with an ideological attitude toward art in general.

A contradiction may seem to exist in Vertov's demand that the kinoks, on the one hand, record "life as it is" without beautifying it, while, on the other, they were to propagate the communist world view. Vertov did not believe that these two commitments excluded each other; rather, that they reflected the dialectical process of the evolution of a socialist society. The true communist artist, Vertov claimed, must face reality "as it exists," neither hiding from facts nor masking problems.

But Vertov's artistic impulse eventually proved stronger than his social one. (He would have denied that the two impulses could be separated and argued that his formal innovations were superior means of persuasion in support of the Revolution.) Though maintaining their basis in recorded actuality, his films moved ever more toward aesthetic, psychological, even philosophical preoccupations. In his feature-length *Kino-Eye* (1924), opening titles announce it as "The First Exploration of 'Life Caught Unawares'" and "The First Non–Artificial Cinema Object, Made Without a Scenario, Actors or a Studio." What follows is a succession of vignettes and anecdotes suggesting investigative journalism not unlike that of CBS-TV's *60 Minutes* cut together to achieve a structural symmetry. The subtitles of his next two features, *Stride, Soviet!* and *A Sixth of the World* (both 1926), suggest the direction his artistic development was taking: *A Symphony of Creative Work* for the former; *A Lyrical Cine-Poem* for the latter.

His *The Man with a Movie Camera* (1929) is one of the densest, most complex and experimental films ever created. An impressionistic montage of Moscow life from dawn to dusk, it more easily fits among the "city symphonies" being made in Western Europe at the time (discussed in Chapter Four) than among the work of most other Soviet filmmakers. Even in the company of avant-garde work, its examination of filmic illusion in relation to reality and its employment of an amazing range of special effects within a complicated overall structure, constitute a daring innovation that places great demands on the viewer. Like Sergei Eisenstein, Dziga Vertov was essentially a formalist, a term that became a rebuke in the 1930s as the rule of Joseph Stalin tightened and "socialist realism" became the only acceptable artistic style.

Compilation

A major new genre of documentary was introduced by Esfir (Esther) Shub. A consummate editor, she influenced both Vertov and Eisenstein; she also, admittedly, learned from their work, insisting that she was, "in the final instance, Vertov's pupil."[4] Beginning in film in 1922, Shub was shortly inspired by Eisenstein's full-blown use of montage in *Potemkin* (1925) to begin her work on compilation films. In her first three features she reconstructed recent Russian history through editing together shots taken from earlier newsreels, home movies, and other sorts of record material she somehow managed to locate. *The Fall of the Romanov Dynasty* (1927) covered the period 1912 to 1917; *The Great Road* (1927), 1917 to 1927; and *The Russia of Nicholas II and Leo Tolstoy* (1928), 1896 to 1912. The first of these is the only one currently in distribution in the United States.

The Fall of the Romanov Dynasty is in four parts: pre-World War I; preparations for the war; the war; and the Revolution. Throughout, narrative intertitles in the past tense are used to identify images and give them emotional coloring, frequently ironic. It begins with "Czarist Russia in the years of the black reaction." There are short sequences on "The Kremlin of the Czars, " "Moscow of the priests," "Police," and the legislative body: "In St.

Petersburg the State Duma, obedient to the Czar, was in session." We then see a prosperous looking rural Russia of clergy and landed aristocracy. There is one shot of village huts, with peasant women at a well, and a scene of "Yoked peasant labor on the lands of the gentry"; but there is much more of court nobility, senators and officials, and the military (army units and the fleet). In a sequence of pointed contrast between aristocrats "on an outing at sea" dancing the mazurka aboard a warship and laborers doing various sorts of manual work, a title makes a joke about sweating being involved in each activity. This is just one instance of a steady intercutting of contrasts between the ruling classes and the people in factories, on farms, and in mines. A surprisingly substantial industrial economy is documented, while "Landless peasants, driven by need, left their homes." "The Czarist regime's prisons," and "Forced labor and exile," are also shown.

"Speculators," "Banks," "Gold," and "Capitalists" are identified as factors leading to war. Following the title "All countries were preparing for war," we see military training, munitions manufactured, and warlike activity in various countries. "Czarist Russia marched in step with world imperialism." With the threat of war "The mobilization took workers from their machines and peasants from the fields."

Scenes of mobilization are followed by dramatic combat footage of World War I, much of it of French and British forces, and some of German. There is also material taken on the Russian front. "Grain fields were burned

The Fall of the Romanov Dynasty (U.S.S.R., 1927, Esfir Shub). Museum of Modern Art/ Film Stills Archive.

by retreating armies"—presumably the czarist Russian army retreating from the Germans.

Following a title that proclaims simply, "1917," is extensive coverage of the uprising that put Alexander Kerensky in power in February of that year. This is shown as a popular revolution, but "The bourgeoisie, striving to use the revolution for its own purposes, seized power," a title explains. Emphasis is given to the continuing dissidence and the parallel government of Soviets of the Workers and Soldiers. Lenin's slogan of "Bread! Peace! Freedom!" is introduced. A title informs us that on March 4 the people learned of the abdication of Nicholas II. We see torn-down czarist emblems and then "Kerensky, leader of the Social Revolutionaries [Social Democrats] and Minister of Justice," along with the leader of the Mensheviks. (The latter were a wing of the Social Democratic Party who believed in the gradual achievement of socialism by parliamentary methods as opposed to the Bolsheviks led by Lenin.) Kerensky is shown pursuing the war; Lenin is shown speaking from a platform to a huge crowd in a square. The final shot is of Lenin in a locomotive tender, shaking hands with someone and smiling happily.

Two immediate reactions to *The Fall of the Romanov Dynasty* seem likely. One is to wonder how in the world Shub managed to obtain all that remarkable footage. An enormous amount of work, including, no doubt, much ingenuity and persistence, must have gone into locating it, even before the cataloging and creative assembling could begin. The other reaction is amazement and pleasure in the vivid sense of time and place, even of the personalities, caught by the camera. It is an astonishing document, full of life and Shub's lively response to that life.

Even though she is clearly justifying the Revolution through showing the background out of which it came, the humanity of the people still comes through, regardless of which side they were on politically. A scene of an aristocratic celebration in Moscow of the 300th anniversary of the Romanov dynasty is fascinating for its interplay of relationships among family members and friends caught and preserved, in some instances without any apparent awareness on their part that their images were being recorded. Imagine how changed our understanding of ancient Rome and the Romans might be if a similar moving picture record had been made in that time and place. Nothing like Shub's films had existed before them and her work remains among the finest examples of the compilation technique.

Shub's contributions were influential in the United States. In the early 1930s leftist filmmakers made what they called "synthetic documentaries" out of newsreels edited for propaganda purposes. This kind of filmmaking would be picked up and used later in "The March of Time" (1935 to 1951) series, in the "Why We Fight" (1942 to 1945) indoctrination series made during World War II, and in countless compiled documentaries made for television since the great success of *Victory at Sea* (1952–1953). A book by Jay Leyda devoted to this kind of filmmaking has the apt and engaging title *Films Beget Films* (New York: Hill and Wang, 1964). The legacy of Shub will be discussed in Chapters Six, Nine, and Twelve.

Epic

The final Soviet documentary pioneer to be considered is Victor Turin. Only one film of his demands attention: *Turksib* (1929), a large-scale seminal feature about the building of the Turkestan-Siberian railway.

Prior to making it Turin had been sent by his well-to-do family to America, where he moved from the Massachusetts Institute of Technology to the Vitagraph Company in New York City before returning to the Soviet Union and entering filmmaking. After the great success of *Turksib* he was rewarded by being given a studio production post, organizing other people's films.

The introductory titles of *Turksib* set forth the economic-geographical problem with which the film and the activity it documents are concerned. Cotton can be raised in Turkestan but "Cotton for all Russia" could be grown there if the wheat needed for the Turkestans' subsistence could be shipped from Siberia, thus permitting Turkestan land planted in wheat to be planted in cotton. The film is constructed in five "acts."

Act I deals with the importance and scarcity of water in Turkestan. Shots of the parched land are followed by a famous irrigation sequence as the snow melts in the mountains and water flows down into the valley. Trickles become streams which become torrents. (This sequence was imitated in the U.S. in King Vidor's fictional *Our Daily Bread*, 1934, and in Pare Lorentz's documentary *The River*, 1937.) Though there is enough water for wheat, there is not enough for cotton.

Act II deals with transportation under the existing outmoded system: camels and mules in Turkestan (with another splendid set piece of a sand storm [simoon]), and horse-drawn sleds in the snow of Siberia. A way must be found to transport Siberian grain south 1,000 miles to Turkestan, we are told.

Act III presents the work of surveying the route: the surveyors, "the advance guard of the new civilization"; a nomad village and its reactions as they arrive; and the work at headquarters in Alma-Ata of planning the route.

In Act IV, "The attack is launched at last"; "Civilization breaks through." It shows actual construction across the desert, including the removal of a huge rocky obstruction ("But still more stubborn is man and the machine"), the frozen north, and nomad tribesmen on their mounts racing alongside a locomotive on the completed track.

Act V recapitulates what has gone before and concludes in a pulsating exhortation that the railroad be completed by 1930, the final year of the First Five Year Plan.[5]

Turksib combines documentary ingredients which had proven effective with others appearing fully for the first time. It includes the distant and exotic, the Flaherty heroic struggle of man against nature. But, whereas Flaherty recorded and celebrated tribal cultures, Turin urged "WAR ON THE PRIMITIVE" (as the large intertitle shouts). For Flaherty, technology represented a threat to what is most human; for Turin it was an extension of human power ("Forward the machines").

Turksib has the same timeliness as Vertov's work. Released before the completion of the railway, it was designed to enlist enthusiasm and support for that effort. It has the vastness of scale of the American epic western (*The Covered Wagon,* 1923; *The Iron Horse,* 1924), which John Grierson, in Britain, would find related to the documentary impulse. And the roots of its epic struggle are in the economics of the modern industrialized world, as are those of Grierson's own first film, *Drifters* (1929). No wonder he especially valued *Turksib;* it was Grierson who prepared the English-language version.

But *Turksib* to me seems even more to look ahead to the documentaries of Pare Lorentz in the United States, dealt with in Chapter Six. *The Plow*

Turksib (U.S.S.R., 1929, Victor Turin). Museum of Modern/Film Stills Archive.

That Broke the Plains (1936) and *The River* (1937) have much more in common with the epic sweep of *Turksib* than do the British documentaries.

FICTION

If generally it seems possible to separate fiction from documentary, hybrids do exist. For example, Gillo Pontecorvo's *The Battle of Algiers* (Italy, 1966) is a fictionalized account of a major clash in the Algerian struggle for independence from France which draws on actual people and events as the basis of its story. Shot on location, using nonactors almost exclusively, it gives the impression that events are being recorded as they occur. A similar example is *The War Game* (U.K., 1966), Peter Watkins's horrifyingly credible account of nuclear holocaust. In addition to such individual films, certain national styles and movements fall into a gray area containing a bit of both documentary and fiction. The British semidocumentaries of World War II are one such body of films. The Italian postwar neorealist films are another. Both will be dealt with later, the former in Chapter Seven, the latter in Chapter Ten. The first of such bodies of fused fiction-documentary work would be the Soviet silent features.

The basic fact setting all Soviet cinema apart from that of the rest of the world was its state support. Filmmakers had to answer not to bankers and the profit motive but to government administrators and the presumed needs of the citizens. This difference, if basic, may not be as great as it appears. Capitalist as well as communist films embody ideology. Both attempt to attract large audiences. The control of contents and forms in both instances is exerted by a "front office," whether those behind the desks are called bosses or commissars. The success of all Soviet films, however, was measured in terms of how well they conveyed the sponsor's message—the extent to which they succeeded in affecting audience attitudes and behaviors in conformance with the sponsor's wishes. In this respect they were profoundly different. Given government sponsorship and indoctrinational goals, even Soviet fiction films contained many aspects of subject, purpose, form, production method, and resultant aesthetic experience and social effect that would come to be associated almost exclusively with documentary elsewhere.

If there were sufficient space, the documentary aspects in the fiction films and theoretical writings of the three greatest Soviet silent film masters—Sergei Eisenstein, V.I. Pudovkin, and Alexander Dovzhenko—could be considered. Since there isn't, the work of one of them will have to suffice. Eisenstein's is exemplary, and the most influential of the three. It is also closest to documentary.

Eisenstein started his artistic career in the theater, coming under the influence of a great experimental director, Vsevolod Meyerhold. He bounced out of theater into film after he produced a play in 1924 entitled *Gas Masks,* performed by workers and staged in a real Moscow gas factory. Instead of replacing "art" with "life," as he had intended, Eisenstein found that the industrial setting and the performances of nonactors showed up the artificiality of conventions that would have seemed perfectly at home in the theater. He then turned to film as the medium in which art could be made out of materials much closer to life than in the other arts.

What are the documentary-like aspects of Eisenstein's silent films? First, their subjects are all related to actual life lived recently or presently being lived. They are about people in relation to their institutions. Their concerns are social, economic, and political. *Strike* (1925) deals with a labor protest and the smashing of it in czarist Russia. *Potemkin* (1925) is based on the mutiny of the crew of an armored cruiser in the abortive 1905 revolution. *October/Ten Days That Shook the World* (1928) is a recreation of the Bolshevik seizure of power in St. Petersburg (Leningrad), the storming of the Winter Palace, and the takeover from the Kerensky government. *The General Line/Old and New* (1929) is about an agricultural collective in the new state; it is like an expansion of a "Kino Pravda" report (with the same emphasis on machines, in this case a tractor and a cream separator).

The purpose of these Eisenstein films is to inform and involve emotionally the Soviet public regarding: (1) the conditions and events leading to and justifying the Revolution; (2) the heroic struggle of the revolutionary

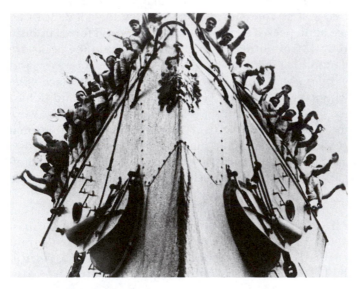

Potemkin (U.S.S.R., 1925, Sergei Eisenstein). Museum of Modern Art/Film Stills Archive.

forces during it; and (3) the positive and constructive efforts of the new state following it. The appeals of these films are perhaps first to a general humanism and then to national pride. Their aim is to arouse the people to support the efforts of their government, to make them think as communists—for brotherhood, collective effort, and material progress and against everything that stands in the way of those goals.

Large in scale, the four films are structured along distinctive epic lines. Their plots consist of events that affect the whole nation. Their characters represent classes and localities more than individual human beings—the masses become the hero. Like *Turksib, Potemkin* has five acts. If that makes it like a classical tragedy, as Eisenstein suggested, it is a tragedy with only a chorus; it is not about particular men or women of high station as in the Greek plays. (Incidentally, the acts are one reel each in length [about 15 minutes], allowing the pause for reel change to come at the end of each should no changeover projector be available.)

As for Eisenstein's production method, he shot on location and used nonactors. Though he started with actuality, he submitted it to extreme formalistic control and shaping. His work seems to me to represent a fusion of the contributions of two American pioneers: David Wark Griffith, who developed the technique of the narrative fiction film, and Robert Flaherty, of documentary fame. He acknowledged his indebtedness to Griffith; we don't know that he saw Flaherty's films. But Eisenstein began with something close to Flaherty's natural material and applied to it a highly developed Griffith directing and editing technique.

According to his theory of *typage*, Eisenstein would select the person to play a priest, or a ship captain, or a foundry worker whose appearance suggested most strongly that he might perform such a function. What Eisenstein needed was different from Flaherty's getting Nanook to play himself catching a seal, however; performances in Eisenstein's films had to be created according to script requirements. Flaherty could capture his sort of action in sustained wide-angle takes. Eisenstein had to cut his nonactors' performances into bits and pieces to omit evidence of embarrassment and of being out of character. Not only did montage, as Eisenstein conceived it, match the Marxist dialectical process—shots cut together equaling thesis, antithesis, synthesis—rendering it ideal for polemical purposes. In his sort of filmmaking extensive editing was required in order to create performances from the behavior of nonactors. (Pudovkin's *Film Technique and Film Acting* [New York: Lear Publishers, Inc., 1949] is very good on this matter.)

The aesthetic experience and social effects offered by Eisenstein's films finally move them outside the realm of documentary. Take *Potemkin*, for example. For all its documentary elements, it is essentially historical recreation and spectacle—superior Cecil B. De Mille (and Eisenstein's direction of crowds is at least equal to De Mille's). Or, consider *Old and New*, his last silent film. In it he is dealing with a fully documentary, contemporary subject matter, and the actual people on their actual land. Through his imposition of formalism and aesthetic concerns onto this material, the film comes to resemble a fairy tale, a kind of lighthearted myth (and its final intertitles call attention to its happy ending, in reference to Hollywood, surely).

Of course, Flaherty had to blend his art with entertainment in order to make a profit, just as did fiction filmmakers. But if the art of Vertov, Shub, and Turin, of Eisenstein, Pudovkin, and Dovzhenko might include entertainment and earn a profit, it was intended ultimately to make a better-functioning state. Almost all of the great Soviet silent films of the 1920s share documentary impulses and characteristics as defined in this book. The relationship between government and documentary established in the USSR would be picked up later not only by Fascist Italy and Nazi Germany but in the English-speaking democracies of Great Britain, the United States, and Canada, as will be seen.

NOTES

[1]Terry Doyle, "Truth at Ten? Some Questions of Soviet Television," *Sight and Sound*, 53, no. 2 (Spring 1984), 106–14.

[2]Frances Flaherty, "Robert Flaherty: Explorer and Film Maker: The Film of Discovery and Revelation" (mimeographed, c. 1958), p. 2.

[3]The quotes and paraphrases of Vertov's theoretical writing, here and below, are drawn from Vlada Petric, "Dziga Vertov as Theorist," *Cinema Journal*, 18, no. 1 (Fall 1978), 29–44.

[4]Petric, "Dziga Vertov as Theorist," p. 43.

[5]A much fuller analysis of the structure, content, and formal properties of *Turksib*, from which this account is partly drawn, is offered by K.J. Coldicutt, "*Turksib*: Building A Railroad," *The Documentary Tradition*, ed. Lewis Jacobs (New York: W.W. Norton & Company, Inc., 1979), pp. 45–48.

FILMS OF THE PERIOD

1922–1925
"Kino-Pravda" series (Dziga Vertov)

1924
Kino-Eye (Vertov)

1926
Mechanics of the Brain (V. I. Pudovkin)
A Sixth of the World (Vertov)
Stride, Soviet! (Vertov)

1927
The Fall of the Romanov Empire (Esfir Shub)
The Great Road (Shub)

1928
The Russia of Nicholas II and Leo Tolstoy (Shub)

1929
The Man with a Movie Camera (Vertov)
Turksib (Victor Turin)

BOOKS ON THE PERIOD

FELDMAN, SETH R., *Dziga Vertov: A Guide to References and Resources.* Boston: G. K. Hall & Co., 1979. 232 pp.

FELDMAN, SETH R., *Evolution of Style in the Early Work of Dziga Vertov.* New York: Arno Press, 1977.

LEYDA, JAY, *Kino: A History of the Russian and Soviet Film.* New York: Macmillan Co., 1983. 513 pp.

FOUR
BEGINNINGS
European Avant-Gardists and Artistic Experimentation, 1922–1929

It is a curious historical coincidence that at almost exactly the same time, Flaherty in America (*Nanook of the North*) and Vertov in Russia ("Kino Pravda") began laying the groundwork for documentary, and the avant-garde film was starting in Western Europe. Thus the three main aesthetic impulses of film art, its three principal modes—narrative fiction, documentary, experimental—were established by the early twenties. Documentary and avant-garde both emerged out of rebellion against the fiction film, which had become the predominant artistic as well as commercial form.

AESTHETIC PREDISPOSITIONS

The two new artistic tendencies had one thing in common. Their devotees viewed the conventions of the fiction film as limited and limiting. Someone once remarked that the Hollywood movie was like playing a grand piano with one finger. The documentarists and avant-gardists shared a desire to explore more fully the capacities of film as medium—to do what only film could do, or only what film could do best. They wanted to create films different from literary stories told through the theatrical means of actors and sets. They agreed that the fiction film was telling lies about life. They did not agree about much else. For the documentarists, conventional fiction films were not realistic enough; for the avant-gardists, they were too realistic. The former wanted external (objective) facts presented accurately; the latter wanted formal (aesthetic) patterns and inner (subjective) truths presented poetically.

The creative predilection of the documentarians extended out of the detailed accuracy the photographic image offered; the addition of motion in the cinematographic image permitted the recording of yet more of reality, more than was possible in any other means of communication or form of art. In the motion picture, material and physical life could be captured as it was being lived. The *actualités* of Louis Lumière (*Workers Leaving the Factory,* 1895) were the filmic antecedents of the documentary.

The avant-gardists extended out of modern painting. They valued the movement of the moving picture for allowing their visual imagery to become more complex and consistent with twentieth-century conceptions of time as a fourth dimension. In addition, movement enabled the avant-gardists to follow the workings of the mind into dreams, fantasies, and hallucinations, which jumble an incongruous succession of images in a stream of consciousness. Through film they could present abstract patterns in movement or represent a dream-like perception. Their filmic precursor was Georges Méliès (*A Trip to the Moon,* 1902), who offered the marvelous, decorative and painterly world of set-designer's unreality and magician's illusion.

In the traditional arts the interrelationship of space and time was already being explored. In painting, Marcel Duchamp's "Nude Descending a Staircase" (1912) offered an abstracted, stroboscopic view of a person and her activity. The abstraction of cubism, Pablo Picasso's "The Violin" (1913), for example, rests on the idea of an observer moving about to view a subject from various distances and angles. The separate views are then overlaid to try to suggest looking at the subject from different positions all at once. In literature, Marcel Proust, in his multi-volume *Remembrance of Things Past* (1919 to 1925), assumes that the past is always present and that places experienced earlier join with places experienced later. James Joyce, in *Ulysses* (1922), intermingles what is happening to his characters in various parts of Dublin on June 16, 1904, cutting back and forth among them as a filmmaker would, to try to convey a sense of simultaneity and interaction of events and persons.

AVANT-GARDE AND DOCUMENTARY

The first of the avant-garde films were along lines of abstractionism and nonobjectivism. In 1921 two painter friends living in Berlin each began work on short films that might be thought of as the beginning of European avant-garde cinema. Influenced by such aesthetic movements as futurism and cubism, Viking Eggeling, a Swede, and Hans Richter, a German, had been attempting to bring a sense of movement approximating animation into their paintings. Their preoccupations led them from picture scrolls to the motion picture, and Richter's *Rhythmus 21* (1921) and Eggeling's *Diagonal Symphony* (1925) were the result. "Rhythm in painting" is what they said they were after. Richter's film comprises an interacting set of square and rectangular shapes in white, gray, and black; as they change sizes, they seem to move toward or away from the viewer. Eggeling's consists of white abstractions shaped like lyres in shifting relationships with each other against a black screen. These two films might make one think of Piet Mondrian paintings in motion.

Sometimes Mondrian's nonrepresentational, geometric canvases resemble aerial photographs of a city taken from extremely high altitudes so that all we see is the grid of the streets, a block of color that may be a park, and so on. In 1921 two Americans, Charles Sheeler and Paul Strand—the first a painter, the second a photographer—made a film that offered a somewhat similar view of New York City. In their *Mannahatta,* shot mostly looking down from skyscrapers, the city becomes abstract. The streets and buildings appear as patterns of light and shadow. The people, flattened and seen at great distance, exist only as part of the design. Though shown very little in the United States, *Mannahatta* appeared in Paris in a Dadaist program that included music by Erik Satie and poems by Guillaume Apollinaire. It is said to have received an ovation on that occasion,[1] and might be thought of as an embryonic beginning of the "city symphony" films that link avant-garde with documentary and are the main subject of this chapter.

A seminal film that might be added to the works of Richter, Eggeling, Sheeler, and Strand is one by the French painter Fernand Léger. With the technical assistance of an American named Dudley Murphy, Léger made *Le Ballet Mécanique* (1924), exploring the rhythmic relationships of images in motion. In it, the capacity of film for mechanical repetition and its power to animate the inanimate (kitchen utensils, mannequin legs, Christmas ornaments, bottles, printed words, and geometric shapes) are strikingly exploited.[2] Marcel Duchamp's *Anemic Cinema* (1926) is somewhat similar in its intentions.

The second line of avant-garde creation was inspired by psychoanalysis and gave rise to the aesthetic *ism* of surrealism, with its preoccupations rooted in dream and the unconscious. In painting, Salvador Dali, who subsequently worked briefly in film, painted in the surrealist manner. This generally involved more or less realistic representations of objects and persons placed in strange juxtapositions with each other. In literature Proust also relates to this psychoanalytic tendency, with the past affecting the present, as does Joyce, in *Ulysses,* especially in the use of stream of consciousness and in the Nighttown dream play. In film Luis Buñuel's and Salvador Dali's *Un*

Chien Andalou (1929), Buñuel's *L'Age D'or* (1930), and Jean Cocteau's *The Blood of a Poet* (1930) are celebrated examples of these dreamscapes.

Even among Rotha's realist (continental) precursors of documentary there are evidences of these two avant-garde styles. Abstractionism appears in Joris Ivens's first significant film, *The Bridge* (1928). It is related to modernist movements like cubism, futurism, and constructivism. Like much of the later Vertov, whose work influenced Ivens, *The Bridge* converts machinery into art. Camera composition and movement, and edited relationships of shots are designed to bring out the functional and also aesthetic essence of an enormous railway bridge in Rotterdam. There are few people in the film—a workman climbing a ladder and a bridge tender answering a phone and starting machinery that raises and lowers the bridge—and it ends with animated squares à la Richter's *Rhythmus 21.*

Surrealism might be thought evident in Jean Vigo's *Jean Taris, champion de natation* (1931). This study of the aquatic style of a famous French swimmer is notable for its beautiful underwater cinematography in slow motion and a dive back out of the pool at the end. Jean Lods's *Le Mile* (1934), about a runner, employs "ether music," slow motion, and superimpositions. Buñuel's *Land Without Bread* (1932) forces us to look at a devastating reality, the poverty of the Las Hurdes region of Spain, in a way that might be described as having the intense irrational reality of a dream—that is, of being *sur*real.

But it was a third line of avant-garde filmmaking, developing near the

A youthful Joris Ivens with editing equipment used at the time. Museum of Modern Art/Film Stills Archive.

end of the twenties, that fed most directly into documentary. Its aesthetic *ism* was impressionism, and its origins went back to the French impressionist painters at the turn of the century. The style of impressionism also placed emphasis on the space/time relationship; impressionist painting was like looking at life from a fast-moving railway carriage, it had been said. (Of course film provided this actual opportunity; see, for example, Jean Mitry's impressionist *Pacific 231*, 1949, about a powerful locomotive rushing through the French countryside.) The impressionist films resemble the earlier paintings through their quick views and concentration on surfaces and light. What they offer mainly are collected glimpses of city life through a passage of time. Joyce's *Ulysses* might again be thought of as a literary precedent. Eisenstein wrote of that novel, "What Joyce does with literature is quite close to what we're doing with the new cinematography, and even closer to what we're going to do."[3] He further said that if *Ulysses* were ever made into a film, the only men capable of directing it would be Walter Ruttmann or Sergei Eisenstein.[4]

Eisenstein's qualifications for such an assignment were discussed in Chapter Three. Ruttmann directed one of the early "city symphonies," *Berlin: Symphony of a Great City* (1927). It was preceded slightly by *Rien que les heures* (Only the Hours, 1926), about Paris, directed by Alberto Cavalcanti. *Rain* (1929), Joris Ivens's film about Amsterdam, followed. In the space remaining I would like to concentrate on these three seminal works: *Rien que les heures, Berlin,* and *Rain.* At the same time it must be acknowledged that the line they started includes Jean Vigo's À *propos de Nice* (1930), a scathingly satirical study of the famous resort in the manner of Honoré Daumier paintings, Ralph Steiner's and Willard Van Dyke's *The City* (U.S., 1939), to be dealt with in Chapter Six, Arne Sucksdorff's *People of the City* (1947), about Stockholm, and John Eldridge's *Waverly Steps* (1948), about Edinburgh. Many other films could be added to this list.

THREE CITY SYMPHONIES

Alberto Cavalcanti was a Brazilian emigré who became part of the Paris avant-garde in the early 1920s. He began his film career as an innovative set designer for Marcel L'Herbier on such features as *L'Inhumaine* (1923), in collaboration with Fernand Léger, and *The Late Matthew Pascal* (1925), in collaboration with Lazare Meerson.

Rien que les heures is a curious and fascinating mixture of the aesthetic and the social. It deals with Paris from predawn to well into the following night—roughly twenty-four hours. Opening titles promise that we will not be looking at the elegant life but rather at that of the lower classes. Thus the social viewpoint is established. But a philosophical thesis about time and space is also introduced and returned to. At the end we are asked, after we have seen what the filmmaker can show us of Paris, to consider simultaneously Paris in relation to Peking (Beijing). The titles assert that, though we can fix a point in space, immobilize a moment in time, both space and time escape our possession, that life is ongoing and interrelated, and that, without their monuments, cities cannot be told apart.

Mainly the film is devoted to contrasting scenes and changing activities of Paris during the passing hours. In early morning we see all-night revelers still out on deserted streets with the first workers appearing; later, workers at labor; then lunchtime. In the afternoon some people are swimming; work ceases, rest and recreation occupy the evening. Among the views of unstaged actuality are brief, staged fragments. Three slight narratives are developed. The protagonists of all three are female—an old derelict (drunken or ill), a prostitute, a newspaper vendor—all of them pathetic figures. The overall mood of the film seems to me a bit downbeat; there is a sweet sadness, a sentimental toughness about it.

Still, Cavalcanti's viewpoint seems to be one of detachment, perhaps cynicism: "*c'est la vie*," he seems to be saying. Though some concern with social matters is evident, the considerable number and variety of highly stylized special effects—wipes, rapid match dissolves, multiple exposures, fast motion, spinning images, split screens, freeze frames—seem to confirm that Cavalcanti's greatest interest was in artistic experimentation.

Like Cavalcanti, Walter Ruttmann came out of architecture and painting to avant-garde filmmaking in the early 1920s—specifically, in his case, to abstract, geometric forms in motion like those of his mentor, Viking

Rien que les heures (France, 1926, Alberto Cavalcanti). Museum of Modern Art/Film Stills Archive.

Eggeling. A fascination with design is even more evident in *Berlin: Symphony of a Great City* than in *Rien que les heures;* and, incidentally, the former was released so close after the latter that there can be little question of one influencing the other. Unlike *Rien, Berlin* emerged from mainstream commercial cinema. Produced for Fox-Europa Film, its scenario was written by Ruttman and Karl Freund, based on an idea by Carl Mayer. (Mayer had written scripts for *The Cabinet of Dr. Caligari,* 1919; *The Last Laugh,* 1924; *Tartuffe,* 1925; and other notable German silent features.) The cinematography was supervised by Freund (who also had worked on some of the great fiction films of the period including *The Golem,* 1920; *The Last Laugh,* 1924; *Variety,* 1925; and *Metropolis,* 1927; three camera operators are credited. Original music was composed by Edmund Meisel (who had composed a famous score for the German exhibition of *Potemkin*). The editing was done by Ruttmann. Though the camerawork of *Berlin* is dazzling, it is above all an editor's film and Ruttmann is credited as director. We see Berlin, true enough, but it is Ruttmann's Berlin that we see.

The overall organizational basis is temporal; occasionally clocks show the time: 5:00, 8:00, 12:00. The major sequences comprise very early morning (the city coming to life), morning (work and general activity), lunchtime (eating and repose), afternoon (work ceases, recreation takes place), and evening (entertainment and various sorts of diversions). Intertitles indicate "acts" up through four (though a fifth would seem to be intended), but they are much less clearly structured than the five acts of *Potemkin* or *Turksib.*

The criteria for selection and arrangement of material within these acts rests heavily on visual similarities and contrasts. Ruttmann is fascinated with the way things are shaped, the way they move. At any given time the organizing principle may be kinetic (things going up, things coming down; things opening, things closing) or shapes that look alike (people walking in a crowd, a herd of cattle moving, soldiers marching).

There are also topical groupings: workers going to work; children going to school; women cleaning and scrubbing; the various means of transport; people eating lunch; animals feeding at the zoo. The pattern for each scene or subsection within the major sequences/acts is frequently that of an activity starting, increasing in tempo, then coming to a halt. The people are treated much as the objects; both are subjects for visual examination.

Some of the action is staged: a group of merrymakers in the early morning returning from a party; an argument between two men with a crowd gathering; a woman jumping from a bridge to drown, apparently. But mostly life is caught unawares. Much influenced by Vertov, Ruttmann did not follow Vertov's dictum about advancing a social point of view, though at the time he was identified with the political left.

In *Berlin* the rich and powerful are seen in contrast to members of the working classes but no social comment is made. Much less attention is paid to individual persons in *Berlin* than in "Kino Pravda." Machines are as important for Ruttmann as they are for the Soviets, but in *Berlin* they are not shown to have social utility as they are in *Turksib*. Instead, they exist as fascinating, intricate, moving objects. The film's opening proceeds from abstractions of water to what look like polarized images of fast-moving locomotive wheels and railroad tracks beginning a protracted, elaborately cut evocation of a train's early morning approach to a Berlin terminus, which climaxes in a huge closeup on one of the engine's stationary piston wheels after its arrival. Later, the image of a typewriter keyboard is set spinning and metamorphoses into a whirling animated design. *Berlin* strikes most viewers as brilliant and cold, an exercise in cinematic virtuosity.

The exclusively aesthetic preoccupation of Ruttmann represented a severe limitation not only from the Soviet point of view but from that of

A collage of images from *Berlin: Symphony of a Great City* (Germany, 1927, Walter Ruttmann). Museum of Modern Art/Film Stills Archive.

subsequent British documentarians. *Berlin* may, however, have more value as a *document* than do those *documentary* films made with more explicit social biases and programs. What it offers is a visual description composed according to artistic insights and intuitions and the requirements of form. As a result of this film we can know a great deal about the appearance of life in Berlin in 1927.

Joris Ivens, like Louis Lumière, came out of the photographic business. His grandfather was a pioneer Dutch photographer; his father owned a chain of camera shops. After serving an apprenticeship at the Zeiss camera factories in Germany, Ivens returned to Holland in 1926 to become manager of his father's Amsterdam branch.

His *Rain* (1929) is a short, like *The Bridge* (both run 10 to 15 minutes) and unlike *Rien* or *Berlin,* which are short features (45 and 70 minutes, respectively). Perhaps *Rain* is a city sonata. It presents Amsterdam just before, during, and immediately after a shower. Ivens's play with light and shadow and the compositional relationships of shots becomes much more important than in *The Bridge. Rain* is impressionist rather than cubist; lyrical rather than analytical. Its shapes and textures tend to be round and soft rather than straight and hard. It seems a very tactile film.

Rain begins with shots of canals and harbor, roofs, sky, an airplane, streetcar and traffic, sheets hanging on clotheslines, and awnings. The first person we see extends his hand, palm up, to feel rain drops, then turns up

Rain (Holland, 1929, Joris Ivens). Museum of Modern Art/Film Stills Archive.

his coat collar. An umbrella is opened; a window is closed. Throughout, Ivens seems to be asking us to examine images in everyday life—rain on windshields, puddles in streets, umbrellas, reflections—to see the "artistic" in the actual. Fernand Léger once observed, that before the invention of the moving picture no one knew the possibilities latent in a foot, a hand, or a hat. Ivens makes of something as commonplace as an umbrella or a bare window a thing of uncommon beauty and significance.

END OF THE AVANT-GARDE

The avant-garde was killed in part by the expensiveness, complexity, and cumbersomeness of motion picture sound, added in the late 1920s. It was no longer possible for individuals or groups of friends to shoot on weekends, recording images as they found or created them, cutting them together in the evenings using only a pair of rewinds and a splicer, and screening the completed film at a local ciné-club. Now the big studios, with sound stages and synchronous sound recording apparatus, exercised complete domination, not only over production, but over distribution and exhibition as well.

Perhaps at least as contributive to the death of the avant-garde were changing intellectual and artistic interests and attitudes. If the twenties were "roaring" and frivolous, they also nurtured aesthetic innovation. The notion of art for the sake of art, with emphasis on formal experimentation, prevailed in influential circles. The intellectual preoccupations of the thirties, in contrast, were markedly social and political. This decade included a worldwide depression, the rise of fascism, and other misfortunes that culminated in a second world war. In the thirties, art for the sake of society became a rallying cry, and the documentary film replaced the avant-garde film at the center of social and artistic life in many countries.

Before making *Rain*, Joris Ivens had been involved in the politics of the international student movement and had participated in workers' demonstrations, which strengthened his leftward leanings. In his subsequent films Ivens moved away from formal experimentation towards social problems posed in a realistic style. In 1929 and 1932 he visited the Soviet Union. From that point on his films would be made in support of projects on the political left. His work will be encountered again in subsequent chapters, especially Chapter Six.

Ruttmann, too, moved from the avant-garde to the political, but in a different direction. In the late 1930s he lent his talents to the Nazi propaganda ministry. He served as adviser to Leni Riefenstahl on the editing of her *Olympia* (1938), which celebrated the Olympic games held in Berlin in 1936 and subtly supported certain aspects of Nazi mythology. In 1940 Ruttmann made *Deutsche Panzer* (German Tanks) and recorded on film the German occupation of France. The following year he was killed while covering the Russian front for a newsreel.

But of the three city symphonists, Alberto Cavalcanti is the most neatly symbolic figure of transition. He moved from the French avant-garde of the 1920s to the British documentary of the 1930s. Cavalcanti's documentary work will be dealt with in the next chapter.

In concluding this chapter let me make two points about the relationship between British documentary and the avant-garde. One is that in its time, British documentary was considered avant-garde too, and included much experimentation with new forms and techniques as well as with new subjects and purposes. The second is that if it is thought of as an artistic movement, as it can be, British documentary is remarkable within the history of art movements for lasting some twenty years, its influence spreading and extending down to this day. The formal experimentation was encouraged partly to attract artistically talented young persons to documentary filmmaking, and partly to find ways in which social arguments could be made most appealing and convincing. British documentary continued the avant-garde experimentation with shapes in movement; the emphasis of the Soviets and the avant-gardists on machines persisted in Britain. While the addition of sound helped end the avant-garde, it increased the potency of documentary; spoken commentary became one of its hallmarks. British documentary led the way in the creative use of sound in relation to image.

NOTES

[1]Lewis Jacobs, ed., *The Documentary Tradition* (New York: W.W. Norton & Company, 1979), p. 7.

[2]Bruce Jenkins, "The Films of Hollis Frampton: A Critical Study" (Ph.D. dissertation, Northwestern University, 1984), p. 215.

[3]A letter from Sergei Eisenstein to Léon Moussinac published in the latter's *Sergei Eisenstein* (New York: Crown Publishers, Inc., 1970), p. 148.

[4]Marie Seton, *Sergei M. Eisenstein* (New York: A.A. Wyn, Inc., n.d.), p. 149.

FILMS OF THE PERIOD

1921
Mannahatta (U.S., Charles Sheeler and Paul Strand)

1926
Melody of the World (Germany, Walter Ruttmann)
Ménilmontant (France, Dimitri Kirsanoff)
Rien que les heures (France, Alberto Cavalcanti)

1927
Berlin: Symphony of a Great City (Germany, Ruttmann)
The Bridge (Holland, Joris Ivens)

1928
La Tour (The Eiffel Tower; France, René Clair)
La Zone (France, Georges Lacombe)

1929
Finis Terrae (France, Jean Epstein)
Rain (Holland, Ivens)

BOOKS ON THE PERIOD

BÖKER, CARLOS, *Joris Ivens, Film-Maker: Facing Reality*. Ann Arbor, Mich.: UMI Research Press, 1981. 222 pp.

DELMAR, ROSALIND, *Joris Ivens: 50 years of film-making*. London: British Film Institute, 1979. 127 pp.

IVENS, JORIS, *Joris Ivens: The Camera and I*. New York: International Publishers, 1969. 280 pp.

MANVELL, ROGER, ed., *Experiment in the Film*. London: The Grey Walls Press Limited, 1949. 285 pp.

FIVE
INSTITUTIONALIZATION
Great Britain, 1929–1939

While documentary filmmaking was beginning in the 1920s—in America, with films about tribal societies (*Nanook of the North* and *Grass*); in the Soviet Union, with indoctrinational newsreels ("Kino Pravda") and epics (*The Fall of the Romanov Dynasty* and *Turksib*); and in Western Europe, with the city symphonies (*Rien que les heures* and *Berlin: Symphony of a Great City*)—the conceptual origins of British documentary were also taking shape. But not in Britain, and not in film. John Grierson later remarked that "The idea of documentary in its present form came originally not from the film people at all, but from the Political Science school in Chicago University round about the early twenties."[1]

BACKGROUND AND UNDERPINNINGS

Grierson, founder and leader of the British documentary movement, was a Scot. Born in 1898 and raised near Stirling, he was strongly influenced from an early age by the Scottish labor movement and what was then called "Clydeside socialism," emanating from the working-class district along the Clyde River in Glasgow. Most of World War I he spent in the Navy. When he was mustered out in 1919 he entered Glasgow University with other re-turning veterans.

Upon graduation in 1923 Grierson taught briefly in Newcastle-on-Tyne. While there he obtained a Rockefeller fellowship to pursue postgrad-uate research into public opinion and the mass media in the United States. He set sail for America in 1924.

He had chosen the University of Chicago as his base because of its distinguished social science faculty. He also knew and admired the work of Chicago writers like Carl Sandburg, Vachel Lindsay, and Sherwood Ander-son. He was fascinated by the newness and originality of American culture and the ways in which Europeans were being changed into Americans.

This assimilation of foreign immigrants into American culture, and the role the popular press played in their education, occupied much of Grierson's attention. He spent more time on Halsted Street, with its poly-glot population of Germans, Italians, Greeks, Russians, and Poles, than on the Midway campus of the university, he liked to say. As Grierson came to understand the matter, the tabloid newspapers—the "Hearst press" or "yel-low press" as they were called—provided more of these foreigners' educa-tion into citizenship than did the schools, churches, or government.

A book that strongly influenced his thinking at the time was Walter Lippmann's *Public Opinion,* published in 1922. In it Lippmann described how the earlier ideals of Jeffersonian democracy had been rendered inop-erative. Originally the Virginia gentleman, sitting on his veranda reading the two-week-old newspaper brought by packet from Philadelphia, could make up his mind about the issues facing the nation and vote for someone running for public office who would represent his views. Since that time government had gotten big, distant, and complex. The citizen, feeling he could not keep abreast of the information necessary to participate in the decision-making process, had disassociated himself from government. Lipp-mann thought education was the only solution to the problem, but that it was too late for it to take effect in time to keep the democratic system viable. Grierson postulated that what was needed was to involve citizens in their government with the kind of engaging excitement generated by the popular press, which simplified and dramatized public affairs.

As he traveled around the country, Grierson eventually met Lipp-mann. It was Lippmann, Grierson frequently acknowledged, who suggested to him that, rather than the press, he look into the movies. Perhaps they were the form best suited to turn citizens' attention to the decisions that needed to be made in common, and to provide them with a basic education in the factors to be considered.

Clearly the entertainment film was not readily available for these pur-poses. Two filmmakers and films not part of the Hollywood industry sug-gested to Grierson a way to harness the motion picture to the job of educating citizens. One filmmaker was Sergei Eisenstein. Though Grierson would not meet Eisenstein until a few years later, he did gain intimate knowledge of and respect for his *Potemkin* (1925) by helping prepare it for American release. The other filmmaker, Robert Flaherty, Grierson met sometime in 1925. It was to Flaherty's second film, *Moana* (1926), that he first applied the term documentary.

When Grierson returned to England in 1927 he approached another man who would become enormously important in the development of documentary: Stephen (later Sir Stephen) Tallents, Secretary of the Empire Marketing Board. The EMB had been established in 1926 to promote the marketing of products of the British Empire and to encourage research and development among the member states. The broader purpose implicit from the outset was to substitute for the decaying military and political ties of empire the economic ones of a commonwealth of nations. Tallents saw quickly that the motion picture might be a valuable tool in this new and unique governmental public relations endeavor, and that Grierson was exceptionally well qualified to initiate its use.

Employed at first in an unofficial advisory capacity, Grierson surveyed and reported on the use of film by governments abroad. He also set up for EMB personnel screenings of films that seemed to him to provide some suggestions for what would become the documentary film. Along with straight informational and instructional shorts, there were the features of Flaherty, with their detail of the life of traditional cultures. There were the films of the Soviets, which dramatized revolutionary events in order to indoctrinate and educate the Russian people. There were the Hollywood superwesterns, *The Covered Wagon* and *The Iron Horse,* for example, which had attracted Grierson's attention as offering a kind of American screen epic. And, finally, there were the city symphonies of the European avant-garde, which made impressionist art out of urban realities.

THE SYSTEM

Empire Marketing Board

Following Grierson's research into film activities of other governments and the EMB screenings, he and Tallents succeeded in talking the Department of Treasury into backing production of a film by the Empire Marketing Board. *Drifters* (1929) was the result, written, produced, directed, and edited by Grierson. A short feature in length, it dealt with herring fishing in the North Sea. Rather than follow its substantial success with another and then another film of his own, as he certainly might have done, Grierson chose to establish a collective filmmaking enterprise, a sort of workshop and schoolhouse, out of which the British documentary movement would emerge.

In 1930 the Empire Marketing Board Film Unit was established with Grierson as its head. During the four years of its existence it made over one hundred films. Two of them still in active distribution will be discussed later.

Grierson's catchphrase for what the EMB films were designed to do was "to bring the Empire alive." He pursued this purpose by showing one and then another part of the Empire (one region of Britain, one of its colonies, one of its industries) to the rest. He hoped that films of this sort would help citizens of the Empire to more fully understand and appreciate each other, to perceive their interdependencies and value them, and to create a better functioning, more coherent civic whole.

In the production of the EMB films Grierson involved dozens of young people, mostly upper middle class and well educated (many at Cambridge University), who were used to being listened to, as Grierson once put it. They learned not only filmmaking but the sort of social commitment that motivated Grierson. What he wanted films to do was to make the state and the society function better. He thought that collective effort, cooperation, and understanding could lead to a better world—not only better food and better housing, better teeth and better schools, but a better spirit—a sense of being part of a valuable society with room still left for individual satisfactions and eccentricities.

Those who came through this informal but rigorous schooling begun at the Empire Marketing Board included, roughly in the order of their hiring, Basil Wright, Arthur Elton, Edgar Anstey, and Paul Rotha. Stuart Legg and Harry Watt came later, as did Humphrey Jennings. Alberto Cavalcanti joined the group as a sort of co–producer and co–teacher with Grierson. They were paid so little it was laughable, or perhaps weepable at the time, but they were caught up in the excitement of art put to social use. Each had special talents and interests: Wright's were poetic, Elton's technological and scientific, Legg's political, and so on. After absorbing what Grierson had to offer and developing deep and lasting loyalties to his causes and to himself, they could (and did) move out into the world filming for other sponsors, forming other units, training other filmmakers, while still working in common cause.

Concerned with creating filmmakers, Grierson was also concerned with creating audiences for his kind of film. Though documentaries were shown in theaters, theatrical showings were limited. The film industry resisted government filmmaking; distributors and exhibitors said the public didn't want documentaries. In answer, Grierson developed a method of nontheatrical distribution and exhibition. It began with afternoon screenings at the Imperial Institute in London, expanded to include the Empire Film Library for the free loan of 16mm films by mail, and, later, at the General Post Office, came to include traveling projection vans going out into the countryside.

In order to build audience support, film critics on the major papers were recruited in behalf of the movement and Grierson and his colleagues wrote and lectured tirelessly. They were instrumental in founding and guiding three successive journals—*Cinema Quarterly, World Film News,* and *Documentary News Letter*—that served as house organs for documentary.

If Grierson didn't do it all himself, it was mainly his leadership and his manifold activities that brought British documentary into being and caused it to last and grow in its influence. The movement developed a powerful, coherent energy, with Grierson able to direct, to a remarkable extent, the uses to which that energy was put.

General Post Office

In 1933, at the depth of the Depression, the Empire Marketing Board was terminated on grounds of necessary government economy. Tallents moved to the General Post Office as its first public relations officer, on condition that he could bring the EMB Film Unit and the Film Library with him. When the film unit moved to the General Post Office, the new institutional needs were to show government services that provided the means of modern communication. Specifically, the films were designed to increase

John Grierson in the 1930s. Museum of Modern Art/Film Stills Archive.

respect for the work of the GPO, by the population at large and by the GPO workers themselves.

A vast enterprise, the GPO handled not only the mail but the telephone, wireless broadcasting, a savings bank, and a whole host of government services. Here the subjects of the films were reduced from the exoticism and drama inherent in the far-flung reaches of the empire available at the Empire Marketing Board to such subjects as the picayune detail of mail delivery (*Six-Thirty Collection,* 1934; *Night Mail,* 1936). "One remembers looking at a sorting office for the first time," wrote Grierson, "and thinking that when you had seen one letter you had seen the lot."[2]

The drama was found, though sometimes by stretching beyond what might properly seem post office concerns (*The Song of Ceylon,* 1934; *Coal Face,* 1935). Out of the more than one hundred films made by the General Post Office Film Unit came some lovely and lasting ones. Major British documentaries of the thirties will be discussed shortly.

Private Sponsorship

Grierson became restive within the restrictions of governmental budgets and departmental requirements. He began to reach out into private industry as an additional source of funding. He must have been remarkably persuasive in talking industrial leaders into taking his own broad view. Not only did he find sponsors, he convinced them to eschew advertising in favor of public relations. This meant backing films in the public interest—that is to say, films whose subjects Grierson thought needed attention. The oil industry was especially receptive.

Out of a report Grierson made for Shell International on the potential uses of film came the Shell Film Unit, highly respected for its films on scientific and technological subjects. Edgar Anstey was first head of the Shell Unit. He was succeeded by Arthur Elton, who maintained a lifelong connection with films sponsored by the oil industry and developed great skill as a maker of expository films on technical subjects.

Grierson succeeded in getting the gas industry to back an annual film program. The group of films resulting were intended to increase general awareness of problems of pressing concern, to provoke discussion of them, and to suggest attitudes that might contribute to their solutions (*Housing Problems,* 1935; *Enough to Eat?,* 1936). Some of them will be discussed in the following section.

With documentary growing apace, private units were being set up by Grierson alumni to make films for the emerging nongovernment sponsors. In 1937 Grierson resigned from the GPO to set up a central coordinating and advisory agency to put sponsors in touch with producers (and the other way around), oversee production, plan promotion and distribution, and the like. Film Centre was the organization which he (with Basil Wright, Arthur Elton, Stuart Legg, and J.P.R. Golightly) established for that purpose in 1938.

The British system of documentary financing, production, and distribution became a model for subsequent developments in other countries. Many foreign visitors came to London to look into this new use of film—especially from the commonwealth nations and the colonies—and in 1937 Paul Rotha went on a six-month missionary expedition to the United States to show British documentaries and spread the documentary gospel. At the New York World's Fair of 1939 British documentaries were shown to sizeable audiences with evident success.

THE FILMS

Some sixty documentary filmmakers working within what I have called the British documentary system made over three hundred films between 1929 and 1939. Three main lines of subject/purpose/style emerged roughly in the order in which they are dealt with below. First, out of *Drifters* (1929), were the documentaries which undertook to interpret one part of the Empire—one region of Britain, one of its industries, or one part of the government services—to the population at large. Often poetic and experimental, this group included such films as *Industrial Britain* (1933), *Granton Trawler* (1934), *The Song of Ceylon* (1934), and *Coal Face* (1935).

Drifters, Grierson's first film, was the only one of the hundreds of films

Drifters (U.K., 1929, John Grierson). Museum of Modern Art/Film Stills Archive.

which he completely controlled creatively. It has a simple narrative structure. The herring fishermen board their trawlers in the harbor, sail to the North Sea banks, lay the nets, haul in the catch in the midst of a storm, and race homeward to auction the catch at quayside. Rather than evidence of creative genius, it seems to me to represent the work of a brilliant synthesist who had absorbed what was at hand to make the kind of film he wanted to see made. In it are reflections of Flaherty's *Nanook of the North,* with brave men eking out their existence in the face of the elements. Eisenstein's *Potemkin* is even more heavily called upon. In *Drifters,* the loving long takes of a Flaherty are cut up and banged together in Eisensteinian montage to provide a modern dynamism, and the individual accomplishments of Nanook are replaced by the collective efforts of a crew as in *Potemkin.*

It is unlike both models in certain respects, however. Instead of the exotics of Flaherty or the heroics of the Soviets, the drama of *Drifters* is in the everyday workaday. By ending it with the fish being sold at market, Grierson sets the fishermen's work firmly within the context of economic actualities of contemporary Britain. It was the first instance in British cinema in which work had been given this sort of importance and members of the working class presented with dignity rather than as comic relief.

Industrial Britain establishes its thesis at the outset: Though traditional ways of work have changed over the centuries, the success of British industry rests on the skill of its craftsmen. "The human fact remains, even in this machine age, the final fact," the commentator intones. To make it, Grierson invited Flaherty to England. Though given a lot of film, Flaherty shot it all

Industrial Britain (U.K., 1933, John Grierson and Robert Flaherty). National Film Archive/Stills Library.

on the lovely images of traditional craftsmen (glass blowers) and ancient crafts (pottery). The individual faces and gestures that appear ("Look at those hands," exclaims the commentator) are like *Moana* in fragments. Then an intertitle in large letters, "STEEL," advances towards us, accompanied by portentous music. This unexpectedly announces what becomes in effect a separate film, making the point of bigness, collectivity, and internationalization—clearly Grierson's contribution. If *Industrial Britain* represents the contrast between these two filmmakers' approaches, the commentator's stilted style of delivery and the clichéd stock music (including bits of Beethoven) are at odds with both. It was made before the film unit had its own sound recording facilities. Nonetheless, along with *Drifters*, *Industrial Britain* was the most successful and generally liked film to come out of the Empire Marketing Board.

Granton Trawler can be thought of as a shorter version of *Drifters*. It, too, is about herring fishing, but lyric rather than epic in its intentions and form. Grierson himself shot it on a busman's holiday in the North Sea. Edgar Anstey edited it under his supervision (as he had *Industrial Britain*). Later Cavalcanti added sound. The sound track is made up of the rhythmic thumping of the ship's engine, the creaking of its rigging, the cries of gulls, the harsh metallic sound of a winch playing out cable, muffled shouts of the men as they pull the nets, a repeated fragment of a plaintive tune played on an accordion and another whistled, and random and mostly unintelligi-

Granton Trawler (U.K., 1934, John Grierson). Museum of Modern Art/Film Stills Archive.

ble comments from members of the crew. There is no commentary. The sounds were all postrecorded, imitated in fact, in the studio. (One of the "fishermen's" voices is Grierson's.)

Simple as it is, the track strikes me as a remarkably strong component of the picture. This montage of seemingly natural sounds arbitrarily modified and arranged is what would come to be called *musique concrète*. Not only was it an aesthetic experiment ahead of its time, it represents the kind of poetry that can be achieved by a stylized rendering of reality completely controlled by the creator(s). Sounds are laid over a succession of impressionistic views of parts of the ship, the fishermen's activities, and the shifting horizon which becomes vertiginous in high seas. It is as if the makers of the film, and therefore the viewers, were standing on the trawler looking about as their eyes are led to one thing or another while their ears register certain sounds.

The Song of Ceylon, mainly Basil Wright's creation, is one of the accepted masterpieces of British documentary. Sponsored by the Ceylon Tea Propaganda Board, it is remarkable in being so fully and freely a work of art while doing so little to sell the sponsor's product, perhaps even subverting their main goals. *The Song of Ceylon* is remarkable, too, within the canon of British documentary, as a highly personal work and one which emphasizes matters of the spirit. It is a moving hymn to a native people, their work, their ways, and their values in conflict with the imposed requirements of modern commerce.

The Song of Ceylon (U.K., 1934, Basil Wright). Museum of Modern Art/Film Stills Archive.

Formally, in aesthetic terms, *Song of Ceylon* is the most complex and sophisticated artwork of the British documentary of the 1930s. Though it contains exquisite images of a golden time and place, not unlike those of Flaherty's Samoa in *Moana* (1926), Wright's discovered Eden has a discordant sound to it.

The commentary is drawn from a book on Ceylon written by the traveler Robert Knox in 1680. It provides an appreciative description of traditional life, which we see and also hear in reverberating gongs, native music, and rhythmic chanting to the dancing. In the third sequence, entitled "The Voices of Commerce," the discord erupts. Images of the native and traditional are here accompanied by deep whistles of seagoing freighters, Morse code beeping on the wireless, English voices dictating business letters and listing stock market quotations. This medley of sound, plus a musical score suggesting an Eastern modality, composed and conducted by Walter Leigh, was supervised by Cavalcanti. Wright, Leigh, Cavalcanti, and Grierson, to one extent or another, were all involved in the creation of the whole, which can astonish and delight audiences today as much as it did when first shown.

Coal Face, mainly Cavalcanti's creation, continued the formal experimentation with sound in relation to sight, though this time as an exalted tribute to the lives of British miners. Added to Grierson and Cavalcanti on its crew were the poet W.H. Auden and the composer Benjamin Britten, who worked together and separately on subsequent documentaries. *Coal Face* is an evocative combination of factual information laid over lovely im-

Coal Face (U.K., 1935, Alberto Cavalcanti). Museum of Modern Art/Film Stills Archive.

ages drawn from the coal mining regions, of modern discordant music with piano and percussion prominent, of choral speech which at one point ascends into a kind of keening, and of snatches of miners' talk and whistling. The drabness, hardship, and sad poetry of the men's lives, along with their resilience, courage, and dignity, are presented—especially in the poetry of Auden recited and sung by the women's chorus. The commentary ends with the statement "Coal mining is the basic industry of Britain." The last images we see are of an individual miner walking against a background of mining village and pithead at evening.

The second line of British documentary, which began in the mid-thirties, consisted of calling public attention to pressing problems faced by the nation, of insistence that these problems needed to be solved, and of suggestions about their causes and possible solutions. These matters sometimes involved differing political positions and in any case did not relate directly to the concerns of the General Post Office. To produce such films Grierson stepped outside the GPO to enlist sponsorship from large private industries. The subjects included slums (*Housing Problems,* 1935), malnutrition among the poor (*Enough to Eat?,* 1936), smog (*The Smoke Menace,* 1937), and education (*Children at School,* 1937). They consisted of reportage and argument. Sometimes compiled from stock shots and newsreel footage, they were given coherence and rhetorical effectiveness through editing and voice-over commentary.

Unlike the earlier British documentaries, these films are journalistic rather than poetic; they seem quite inartistic, in fact. Yet they incorporate formal and technical experiments. Most notable among these is the direct interview—with slum dwellers in *Housing Problems,* for example—presaging the much later cinéma-vérité method.

Sponsored by the British Commercial Gas Association, *Housing Problems* was made by Arthur Elton, Edgar Anstey, John Taylor, and Ruby Grierson. It begins with the problems and what they look like—"a typical interior of a decayed house"—with a housing expert commenting (voice-over) on how badly the housing functions. Then the film commentator (also voice-over) says "And now for the people who have to live in the slums." The man on camera (no interviewer appears; the interviewees talk directly to the camera) says that they "haven't room to swing a cat around," and describes how uncomfortable and unhealthy his apartment is; two of his children have died. A Mrs. Hill tells us "the vermin in the walls is wicked" (shots of cockroaches crawling on walls are cut in) "and I tell ye we're fed up!"

The commentator says "The more enlightened public authorities have been applying themselves to clearing away slums with energy." We see models of new types of housing, one of them of a housing development at Leeds. "And now let's have a word with Mrs. Reddington," who is living in one of the new housing developments. She tells us how pleased her family is with their new housing; they especially like the new bathroom.

Housing Problems (U.K., 1935, Arthur Elton and Edgar Anstey). Museum of Modern Art/ Film Stills Archive.

Set forth in this bold way *Housing Problems* may not strike you as the innovation it was. Its combination of voice-over housing authority and film commentator with onscreen interviews, of stock footage with models and fresh-shot footage, established the basic format and technique of much television documentary today. The spoken word is used to provide information and analysis and to allow persons to reveal themselves more fully and colorfully than was altogether possible in silent film. The intentions of *Housing Problems* and certainly its effect are quite different from those of *Nanook*. "Kino Pravda," on the other hand, would have benefitted from spoken commentary and spontaneous dialogue.

Shortly after *Housing Problems, Night Mail* (1936) started a third trend, the narrative. Cavalcanti and Harry Watt were the leaders in this new tendency. Watt would go on in a direct line of increasing narrative elements. In *The Saving of Bill Blewitt* (1937), he shaped documentary ingredients of locating shooting, nonactors, and sponsor's message into plot, character, and theme. With *North Sea* (1938) he reached a peacetime height in realistic use of story. This line led to the British semidocumentary feature, a fusion of fact and fiction. Essentially a contribution of the 1940s, it is dealt with in Chapters Seven and Ten. Judging from the evidence of Watt's subsequent films, it is his directorial style that is dominant in *Night Mail,* though he shares director's credit with Basil Wright.

Night Mail is the most celebrated of Watt's prewar films. Recording the journey of a postal train from London to Glasgow, it is an example of "drama on the doorstep," to use a Grierson phrase—everyday and close to home, yet lovely and lasting. It may be the ultimate blend of Grierson's ethic (social purposes) and aesthetic (formal properties). It is a paradigm of propaganda so entertwined with art that the viewer experiences pleasure while absorbing the message (painlessly, effortlessly, and probably even unconsciously). What this film is saying is simply that: (1) mail delivery is a large and complicated undertaking requiring the attention of the national government on behalf of all of us; (2) this government service is a splendid thing involving speed, efficiency, and intricate processes faultlessly learned and carefully regulated; and (3) the government employees who perform these multifarious and interesting tasks for us are a pretty good bunch, patient and caring but not without an occasional irritability or a little joke.

Within this slight odyssey of a working journey, expository and poetic sequences alternate. The poetic interpolations include the rhythmic montage of the mail bags discharged and picked up by the speeding train, and the climb up into Scotland, "Past cotton grass and moorland boulder, shoveling white steam over her shoulder." These latter words are a passage of verse written by Auden. (Grierson himself speaks two passages after the train enters Scotland, including the final one; Stuart Legg speaks the rest.) As in *Coal Face,* the words are combined with the music of Britten; sound supervision is again by Cavalcanti. Interlaced with Auden's poetry is a fac-

Night Mail (U.K., 1936, Basil Wright and Harry Watt). Museum of Modern Art/Film Stills Archive.

tual, statistical commentary, as if from the General Post Office itself, and the dialogue of the postal workers' conversations with each other while doing their jobs. This melange of sound, as diverse in its components and complex in its assemblage as that of *The Song of Ceylon,* accompanies the visuals in a manner that makes *Night Mail* a lively and seemingly effortless description and explanation of the workings of the postal special on its nightly run.

GRIERSON AND FLAHERTY

In eighteenth-century England, the essayist Joseph Addison, in his *Lives of the Poets,* complimented Alexander Pope by writing that in his poetry "New things are made familiar, and familiar things are made new." In the films of Robert Flaherty it seems clear that he was attempting to make the unfamiliar familiar, to discover and reveal, as he put it, what was distant and past. In the films produced under John Grierson, on the other hand, the attempt was to find new meanings and excitements in the familiar through applying the creative treatment of actuality, as Grierson put it, to the close-to-home workaday modern world. Flaherty and Grierson represent two poles in the documentary tradition between which any documentary filmmaker has to find a place. Incidentally, both men—the Irish-American, whom Grierson once described as "a sort of handome blond gorilla," and the small wiry Scot—had considerable personal magnetism and charm. How extraordinary and yet appropriate that these two should have become friends and antagonists, loving each other while hating each other's ideas. Their seminal arguments were carried on in long evenings of talk and drink in what Grierson once described as "a dialectical pub-crawl across half the world."[3]

Flaherty, the artist, was a practical artist in many ways. Determined and persuasive, he could talk big business and big government into paying for his artistic statements. His concern was with showing the world as he saw it, which is one way of understanding the artist's job; sometimes it is argued to be the only thing the artist should be expected to do. The artwork may bring about social change but it is not created to effect that end. So it was with Flaherty.

Grierson, for his part, said: "I look on cinema as a pulpit, and use it as a propagandist."[4] He was, however, a very discerning and sophisticated propagandist who realized the utility of beauty in selling ideas—and recognized it when he saw it, incidentally. His reviews of fiction feature films (collected in *Grierson on the Movies,* Forsyth Hardy, ed. [London: Faber and Faber, 1981]) are exceptionally sensitive, informed, and articulate. In his own filmmaking, however, he was primarily concerned with social engineering—with making the institutions of society function better on behalf of all the people—and used every means available, including art, to achieve that end. Art in British documentary of the 1930s was used mainly when it could contribute emotional depth to intellectual argument.

Grierson's goals were always social, economic, and political. He saw British documentary from the beginning as an anti–aesthetic movement. Art for him was "the by-product of a job of work done"—not beauty as a good in itself, or the aesthetic experience as enriching and broadening. Nor was he interested in films that offered information or insights along with beauties which contributed to sympathetic understanding, unless they led to action.

Perhaps this fundamental aesthetic/ethical divergence between the Flaherty and the Grierson positions can best be amplified by quotations— a short one from Frances Flaherty, acting as her husband's medium, and a long one from Grierson, summing up the relationship between Flaherty and himself as he saw it. Here is Frances Flaherty:

> A Flaherty film is not a documentary, because a documentary film is precon-ceived. The great documentary movement fathered by John Grierson is all preconceived for educational and social purposes. The Russians precon-ceived their films for political purposes. Hollywood preconceives for the box-office. None of these is simply and purely, freely and spontaneously, the thing itself, for its own sake. In other words he had no axe to grind.[5]

It is interesting, of course, that the films of the man frequently called the father of documentary are disassociated from that mode. The matter of whether Flaherty had no preconceptions, "no axes to grind," was discussed in Chapter Two.

Now to Grierson, and his views of Flaherty's position in relation to his own:

> The history of the documentary film so far as I personally have been con-cerned with it has derived in part from my own theoretical deviation from Flaherty; but I ought also to add that we have been the closest of friends for twenty years and that no difference of opinion has affected our complete dependence on each other. In the profoundest kind of way we live and pros-per, each of us, by denouncing the other.
> Flaherty's approach to documentary in *Nanook* and *Moana* in the early 'twen-ties was a naturalist's approach. He was in revolt against the synthetic dramas of Hollywood. He believed that the film camera was denying its destiny in shutting itself up inside the studios; that its destiny was to get about on the earth, and be the means of opening the end wall of the theater on the whole wide world. . . . All this, of course, was very sensible and exercised an enor-mous influence on those of us who were thinking our way to the film of re-ality.
> The influence of Flaherty's outlook was the greater because of the highly refined personal talent he brought to his observation. No eye was clearer, nor, for that matter, more innocent. [Arthur Calder-Marshall borrowed this

characterization for the title of his biography of Flaherty: *The Innocent Eye.*]
He was by nature a poet ... He could see things with great simplicity, and
everything he touched found added grace at his hands.... In any estimate,
Flaherty has been one of the greatest film teachers of our day, and not one
of us but has been enriched by his example—and I shall add, but has been
even more greatly enriched by failing to follow it.

I have said that Flaherty was innocent. He was all too innocent. His revolt
was not just against the synthetics of Hollywood; there was at the same time
a revolt more dangerous: against the very terms of our actual and present
civilization. Flaherty's choice of themes was significant. It was primitive man
in Labrador or primitive man in Samoa or primitive man in the Aran Islands,
or primitive man in industry, or primitive man, in the significant person of
romantic youth, taming elephants in India. Flaherty would be shocked all over
again to hear me say so; for he would maintain, with his usual great distinction, that the beauties they enact are age-old beauties and therefore classical.
I merely make the point that his people and his themes are noticeably distant
from those which preoccupy the minds of mankind today, and that if they
were not so notably distant Flaherty would make them so.

But there is a problem of the Eskimo that is all too close to our own problems,
as our technological civilization marches northward in Asia and America and
takes him in. His hunting grounds today are scientifically observed, and his
economy is progressively planned. He is subjected to the white man's religion
and the white man's justice and the white man's misunderstanding of polygamy. His clothes and his blankets most often come from Manchester, supplied
by a department store in Winnipeg, which, incidentally, has the public health
of the Eskimo on its conscience. Some hunt by motor boats, and some travel
by air. They listen to fur prices over the radio, and are subjected to the fast
operations of commercial opportunists flying in from New York. They operate tractors and bulldozers, and increasingly the northern lands, and with
them the Eskimos who inhabit them, become part of our global concerns.

Our contrary approach to documentary has been so different as to appear
sometimes all too practical and all too materialistic and, in the sense of plain
sailing, all too plain. We have not denied the fine first principles of Flaherty's,
though, but rather have given them a different application. We have struck
out, against every temptation, and not without a grim measure of self-disci-
pline, against the attraction of both romance and commerce, to the here and
now of our own society. We have sought not the residuum of the ancient
beauties, but the beginnings of new ones in the somewhat unlikely milieu of
the chaotic present. We have believed with persistence that the first and last
place to find the drama of reality is in what men today are doing and thinking
and planning and fighting for. We have indeed found our field of observation
and the·rough patterns of our work in the clash of forces inside our own
metropolitan community.[6]

Like Flaherty, who had been a geologist and explorer, Grierson came
to film from another field, social science. Whereas Flaherty wanted to use
film to discover and reveal little known people and places, Grierson wanted
to use film to enlighten and shape the modern, complex, industrialized society in which most of us live.

Flaherty was a highly personal filmmaker who worked alone initially
and always attempted to control every phase of his films. Grierson, who

directed only one film himself, established documentary film units within which dozens of others were created.

In *Industrial Britain* (1933), the credits for which read "Production Grierson-Flaherty," Flaherty came into brief contact with the early stage of British documentary. Then he went on his individual way to make *Man of Aran* (1934), a project Grierson helped set up, incidentally, leaving Grierson to the production and supervision of a host of other documentaries.

GRIERSON'S CONTRIBUTION

It is for his multifaceted, innovative leadership that Grierson is to be most valued. As a theoretician he articulated the basis for the documentary film, its form and function, its aesthetic and its ethic. As a teacher he trained and, through his writing and speaking, influenced many documentary film-makers, not only in Britain but throughout the world. As a producer he was eventually responsible to one extent or another for thousands of films, and played a decisive creative role in some of the most important of them. And almost all his life he was an adroit political figure and dedicated civil servant. Even when not on government payroll, his central concern was always with communicating to the people of a nation and of the world the information and attitudes he thought would help them lead more useful and productive, more satisfying and rewarding lives.

More than any other person, Grierson is responsible for the documentary film as it has developed in the English-speaking countries. The use of institutional sponsorship, public and private, to pay for his kind of filmmaking, rather than dependence on returns from the box office, was one key Grierson innovation. A second, that complemented the first, was nontheatrical distribution and exhibition—going outside the movie theaters to reach audiences in schools and factories, union halls and church basements, and elsewhere.

The three hundred or more British documentaries (made during the ten years between *Drifters* and Grierson's departure for Canada in 1939) and the system that spawned them became models for other countries. If many of those 300 films were dull and transient in their significance—only the exceptional have been dealt with here—such an opinion would not have disturbed Grierson. His strategy involved a steady output of short films presenting a consistent social view—a constant reinforcement of certain attitudes, not unlike the strategy of today's makers of television commercials. Each film dealt with a small piece of the larger argument. It may seem ironic that conservative institutions were talked into paying for what was overall and essentially the presentation of a socialist point of view. But the desperateness of the economic situation during the Depression had to be acknowledged even by the Tories in power. Perhaps the subject matter of the films about work and workers that Grierson talked them into sponsoring was, or was made to seem, obligatory.

The attitudes of those films were always positive; problems could be solved by combined good will and social action. Though never acknowledged publicly, it seems to be true that the films were seen mostly by middle and upper classes rather than by the working classes whom they were mostly about. Opinion leaders were thus reached who may have been persuaded or encouraged by the films to take a Griersonian view of the world.

One of the requisites for the success of the Grierson enterprise was the idea of consensus. The documentary films did not advance partisan political positions; they stayed within what the two major political parties, Conservative and Labour, might agree upon. Nor did the documentary filmmakers attach themselves publicly to a political party. At the same time, the subjects and attitudes evident in the steady flow may have contributed to some extent to the sweeping Labour victory in 1945, at the end of the war.

In any case, Grierson once hinted that he thought the documentaries of the thirties had helped prepare the British people for the collective effort soon to be required of them in wartime. Perhaps, without the documentary movement there might have been responses other than the heroic national effort that began once the bombs started to fall. Before dealing with World War II in Britain, however, let's have a look at the parallel, if ultimately contrasting, documentary developments in the United States during the 1930s.

NOTES

[1]John Grierson, *Grierson on Documentary*, ed. Forsyth Hardy (Berkeley: University of California Press, 1966), p. 289.

[2]Grierson, *Grierson on Documentary*, p. 21.

[3]Gary Evans, *John Grierson and the National Film Board* (Toronto: University of Toronto Press, 1984), p. 45.

[4]John Grierson, "Propaganda: A Problem for Educational Theory and for Cinema," *Sight and Sound*, 3, no. 8 (Winter 1933–1934), 119–21.

[5]Frances Flaherty, "Robert Flaherty: Explorer and Film Maker" (mimeographed, c. 1958), p. 1.

[6]John Grierson, "Postwar Patterns," *Hollywood Quarterly*, 1, no. 2 (January 1946), 159–65.

FILMS OF THE PERIOD

1929
Drifters (John Grierson)

1933
Aero-Engine (Arthur Elton)
Contact (Paul Rotha)
Industrial Britain (Grierson and Robert Flaherty)

1934
Granton Trawler (Grierson and Edgar Anstey)
Shipyard (Rotha)
The Song of Ceylon (Basil Wright)
Weather Forecast (Evelyn Spice)

1935
B. B. C.—The Voice of Britain (Stuart Legg)

Coal Face (Alberto Cavalcanti)
Housing Problems (Anstey and Elton)
Workers and Jobs (Elton)

1936
Enough to Eat? (Anstey)
Night Mail (Harry Watt and Wright)

1937
Line to Tschierva Hut (Cavalcanti)

The Saving of Bill Blewitt (Watt)
We Live in Two Worlds (Cavalcanti)

1938
North Sea (Watt)

1939
Transfer of Power (Geoffrey Bell)

BOOKS ON THE PERIOD

ALEXANDER, DONALD, *The Documentary Film*. London: British Film Institute, 1945. 9 pp.

ANSTEY, EDGAR, "Development of Film Technique in Britain," *Experiment in the Film*, ed. Roger Manvell. London: The Grey Walls Press Ltd., 1949. pp. 234–65.

THE ARTS ENQUIRY, *The Factual Film*. London: Oxford University Press, 1947. 259 pp.

BEVERIDGE, JAMES, *John Grierson: Film Master*. New York: Macmillan Publishing Co., Inc., 1978. 361 pp.

COMMISSION ON EDUCATIONAL AND CULTURAL FILMS, *The Film in National Life*. London: George Allen and Unwin Ltd., 1932. 204 pp.

ELLIS, JACK C., *John Grierson: A Guide to References and Resources*. Boston: G. K. Hall & Co., 1986. 262 pp.

GRIERSON, JOHN, *Grierson on Documentary*, ed. Forsyth Hardy. Berkeley: University of California Press, 1966. 411 pp.

HARDY, FORSYTH, "The British Documentary Film," *Twenty Years of British Film 1925–1945*, eds. Michael Balcon and others. London: The Falcon Press Limited, 1947. pp. 45–80.

HARDY, FORSYTH, *John Grierson: A Documentary Biography*. London: Faber and Faber Limited, 1979. 298 pp.

HOGENKAMP, BERT, *Deadly Parallels: Film and the Left in Britain 1929–39*. London: Lawrence and Wishart Publishers, 1986. 240 pp.

LOVELL, ALAN AND JIM HILLIER, *Studies in Documentary*. New York: The Viking Press, Inc., 1972. 176 pp.

LOW, RACHAEL, *The History of the British Film 1929–1939: Documentary and Educational Films of the 1930s*. London: George Allen & Unwin Ltd., 1979. 244 pp.

LOW, RACHAEL, *The History of the British Film 1929–1939: Films of Comment and Persuasion of the 1930s*. London: George Allen & Unwin Ltd., 1949. 256 pp.

LYLE, VALDA, TOM POLITIS, AND ROSS STELL. *Stanley Hawes: Documentary Filmmaker*. Sydney: WEA Film Study Group, 1980. 96 pp.

MACPHERSON, DON, in collaboration with Paul Willemen, eds., *Traditions of Independence: British Cinema in the Thirties*. London: British Film Institute, 1980. 226 pp.

ORBANZ, EVA, *Journey to a Legend and Back: The British Realistic Film*. Berlin: Verlag Volker Spiess, 1977. 213 pp.

ROTHA, PAUL, *Documentary Diary: An Informal History of the British Documentary Film, 1928–1939*. New York: Hill and Wang, 1973. 304 pp.

ROTHA, PAUL, *Rotha on the Film*. London: Faber and Faber Ltd., 1958. 338 pp.

SUSSEX, ELIZABETH, *The Rise and Fall of British Documentary: The Story of the Film Movement Founded by John Grierson*. Berkeley: University of California Press, 1975. 219 pp.

WATT, HARRY, *Don't Look at the Camera*. London: Paul Elek, Ltd., 1974. 197 pp.

SIX
INSTITUTIONALIZATION
United States, 1930–1941

In Great Britain, documentary began in order to meet needs of the government. Alongside the Grierson movement was a small production effort out of the extreme left. In 1934 the (British) Workers' Film and Photo League was established. It produced "Workers' Newsreels," which lasted to a fourth edition before ending in 1935, *March Against Starvation* (1936), and subsequent "story documentaries." This production never attracted the attention of a wide public, nor did the people involved in it become part of the main line documentary movement, for the most part.

In the United States the situation was different. From its outset, American documentary was deeply involved with political positions, generally on the left, and faced up to the central issues of the 1930s, including the Depression, unemployment and poverty, unionism, and the growing threat of fascism abroad. Filmmakers who began their work in leftist organizations moved over into the mainstream.

Films were made by U.S. Marxist groups beginning in the early thirties. In the mid-thirties "The March of Time" series, an offshoot of *Time* magazine, began. At the same time, federally sponsored documentary production commenced. In the late thirties large-scale nongovernment documentaries took their place alongside the government ones. These four developments will be dealt with in this chapter.

FILM ON THE LEFT

In 1930 the (U.S.) Workers' Film and Photo League was established in New York City. Its goal was to train filmmakers and photographers to produce media materials that would present the "true picture" of life in the United States; that is, from the Marxist point of view—a picture not revealed by the news services, the newsreels, or the capitalist press. Among its listed advisors or associates were: Margaret Bourke-White and Ralph Steiner, photographers, the former subsequently worked for *Life* magazine, the latter became a documentary filmmaker; Elia Kazan, actor and, later, stage and screen director; Elmer Rice, playwright; Burgess Meredith and James Cagney, actors; Slavko Vorkapich, film theorist and montage expert. The Film and Photo League (it dropped Workers' from its title, as did the League in London) produced such topical films as *Winter* (1931), *Hunger* (1932), and *Bonus March* (1932).

An increasing schism in this leftist group developed between those who wanted to stick to straight agit-prop newsreels and polemical films and those who thought the cause of revolution (or of social progress—political aims varied from person to person) could best be served by films with greater aesthetic value and emotional appeal. The latter contingent argued that through film artistry they might in fact be able to persuade the unpersuaded, whereas the standard and obvious forms of propaganda being used were mainly preaching to the already converted.

In 1934 three key members—Leo Hurwitz, Ralph Steiner, and Irving Lerner—left the Film and Photo League to form Nykino (evidently a Russianized abbreviation for New York cinema; a leftist film organization named Kino existed in London). Its *Pie in the Sky* (1934), by Elia Kazan, Molly Day Thatcher, Ralph Steiner, and Irving Lerner, became its first publicized release. It is a whimsical spoof of the promises of religion for life in the hereafter in place of food for present hunger on earth. Nykino would subsequently become Frontier Films, whose work will be dealt with later under Nongovernment Documentaries.

THE MARCH OF TIME

Like the developments on the political left from the Workers' Film and Photo League, another development, on the political right (or center at least), stood apart from the mainstream of American documentary, but would be very influential in relation to it, and to British and Canadian documentary as well. Entitled "The March of Time," this monthly film series offered a new and distinctive kind of screen journalism, a cross between the newsreel and the documentary. Sponsored by Time-Life-Fortune, Inc., headed by Henry Luce, it was preceded by a weekly radio series of the same title. Roy Larsen of *Time* was responsible for the initiation of both series; Louis de Rochemont became the principal creator of the film series. It is the American prototype for the "compilation documentary," pioneered by Esfir Shub in the Soviet Union (see Chapter Three).

"The March of Time" had the most substantial and sustained success of any documentary-like material prior to television. It was advertised on movie marquees and I can remember my family frequently being more attracted by its promise than the feature it accompanied. At its peak, in the late 1930s and the years of World War II, it was seen in the U.S. alone by over twenty million people a month in 9,000 theaters. It was distributed internationally as well.

Though originating from a conservative organization, the MOT was identified with a liberal stance, more so than *Time* magazine. This was particularly true in foreign affairs; the films tended to be more conservative or erratic on domestic issues. Still, while fiction features in the thirties ignored or dealt only covertly with the Depression, MOT acknowledged the bread lines, unemployment, and the political demagoguery it gave rise to (*Huey Long*, 1935; *Father Coughlin*, 1935; *Strikebreaking*, 1935; *U.S. Unemployment*, 1937). Internationally, while the newsreels avoided controversial political and military developments, MOT tackled the machinations of Hitler, Stalin, Mussolini, and Tojo (*Nazi Conquest—No. 1*, 1938; *The Mediterranean—Background for War*, 1939; *Japan—Master of the Orient*, 1939; *Newsfronts of War—1940*, 1939).

Along with its energetic innovations, the success of "The March of Time" was fueled by the controversy it aroused and by its press agentry. One of the most politically controversial films in the history of American cinema was MOT's *Inside Nazi Germany* (1938). It examined in some detail (16 minutes): (1) the regimentation of the German people; (2) the control and consolidation of nationalistic allegiances; and (3) the preparations being made for future military and economic expansion. This was at a time when the majority of the American public was still strongly isolationist and the government maintained a careful impartiality.

A standard format for "The March of Time" was worked out early and varied little, regardless of subject. The fixed form may have been necessitated by the pressures of monthly production with modest resources; it must have also come to seem desirable given the considerable popularity of the series in the form in which it was offered. One of the most important ingredients was the voice and delivery style of its commentator, Westbrook van Voorhis. His "Voice of Time" (sometimes irreverently referred to as the "Voice of God") was deep and commanding, ominous and reassuring at the same time. Spoken words carried the weight of the communication; the footage (largely stock), music (obvious and clichéd), and sound effects (sparse and highly selective) were cut to them. Often the pictures were given their meaning by the words, as part of "the dramatization of the news" that MOT practiced. An extreme closeup of a face and mouth at a telephone becomes "An angry refusal"; a long-shot of a city street at night with a few electric signs becomes "That evening Shanghai is tense" (both instances from *War in China*, 1937). Editing was the key. The pace is fast, with a hard rhythmic impact; a great deal of information is presented, dramatically to capture the attention of the popcorn-chewing Friday night audience.

Structurally, each issue has four parts, with titles announcing each part. The first establishes the magnitude and urgency of the problem being dealt with. The second offers a historical survey of its origins and causes. Part three presents the immediate complications, confirming its newsworthiness. The concluding part looks to the future, stressing that the problem is a matter for continuing and serious concern.

No doubt its fixed style and approach had something to do with its eventual demise in 1951 (along with the competition of television and the rising costs of production). "The March of Time" remains, however, a large event in the history of popular American culture. Its influence has extended down to much of the documentary and public affairs programs on television today.

League of Nations, "The March of Time" series (U.S., 1936, Louis de Rochemont). Museum of Modern Art/Film Stills Archive.

GOVERNMENT DOCUMENTARIES

The Film and Photo League and "The March of Time" were precedents of sorts, but documentary in the institutional or Griersonian sense—involving and educating citizens in the affairs of the nation—began in June of 1935, in Washington, D.C. At that point Rexford Guy Tugwell, head of the newly-established Resettlement Administration, made a decision to interpret its program and objectives through motion pictures.

A former University of Chicago professor, Tugwell was one of the "brain trust" collected by President Franklin Delano Roosevelt to implement his New Deal. Roosevelt gathered around him the best minds he could find—many of them from the universities—to help solve the problems presented by the Depression. He established them in a number of separate agencies, often overlapping and competing with each other. The "alphabet soup" of those days included the NRA (National Recovery Administration), PWA (Public Works Administration), WPA (Work Projects Administration), and CCC (Civilian Conservation Corps). The Resettlement Administration was one of the agencies clustered around the Department of Agriculture. It was intended to aid those farmers who were being forced off their land by low crop prices compounded by the dreadful drought in the West and Southwest that had caused a Dust Bowl.

Into Tugwell's office came a movie critic named Pare Lorentz, whose wife was vaguely related to the president. Lorentz was a combination of New York liberal (where he was established) and West Virginia populist (where he was born and raised). He convinced Tugwell that what was needed was a new kind of dramatic/informational/persuasive movie. (Lorentz disliked the word documentary and much of Grierson's work in England for being too schoolteacherish. "Films of Merit" was Lorentz's term for what he would produce.)

Out of that conversation came *The Plow That Broke the Plains* (1936), an indictment of the lack of planning that caused the Dust Bowl. In its present version of twenty minutes, *The Plow* shows the historical origins of the problem and its present magnitude and urgency. Originally, a final sequence dealt with the "beltville communities" being proposed by the Resettlement Administration. These beltvilles were to be established adjacent to industrial towns and cities, such as Detroit. The rural dispossessed, when moved there, would be able to farm small plots of land and work part-time in the factories. Shortly after the release of the film, the Resettlement Administration became part of the Department of Agriculture; subsequently its name was changed to the Farm Security Administration. The beltville concept was never fully realized.

Lorentz, who had no prior film production experience, wrote and directed *The Plow*. As cinematographers he hired Paul Strand, Ralph Steiner,

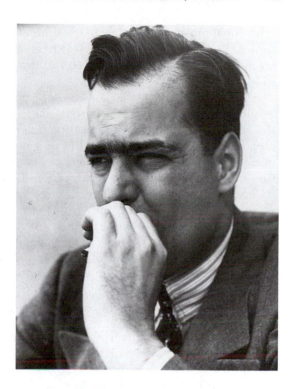

Pare Lorentz in the 1930s. Museum
of Modern Art/Film Stills Archive.

and Leo Hurwitz. Strand and Steiner had backgrounds in still photography; all three had been active in the Film and Photo League. When they began shooting out in the field, with Lorentz remaining in Washington, they were frustrated by the lack of clarity in their instructions. To compensate for this, and to give them some guidelines for shooting, they drafted a script. The film as they conceived it was to be about the devastation of the land and the hardships of the people caused by exploitative capitalism. This was not an economic-political stance Lorentz was prepared to take (nor would the government have welcomed it) and dissension and cross-purposes resulted.

Lorentz hired an editor to assist him and with her help, learned to edit. He assembled the footage according to a rough outline and began writing the commentary. Virgil Thomson, whom he had known in New York, was hired to compose the score. Working together, in hours upon hours of shaping and reshaping, they combined images and music with commentary and sound effects. It was Thomson's idea that his music should have an operatic balance with the rest of the film. In fact, his score—which exists virtually as he wrote it for the film as a suite in the standard orchestral repertoire—tends to outweigh the visuals. Thomson was in full professional stride; Lorentz was learning filmmaking. The score is drawn mostly from traditional music appropriate to the time and indigenous to the place being shown. The tango over the final sad spectacle of the caravans of Okie jalopies moving westward is an inspired instance of the use of music in relation to images.

Unlike Grierson, who always determined in advance how his films would reach their audience, Lorentz had failed to set up distribution for the completed film. In his innocence he evidently had assumed that if he created a fine piece of work, a film of merit, others would be eager to acquire it for distribution. He might have been forewarned of the Hollywood film industry's resentment of government film production by the resistance he had met in trying to obtain footage from fiction features of covered wagon trains. It was finally only with the help of veteran director King Vidor that he obtained what he needed. Accordingly, *The Plow That Broke the Plains* was not shown as widely as it might have been. It received what distribution it had largely because of glowing reviews. Theater patrons would ask local exhibitors when the film was going to be shown. The Rialto Theatre in New York City publicized its showing by proclaiming it as "The picture they dared us to show!"

Lorentz was discouraged by the inadequate distribution, exhausted from the hard work and frustrations of production, and in debt for the money he (and his wife) had invested in the film to complete it. (His original bid on the cost was an unrealistic $6,000.) In that dismal mood, he went to Tugwell's office to say goodbye. As part of his farewell, he suggested another film that should be made—one about flooding in the Mississippi valley. Lorentz's enthusiasm for this project convinced Tugwell to allow him to pro-

The Plow that Broke the Plains (U.S., 1936, Pare Lorentz). Museum of Modern Art/Film Stills Archive.

duce yet another government film, *The River* (1937), backed by the Farm Security Administration.

While the Resettlement Administration, which had sponsored *The Plow,* had intended to resettle people forced off their land, the Farm Security Administration was attempting to keep them on their land. *The River* was a compelling plea for national flood control and soil conservation. Whereas *The Plow* offered the beltville communities as alternatives to Dust Bowl deserts, *The River* showed the Tennessee Valley Authority as a way to make ravaged land and economically depressed communities viable. The film also counteracted the public relations campaign being conducted by private utilities to keep government out of electric power. If it is now generally agreed that the TVA is a remarkable and salutary instance of the government undertaking an activity heretofore in the hands of private corporations, it remains an experiment that has never been repeated.

Lorentz again wrote and directed. For *The River* the cinematographers were Stacy Woodard, Floyd Crosby, and Willard Van Dyke. Woodard had been producing a series of nature films called "The Struggle to Live." Crosby had worked on the Murnau-Flaherty *Tabu* (1931), would have a long association with Lorentz, and went on to fiction features (for example, *The Brave Bulls,* 1951, and *High Noon,* 1952). Van Dyke had studied still photography with Edward Weston; he was marginally involved with political film-making on the left and would become a fine documentary maker in his own right. Though there was no political contention this time, there seems to have been the same uncertainty on the part of the cameramen (and maybe on the part of Lorentz) as to exactly what kind of footage was wanted. The music was by Virgil Thomson, again using folk and traditional music; for example, "Go Tell Aunt Rhody" and "There'll Be a Hot Time in the Old Town Tonight." The orchestral suite arranged from *The River* is less often performed than *The Plow* suite. *The River* music is more fully integrated with the visuals; the edited images are its equal in aesthetic weight.

Lorentz's lyric commentary for this film is now classic; its blank verse litany of the names of rivers and towns has often been imitated and sometimes parodied. For example:

> We built a hundred cities and a thousand towns:
>   St. Paul and Minneapolis,
> Davenport and Keokuk,
>   Moline and Quincy,
> Cincinnati and St. Louis,
>   Omaha and Kansas City. . . .

Or, again:

> Down the Judith, the Grand, the Osage and the Platte;
> The Rock, the Salt, the Black and the Minnesota;
> Down the Monongahela, the Allegheny, Kanawha and Muskingum;

The Miami, the Wabash, the Liking and the Green;
The White, the Wolf, the Cache, and the Black;
Down the Kaw and Kaskaskia, the Red and Yazoo.
Down the Cumberland, Kentucky and the Tennessee. . . .

It is possible that *The River* has been seen by as many people as any film ever made. Lorentz this time took pains to set up proper distribution and it was shown in more than 5,000 theaters. It has remained in active nontheatrical distribution ever since—shown in schools, to various sorts of adult groups, and on public television—not just as a historical curiosity but as a statement of an ongoing ecological problem and as an epic poem. The only negative criticism frequently leveled at it is that, following its moving evocation of the history of this big country, its people, and its natural re-sources, it adds a commercial. The last six minutes on the TVA are much weaker; even the photographic quality drops, with some stock shots being used. Unlike the best of the British documentaries, in which the propaganda becomes an indissoluble part of the whole, here the sponsor's message seems tacked on. The first twenty-four minutes are unrivaled, however. Lav-ishly praised at the time of its release, *The River* has come to be considered a masterpiece of the screen.

On the basis of its success, Lorentz was able to persuade the Roosevelt administration (with the backing of the president himself, who is reported

The River (U.S., 1937, Pare Lorentz). Museum of Modern Art/Film Stills Archive.

to have loved the film) to set up the United States Film Service in 1938. It was to make films propagandizing the policies and activities of all departments of the government.

The first of the U.S. Film Service productions was *The Fight for Life* (1940), produced for the U.S. Public Health Service. Written and directed by Lorentz, it was based on a book by Dr. Paul de Kruif, a writer who popularized scientific and medical subjects. It is about the work of the Chicago Maternity Center in providing prenatal care for mothers and delivering babies in the homes of poor families. It was photographed by Floyd Crosby. The music, composed by Louis Gruenberg (who shortly before had written the score for John Ford's *Stagecoach*), was innovative, including the use of blues while the young doctor wanders the city streets at night. Its cast mixed nonactors with actors, including Will Geer (subsequently of the long-running television series *The Waltons*).

Feature-length, half dramatic and half documentary, *The Fight for Life* is what would come to be called a semidocumentary. It was made a little before Harry Watt's *Target for Tonight* (1941), the British wartime prototype for the form (dealt with in Chapter Seven). It might be considered a precursor for Hollywood postwar semidocumentaries like *The House on 92nd Street* (1945), *Boomerang* (1947), and *Call Northside 777* (1948) (to be discussed in Chapter Ten). In attempting to heighten the drama and engage the emotions, Lorentz made childbirth a frightening experience. When the film was completed and rushed to the White House for viewing on New Year's Eve, 1939, Franklin Roosevelt showed little enthusiasm for it. Eleanor Roosevelt

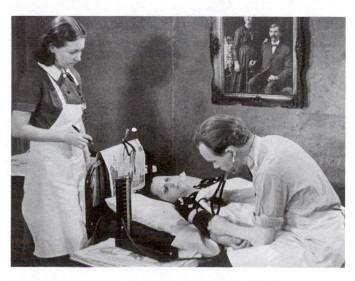

The Fight for Life (U.S., 1940, Pare Lorentz). Museum of Modern Art/Film Stills Archive.

is said to have remarked, in her gentle way, "Surely there's something good to be said about having a baby," having given birth to a number of sons herself. It was not very widely shown. In Chicago it was banned by the police censorship board, though it was made there.

On the other hand, *Power and the Land* (1940), the next production, was distributed by RKO to nearly 5,000 theaters. It was so well received that it continued being reissued into the late 1940s, with its maps being updated to show the number of farms currently receiving electric power. It was produced for the Rural Electrification Administration and the Department of Agriculture. Joris Ivens, the Dutch documentarian now living in the U.S., directed and Helen van Dongen, his then wife and expert documentary editor, edited. Cinematography was by Floyd Crosby and Arthur Ornitz; the commentary was written by poet Stephen Vincent Benet; music was composed by Douglas Moore, composer of *The Ballad of Baby Doe.*

Power and the Land pursues its objective of persuading farmers to organize rural cooperatives to obtain government power by showing the Parkinson family on their farm in southwestern Ohio. We see them at work, before they have electricity and afterwards. The contrast in the greater ease and comfort electric power provides these decent and hardworking people with whom we have become acquainted is a simple and effective argument. At

Power and the Land (U.S., 1940, Joris Ivens). Museum of Modern Art/Film Stills Archive.

the same time, Ivens offers an affectionate picture of this farm family and family farm as it would strike a sensitive and sympathetic visitor. With deft and poetic strokes, he documents for other cultures and later generations a kind of life and economy that no longer exists.

The next production, *The Land* (1941), was written and directed by an even more famous documentary pioneer, Robert Flaherty, returning to America after a decade in Britain. It too was edited by Helen van Dongen. Cinematography was by Irving Lerner, Douglas Baker, Floyd Crosby, and Charles Herbert; the music was composed by Richard Arnell; the commentary was written and read by Flaherty.

Produced for the Agricultural Adjustment Agency (AAA) of the Department of Agriculture, this is what the French would call a *film maudit*— a cursed film. Its initial purpose was along the lines of *The Plow That Broke the Plains* and *The River:* to encourage the careful and controlled use of our agricultural resources. During its production, United States foreign policy shifted from a strict neutrality in the second World War to support of Britain standing alone against Nazi Germany. A lend-lease program had been instituted and our promise to become "the breadbasket of democracy" required that agricultural production be increased by any means available. *The Land* works against itself (not unlike the earlier *Industrial Britain,* with Flaherty pursuing one line and Grierson another). The commentary argues that intelligent and scientific agricultural practices and modern machines

The Land (U.S., 1941, Robert Flaherty). Museum of Modern Art/Film Stills Archive.

will make the land even more productive. The images, however, of the despoilation created by cutting down the timber and cultivating all of the available land, like those of *The Plow* and *The River,* carry the dramatic weight. The images may represent Flaherty's true uneasiness concerning what he had discovered about the land and the people on it in this first film about his own country.

In any case, before *The Land* was completed, Congress, now alienated from the New Deal by Republican victories at the polls in 1940, decided that government film production was needless and, indeed, un–American. The U.S. Film Service was not exactly abolished since it had never really been approved. It had worked out of the administrative branch, with funds allocated for individual films. Now, not only were no funds for the Film Service appropriated by Congress, legislation was passed that forbade tucking film production costs into other budgets. *The Land* was never shown in the theaters. Its only source of nontheatrical distribution was the Museum of Modern Art Film Library, where it could be obtained for film study purposes only, like the Nazi propaganda film *Triumph of the Will.*

The reasons offered by Lorentz's biographer, Robert Synder, for the termination of the United States Film Service are these: (1) antagonism and antipathy in Congress to the New Deal; (2) lack of support from the executive branch (Roosevelt was now preoccupied with international issues); (3) opposition by the public and Congress to propaganda activities by the government (portrayal of southwestern and western states as deserts in *The Plow That Broke the Plains* provoked considerable outcry at the outset); and (4) opposition from Hollywood.[1]

In summarizing Lorentz's contributions, a number of things can be said. He established American precedent for the government use of documentaries, which would be continued during World War II (by the Armed Forces and the Office of War Information) and afterwards (by the United States Information Agency). From Lorentz's efforts five large and important films resulted, the first three of which he directed: *The Plow That Broke the Plains* (1936), *The River* (1937), *The Fight for Life* (1940).

In *The Plow* and *The River,* Lorentz developed an original, personal style of documentary that also became a national style. (Similarities can be seen in films by others: *The City,* 1939, and *And So They Live,* 1940, for example, to be dealt with in the next section.) In his two mosaic patterns of sight (carefully composed images shot silently) and sound (symphonic music, spoken words, noises), no one element says much by itself. Together they offer a form and content resembling epic poems. They seem close to the attitudes of American populism and are rooted in frontier tradition. The sweeping views of a big country and the free verse commentaries with their chanted names and allusions to historic events make one think of Walt Whitman. The use of music is quite special, with composer Virgil Thomson sharing more fully than usual in the filmmaking process.

In contributing two lasting masterpieces to the history of documentary, Lorentz joins a very select company: the artists of documentary. (Flaherty and Humphrey Jennings, the latter to be considered in Chapter Seven, would be other members of that company.) Some would argue that *The River* is the finest American documentary to date—aesthetically and in terms of expressing the American spirit.

Lorentz's major limitations appear most sharply in the light that Grierson would cast on them. First, Lorentz relied on the impermanent partisan support of the party in power. He had the backing of President Franklin Roosevelt and the films were associated with Democratic policies. When the balance in Congress shifted to Republican, the United States Film Service was not allowed to continue. Second, even within that New Deal context, Lorentz opted for a few big films sponsored by agencies related to one department (four of the five films were on agricultural subjects), rather than many smaller films from various departments that would have broadened the base of sponsorship and made for a steady flow of film communication. Third, he was creating art at public expense—making personal films à la Flaherty—with no real commitment to public service. Finally, Lorentz remained aloof in Washington. He made no efforts to seek sponsorship for documentary filmmaking outside the government. He had no real connection with the New York City documentarians responsible for the nongovernmental documentaries of the 1930s (to be dealt with in the next section) though some of them had worked with him on the government films.

On the other hand, the situation was not the same here as in Britain. If Lorentz could not establish a film unit, he could not follow through on the other things Grierson called for. The government of the United States *is* highly partisan; we do not have the centuries-old tradition of public servants working outside the party as in England. It is not clear whether Grierson could have done any better here than Lorentz did; Grierson's criticisms tend to ignore the central differences of government structure and tradition.

However one chooses to look at the matter, the closing of the U.S. Film Service proved a great waste and inefficiency. Shortly after its demise, the United States entered World War II and government filmmaking on a vast scale had to be started from scratch.

NONGOVERNMENT DOCUMENTARIES

Paralleling the work of Pare Lorentz and the United States Film Service were the documentaries of private and commercial sponsorship. "The March of Time," already discussed, was the most conspicuous success, playing in theaters from 1935 and on with increasing popularity. In 1937, Nykino, discussed at the beginning of this chapter, metamorphosed into Frontier Films, which would represent those committed to art on behalf of social action rather than the more doctrinaire party-liners of the Film and Photo League.

Among the persons associated with Frontier Films either actively or as advisors, were John Howard Lawson, Elia Kazan, Leo Hurwitz, Herbert Kline, Ralph Steiner, Joris Ivens, Malcolm Cowley, John Dos Passos, Lillian Hellman, Archibald MacLeish, Lewis Milestone, Clifford Odets, Willard Van Dyke, and Paul Strand. The mainstays were Strand, Hurwitz, and Steiner. Frontier Films hoped to be an alternative to "The March of Time." Films produced under its auspices will be considered shortly.

The nongovernment documentaries of the 1930s offer a catalogue of the most significant contemporary problems and issues—with a bias to the left in their selection and treatment. The largest block of privately-sponsored documentaries matched "The March of Time"'s concern with the growing menace of fascism in Europe and of Japanese imperialist conquest in Asia. A number of films were made about the Spanish Civil War (1936 to 1938), in which General Francisco Franco's Moorish legions, backed by Nazi Germany and Fascist Italy, were pitted against the Republican Loyalists, backed by Communist Russia and volunteers from many nations. All of the films supported the Loyalist cause. From Frontier Films came *Heart of Spain* (1937, Herbert Kline and Geza Karpathi) and *Return to Life* (1938, Henri Cartier-Bresson and Herbert Kline). From Contemporary Historians, Inc., formed in 1937 by a group of writers that included John Dos Pasos, Ernest Hemingway, Archibald MacLeish, and Lillian Hellman, came *The Spanish Earth* (1937).

The most ambitious and widely seen of the Spanish Civil War films, *The Spanish Earth,* was directed by Joris Ivens. Cinematography was by John Ferno (formerly Fernhout), editing by Helen van Dongen. Narration was written and read by Ernest Hemingway. Music was arranged by Marc Blitzstein (a student of Arnold Schoenberg) and Virgil Thomson from Spanish folk melodies. It is a short feature in length (54 minutes).

A slight narrative links the village of Fuentedueña and Madrid. A farm boy, Julian, serving in the Loyalist army, returns home from the city to the village on a three-day leave. The front—extending along a line west of the two locations—has different kinds of terrain and fighting: the open countryside of hills and farm land with infantry and tanks moving forward; Madrid with artillery shelling by Loyalists and Rebels (as Franco's forces are called throughout) and aerial bombardment by the latter; and the road connecting Madrid and Valencia with a crucial bridge subjected to attack and counterattack. The political positions represented are dealt with midway in the film, largely through commentary and paraphrasing of military and civilian leaders speaking to Loyalist gatherings in Madrid and Valencia.

The narration for the film is quite distinctive. Hemingway talks about the images we are seeing as if we were sitting together watching home movies. "I can't read German either," he says, as we see embossed words on pieces of a Junker bomber shot down by a Loyalist fighter plane. The Loyalists are identified as *the people,* as opposed to Franco and his foreigners—Germans, Italians, Moorish mercenaries, and the Civil Guard. Hemingway's words are supported by shots of the people with closeups of faces: soldiers, weeping women, children. The informality and democratic nature of this citizen army are evident, as well as their camaraderie and solidarity. We never see the Rebels; they remain a faceless enemy.

The farmers of Fuentedueña are constructing an irrigation ditch in order to produce more food to feed Madrid. (There are echoes here of *Turksib,* described in Chapter Three.) "For fifty years we've wanted to irrigate," the narrator tells us, "but *they* held us back." The irrigation project connects the Loyalists with food and life; "they" (the fascists), are only interested in sporting (using the land for hunting) and death. The effects of a fascist air raid on a village suggest the famous Picasso painting, *Guernica.* The film ends with water beginning to flow through the irrigation ditch onto the land: the Spanish earth.

As for films dealing with China's defense against Japanese aggression, which began with the invasion of Manchuria in 1931 and continued until

The Spanish Earth (U.S., 1937, Joris Ivens). Museum of Modern Art/Film Stills Archive.

1945, Frontier Films made *China Strikes Back* (1937). Harry Dunham directed; Jay Leyda and Sidney Meyers were among others involved in its production. This film offered sustained coverage of the Chinese 8th Route Army, its guerilla tactics, educational program, relation with the peasants, and efforts toward the unity of Free China against the invading Japanese. (This was the Communist force, with Mao Tse-tung among its leaders. At the time, the only Chinese political entity Americans knew of was Chiang Kai-shek and his supporters.) Contemporary Historians produced *The Four Hundred Million* (1939). The title refers to the size of China's population. It was directed, shot, and edited by the Dutch trio—Ivens, Ferno, van Dongen. Commentary was written by Dudley Nichols (best remembered for his scripts of films directed by John Ford) and spoken by Fredric March. Music was composed by Hanns Eisler.

Films were made about the Munich crisis of 1938. The crisis was resolved by Prime Minister Neville Chamberlain of Great Britain agreeing with Reichkanzler Adolph Hitler that Germany might annex the Sudetanland section of Czechoslovakia without interference from Britain. *Crisis* (1938) was produced and directed by Herbert Kline; it was co-directed and photographed by the Czech Alexander Hackenschmied (who would become Hammid after emigrating to the U.S.). The same pair created *Lights Out in Europe* (1938). In 1940 "The March of Time" released a feature-length compilation summarizing the European situation entitled *The Ramparts We Watch*.

As for nongovernment documentaries on domestic subjects, most of those had "progressive tendencies" and dealt with issues of particular interest to the political left. The 1930s were years of considerable labor unrest and progress, of union building and union busting, and a number of films were made in support of unionism. For example, three were produced by Frontier Films. *People of the Cumberland* (1938) is about an isolated people of pioneer English and Scottish ancestry working in the coal mines of Appalachia and their emergence from poverty and backwardness to social consciousness and action. The work of Miles Horton and The Highlander School is featured in the film. It was directed by Elia Kazan and photographed by Ralph Steiner. *United Action* (1939) is a record of the organization of the United Auto Workers-Congress of Industrial Organizations (UAW-CIO) and the strike in Detroit against General Motors in 1939.

The feature-length *Native Land* was Frontier Films' magnum opus (and swan song). Production of it began in 1939 but it wasn't released until 1942. It was based almost entirely on the investigation and conclusions of the U.S. Senate Robert Lafollette Committee on Civil Rights and on other labor documents. It dealt with workers' rights and unionism and was part actuality footage and part dramatization. Direction and script were by Leo Hurwitz and Paul Strand; cinematography was by Strand; music by Marc

Native Land (U.S., 1942, Leo Hurwitz and Paul Strand). Museum of Modern Art/Film Stills Archive.

Blitzstein. Paul Robeson narrated. Howard da Silva, among the actors in the cast, played a pitiable labor spy in the pay of management.

Municipal planning was another subject dealt with. *A Place to Live* (1941) is a cogent little film about slum clearance in Philadelphia. *The City* (1939) is a trenchant big one. A hit at the New York World's Fair of 1939, it was produced for the American Institute of Planners by American Documentary Films, set up by Ralph Steiner and Willard Van Dyke, who co-directed and co-photographed this film. (When Van Dyke and Steiner left Frontier Films on ideological grounds, this sponsored project left with them. This incident caused a serious and lasting breach among various film-makers who had been involved with Frontier Films.) The scenario was written by Henwar Rodakiewicz from an original outline by Pare Lorentz; the commentary was written by cultural historian Lewis Mumford and spoken by actor Morris Carnovsky. The music score was by Aaron Copland.

The City promotes the concept of the planned greenbelt communities detached from urban centers. It has a five-part historical organization: (1) In the Beginning—New England (a rural community dating from the eighteenth century); (2) The Industrial City—City of Smoke (Pittsburgh); (3) The Metropolis—Men into Steel (Manhattan); (4) The Highway—The Endless City (Sunday traffic congestion in New Jersey and the environs of New York City); (5) The Green City (shot in Radburn, N.J., and Greenbelt, Md.).

John Grierson, who was himself working on a film about city planning at the time (*The Londoners*), much admired the keenness of observation, the rhythm, and the energy of *The City*. In "the sort of analysis one producer expects of another," he had this to say of its weaknesses:

Steiner and Van Dyke, under suasion no doubt, try to tell us they are all against metropolitan madness, that they are sick of its nervousness, its wasted energies, its dangers, its damnations. They describe what they say is their road to heaven. It is, first of all, the rural paradise we have lost; and it is true enough that the rustic swinging with the seasons produced a harmonious art of life. But there is something wrong about the Steiner-Van Dyke paradise. There are fine shapes but no applejack. Van Dyke, as an old villager himself, might at least have remembered the smells that go with it.

The road to heaven twists. What is it now but a Washington suburb—neat and clean and tidy and utterly antiseptic, with all the citizens practicing to be acrobats? No smells here either. . . .

What I am getting at is that I do not believe Steiner and Van Dyke believe a word of it any more than I do; and I have the proof of it the moment they shoot these children on the sidewalk, those domestic jalopies on the metropolitan road, the clamor of the industrial scene, or the open sesame of the automat. Like myself, they are metropolitans. Their cameras get an edge on and defeat their theories.[2]

The City (U.S., 1939, Ralph Steiner and Willard Van Dyke). Museum of Modern Art/Film Stills Archive.

The Depression and unemployment are touched upon in a number of films. *Valley Town* (1940) concerns the problem of technological unemployment. Sponsored by the Sloan Foundation, it was produced jointly by the Educational Film Institute of New York University and Documentary Film Productions. Willard Van Dyke directed. Cinematography was by Roger Barlow and Bob Churchill; editing was by Irving Lerner. The score was composed by Marc Blitzstein. A dark view of a depressed American industrial community, it has an English predecessor in *Eastern Valley* (1937), a film made by some of Grierson's co-workers.

Valley Town offers a partial solution to the bitter problem it examines. But, as with many of the American films of this era, the hopeful ending seems like whistling in the dark, tacked on to meet the sponsor's requirements without much conviction on the part of the film's makers. The impression that remains after viewing it is of the terrible meaning in individual human terms of an impersonal and vast economic system that has somehow gotten out of joint.

Aesthetically and technically *Valley Town* is remarkable for a number of reasons: the extraordinary force and effectiveness of its photographic

Valley Town (U.S., 1940, Willard Van Dyke). Museum of Modern Art/Film Stills Archive.

images and its daring use of soliloquy, even of sung soliloquy, in an effort to heighten the feeling of its contents. It makes one think of the words and music of Bertolt Brecht and Kurt Weill in *The Threepenny Opera* and their other music dramas with social meanings.

From the same sponsor and producer as *Valley Town* came *And So They Live* (1940) and *The Children Must Learn* (1940). Their subject is the kind of education needed to alleviate some of the hardships of poverty-stricken rural areas of Appalachia. The former was directed by John Ferno and Julian Roffman, the latter by Willard Van Dyke. In *And So They Live,* the filmmakers' affection for the Appalachian family, chosen as exemplary of many such families, shines through. There is a beguiling simplicity to their argument: what this family has is in touching contrast to what they need; the sparse commentary suggests merely that life ought to be made better for these gentle people.

But perhaps the beauty and dignity of this family and of their relationships with each other undercut the argument—particularly in the lengthy and lovely final scene of the family together in their cabin in the evening. Their situation may have looked somewhat enviable—like that of Flaherty's people—to persons feeling harrassed by complex lives and unsatisfactory relationships. The film may be stronger as a document (Flaherty) than as a

And So They Live (U.S., 1940, John Ferno and Julian Roffman). Museum of Modern Art/ Film Stills Library.

documentary for social change (Grierson). Perhaps this is true of many U.S. documentaries.

Another, somewhat related film, *One Tenth of a Nation* (1940), is about the need for better schooling for the Southern Negro. It was the most widely seen of several films dealing with the problems of black Americans. Henwar Rodakiewicz and Joseph Krumgold co-produced and co-directed.

In concluding this section, a number of generalizations can be made about the nongovernmental American documentaries of the 1930s. First of all, if the filmmakers often took bold positions on social matters, they had continuing difficulty finding backing for their statements. The pattern was one of a big, fine film for which funding was somehow found, followed by inadequate distribution and exhibition, leading to the sponsor's disenchant-ment and the filmmaker's scrambling to try to find sponsorship for the next film.

Second, because of the uncertainty of sponsorship, there was no steady flow of smaller films reaching interested audiences and little rein-forcement of the ideas presented. Too frequently only those persons who already agreed with the filmmakers' positions saw the films or even learned of their existence.

Third, and related to the second point, rarely is the propaganda mixed with the artistic form in a smooth blend. The sponsor's message may ob-trude. On the other hand, sometimes the pleasures of form seem to be work-ing against the content and evident intention of the film. The liveliness and humor of the New York City sequence in *The City* is much more engaging than the blandness of the greenbelt sequence; the loveliness of much of *And So They Live* makes the Appalachian situation seem one that should be preserved rather than changed.

Though he never contributed to organizing American documentary filmmakers, Robert Flaherty may have been their unacknowledged bell-wether. Often they seemed to be following the Flaherty way more than the Grierson method.

AMERICAN AND BRITISH DIFFERENCES

Documentary in the United States didn't really begin until seven years after documentary in Great Britain. American documentary did not grow out of British documentary, though it may not have begun when it did if there had not been the British precedent. Connections between the two national groups of documentary makers were not made until the late thirties. Some have felt that it would have been better if we had learned from the British. Given the differences in our geographies, histories, and national tempera-ments, perhaps we couldn't have.

Filmmakers

One striking difference was that in Britain there was one production center; out of London came films of all kinds, and documentary was part of general film activity. In this country there was Washington, D.C., where the government documentaries were produced, New York City, where the nongovernment documentaries were produced, and Los Angeles, which produced all of the fiction entertainment films but virtually no documentary. The filmmakers in the three American centers had comparatively little contact with each other.

There were also differences in leadership. In this country, Pare Lorentz was the only one in a position to be a Grierson. De Rochemont, the other possible candidate, wasn't really a maker of documentaries and identified himself more with the newsreel and the theatrical film industry than with the documentarians. But Lorentz was not Grierson. In spite of a shared capacity for drink and talk late into the evening—prerequisites, generally, for documentary making it sometimes seems—Lorentz was more of an individual filmmaker. He demonstrated no particular aptitude for administration or political maneuvering. As in Britain, many of those who would become American documentarians had developed their craft working on government films. The credits of *The Plow* and *The River* contain many of the significant names in American documentary of the 1930s. But Lorentz never attracted a band of loyal colleagues. Without strong leadership, the filmmakers competed with each other in trying to put films together. No sense of collective endeavor developed in this country as it had in Britain.

Political persuasions took on different importance and different forms in the two bodies of filmmakers. American documentarians were highly political, and sectarian squabbling divided New Dealers from socialists, Trotskyites from Stalinists, and so on. In one sector there was the running contention regarding whether to follow Communist Party discipline, which was anti–aesthetic and exclusively in favor of the agit-prop, or to move along lines that permitted more individual and artistic freedom. In general, American documentarians seemed to not consider the need for consensus sufficiently; instead, each stood on principle and—like French politics, with a party for each point of view—they remained fragmented, never achieving the unity of purpose of the British documentary movement.

Sponsorship and Distribution

No one in this country systematically developed industrial sponsorship for documentary as Grierson had done. It was as true here as it was in Britain that business and industrial money was really the only money outside government accessible and sufficient for a program of film production; and business, like government, had reason to communicate with the public. American industry could see the value of advertising goods and services and of promoting corporate images. But the idea that businesses might back films in the public interest or support worthwhile causes seems to have never occurred or been persuasively presented to business leaders.

Instead, American nongovernment documentaries relied on backing from a few philanthropic foundations and, for the most part, contributions from individuals, usually on the left politically and frequently in the arts. As a result, production of documentaries in the U.S. in the 1930s was sporadic. The filmmakers seem to have sometimes been irresponsible in regard to the sponsors' interests, following their own notions of what was needed once the money was obtained. A wake of ill-feeling on the part of the sponsors was left behind on a number of productions.

After their films were made—some big and fine, as has been indicated—American documentarians seemed strangely indifferent to or inept at obtaining adequate distribution for them. Their sense of achievement too often seemed confined to the satisfactions of making the films.

Nor had an effective system of nontheatrical distribution-exhibition been established (as had been in Britain). Documentaries were shown, for the most part, in art-type theaters in a few big cities.

Films

The major differences between American and British documentaries of the thirties seem to grow out of contrasting political positions. The American films are rooted in populism, the British in socialism. The populists, represented in the People's Party around the turn of the century, felt that government should control tendencies toward monopoly (the monopolistic and exploitative excesses of capitalism), but that its function should end there. Populism began among American farmers in the country; socialism, among factory workers in European cities. Agrarian subject matter and influence are very strong in the American films (this despite the fact that by the mid-thirties most Americans were living in cities); urban and industrial subjects predominate in British documentary. In the American films, the importance of the people and the sacredness of the individual receive considerable emphasis. In the British films, collective effort through government, with government leadership, is stressed.

Certain other differences—some of them related to these fundamentally different political stances—are evident in the films described in the last two chapters. The American films seem more romantic, more emotional in the appeals used. They seem related to populist leader William Jennings Bryan's famous "Cross of Gold" speech of 1891. The appeals of the British films seem, in comparison, more reasoned and objective, rooted in evidence and argument. The work and working class of the British films seem different from the labor and people of the American films.

The romantic and emotional led to the poetic rather than the expository. In general, American documentaries of the thirties may have been more "aestheticky," to use a Grierson word, than the British. "The March of Time," of course, is an exception to this generalization. Grierson seemed to value it (he imitated it, in fact, in films he produced in Britain and later in Canada) more than he did *The River* and *The City.*

Perhaps also related to populism is the tendency of American films to be large in scale. Ours is a big country, we seem to be saying, so we make big statements in big films. We employ hyperbole rather than the characteristic British understatement. After all, we are the country of the legendary giant lumberjack, Paul Bunyan, who could cross Minnesota in a single stride. In *The River* the vistas of the land are vast; in *Night Mail* the countryside seems cozy by comparison. Even *The Fight for Life* suggests a city and problems larger than those of *Housing Problems. North Sea* reduces the terrors of the Atlantic to the domestic situations aboard the crippled trawler and in the wireless station at Wick.

Another difference is that American documentaries tend to gravitate towards the historical and to use before-and-after arguments. *The City* moves from eighteenth-century rural New England to twentieth-century urban New York; *Power and the Land* from the farm before electricity to the farm after it. Frequent reference is made to tradition and folk history. It may be that Americans felt themselves lacking in tradition; after all, education, art, and even fashion looked to Europe. In the 1930s we began to discover what it was to be American; that, in fact, there was such a thing as a national heritage. The murals painted by WPA artists in post offices across the country confirm this impulse. Also, the New Deal, accused in some quarters of being a kind of creeping socialism, tended to attach itself to American tradition, suggesting that cooperation with government was as American as apple pie.

As for contemporary subjects, as has been pointed out, American films faced the Depression, rising fascism, and Japanese conquest head on. Some fine, strong films were made on those subjects. With Grierson's dependence on consensus, sponsors couldn't be found to back such statements. I doubt that he tried because they were divisive subjects. Coherence and continuity were important in Grierson's conception of what British documentary and Britain itself needed. In spite of talk about films being in the forefront of policy, main line British documentarians made no directly *political* films. Rotha's little "poster film," *Peace of Britain* (1936), backing the League of Nations, would be the exception that proves the rule.

Finally, there are the sorts of aesthetic experiences and effects on social attitudes being offered. On the aesthetic side the United States certainly need not be apologetic. *The Plow That Broke the Plains, The River, Power and the Land, The City,* and *And So They Live* are as lovely and lasting as anything the British made. On the side of social and educational effectiveness, what

Grierson called propaganda, perhaps none of these matched *Night Mail* or *Housing Problems.* Though there is no way to test such an opinion empirically, American documentary as a whole seems to have had less influence on national life than British documentary. "The March of Time" might make a claim in this respect. But "The March of Time" was not consistently advancing anything in particular except, perhaps, an antifascist, prowar international position beginning in the late 1930s.

CONCLUSION

At the end of the 1930s some efforts were made to organize American documentary along British lines. Mary Losey (sister of feature-film director Joseph) was a key figure in them. She had met Grierson and been stimulated by his work on a trip to London in 1938. On her return "she set to work after the Grierson pattern to organize the jangling sects of American documentary into a purposeful group," as Richard Griffith put it.[3] An Association of Documentary Film Producers (its British model was the Association of Realist Film Producers) was established in New York City in 1939. The A.D.F.P. membership included, "with the conspicuous exception of Pare Lorentz," Mary Losey noted, "all the producers of documentary today"[4]— some sixty full members, roughly the same number of documentary makers as in Britain. Even Flaherty became part of this group on his return from Britain in 1939 to begin production of *The Land.*

In that year Mary Losey established an American Film Center, modeled after Film Centre in London, with support from the Rockefeller Foundation (with which Grierson had close ties). Her intention was to use it as a base "to attack the citadels of sponsorship and distribution," wrote Griffith.[5]

Alas, these efforts were too little and too late. Following the United States entry into World War II in 1941, the members of the Association of Documentary Film Producers were scattered about the globe. That organization was disbanded in 1942. American Film Center ended a few years later, owing to a lack of financial support and divisive differences in point of view among producers and Film Center personnel. "What a people, what a people," Grierson once remarked about Americans, in a mixture of affection and exasperation.

With the war, the groups on the far left that had culminated in Frontier Films lost their principal reason and means for being. The political situation was now that of a common front, with the United States fighting fascism alongside communist Russia. During the war there was a virtual cessation of private documentary production, and documentary filmmakers all made government films of one sort or another. In 1943 Frontier Films was disbanded.

The war would profoundly affect British and American documentary. Since the British were first into the war, as they had been first into documentary, we will return to Britain in the next chapter.

NOTES

[1]Robert Snyder, *Pare Lorentz and the Documentary Film* (Norman: University of Oklahoma Press, 1968), p. 176.

[2]John Grierson, *Grierson on Documentary*, ed. Forsyth Hardy (Berkeley: University of California Press, 1966), pp. 218–20.

[3]Paul Rotha in collaboration with Sinclair Road and Richard Griffith, *Documentary Film* (New York: Hastings House Publishers, 1970), p. 309.

[4]Mary Losey, "Documentary in the United States," *Documentary News Letter,* 1 (May 1940), p. 9.

[5]Rotha, *Documentary Film*, p. 309.

FILMS OF THE PERIOD

1935
"The March of Time" series began (Louis de Rochemont)
The Wave (Paul Strand and Fred Zinnemann)

1936
The Plow That Broke the Plains (Pare Lorentz)

1937
China Strikes Back (Harry Dunham)
Heart of Spain (Herbert Kline)
The River (Lorentz)
The Spanish Earth (Joris Ivens)

1938
Crisis (Kline)
The Four Hundred Million (Ivens)
People of the Cumberland (Elia Kazan)
Return to Life (Kline)

1939
The City (Ralph Steiner and Willard Van Dyke)
Lights Out in Europe (Kline)

1940
And So They Live (John Ferno and Julian Roffman)
Power and the Land (Ivens)
The Ramparts We Watch (de Rochemont)
Valley Town (Van Dyke)

1941
The Fight for Life (Lorentz)
The Land (Robert Flaherty)
A Place to Live (Irving Lerner)

1942
Native Land (Leo Hurwitz and Paul Strand)

BOOKS ON THE PERIOD

ALEXANDER, WILLIAM, *Film on the Left: American Documentary Film from 1931 to 1942*. Princeton, N.J.: Princeton University Press, 1981. 355 pp.

BÖKER, CARLOS, *Joris Ivens, Film-Maker: Facing Reality*. Ann Arbor, Mich.: UMI Research Press, 1981. 222 pp.

CAMPBELL, RUSSELL, *Cinema Strikes Back: Radical Filmmaking in the United States, 1930–1942*. Ann Arbor, Mich.: UMI Research Press, 1982. 398 pp.

DELMAR, ROSALIND, *Joris Ivens: 50 Years of Film-making*. London: British Film Institute, 1979. 127 pp.

FIELDING, RAYMOND, *The March of Time, 1935–1951*. New York: Oxford University Press, 1978. 359 pp.

IVENS, JORIS, *The Camera and I*. New York: International Publishers, 1969. 279 pp.

MACCANN, RICHARD DYER, *The People's Films: A Political History of U.S. Government Motion Pictures*. New York: Hastings House, Publishers, 1973. 256 pp.

SNYDER, ROBERT L., *Pare Lorentz and the Documentary Film*. Norman: University of Oklahoma Press, 1968. 232 pp.

ZUKER, JOEL STEWART, *Ralph Steiner, Filmmaker and Still Photographer*. New York: Arno Press, 1978. 453 pp.

SEVEN
EXPANSION
Great Britain, 1939–1945

On September 1, 1939, German Panzer divisions rolled across the Polish border and Stuka dive-bombers took to the skies. On September 3, Prime Minister Neville Chamberlain announced over BBC radio that a state of war existed between Great Britain and Germany. His announcement was followed by the accidental setting off of air raid sirens.

At the time, the British entertainment film industry was dominated by Americans. Gary Cooper, Greta Garbo, James Cagney, and Bette Davis commanded the popular audience. French and, to a lesser extent, Soviet films attracted the discriminating in London. British features lacked distinction and a specifically national tradition such as French poetic realism or the American genres of western, gangster, and musical. Of course there were isolated exceptions—films of Alfred Hitchcock (*The Lady Vanishes,* 1938), or Anthony Asquith (*Pygmalion,* 1938), or a young Carol Reed (*Bank Holiday,* 1938), for example. But in general the public took British features as second best to Hollywood. The intellectuals were completely indifferent to them.

Documentary, on the other hand, though relatively small in terms of money and audience, had established film as a means of social and scientific communication with hundreds of short films of fact and opinion. It had prestige among the intellectuals and fit in with thirties' ideas about art in relation to society. A movement with trained and skilled workers, it offered a distinct style as well as purpose, and innovations in form and technique that were arguably Britain's most important contribution to the development of film.

Further, with the outbreak of war, when the needs of the nation were paramount, British documentary's identification with government from its beginnings became especially significant. The government film unit at the Empire Marketing Board and then at the General Post Office, had been training ground and trend setter, and had offered means of national expression in an exact sense. With the war, the GPO Film Unit became the Crown Film Unit (in 1940), serving all departments of government. Wartime documentaries would be made by the veteran documentarians plus new recruits.

Following the declaration of war (in spite of the accidental air raid sirens) it was some time before Britain was engaged in actual combat. There was a period of "phoney war," as it was called, the "sitting war" or "Sitzkrieg," as someone dubbed it in reference to the Germans' *Blitzkrieg* (lightning war). Poland was defeated before either France or Britain, bound to it by mutual defense treaties, could come to its aid. Six months passed between the fall of Poland and the beginning in Denmark and Norway of the German drive in Western Europe.

EARLY DAYS

The first film job immediately evident was to record the events of war. For this purpose the five English newsreel companies pooled their resources for what would soon become a mammoth task. This provided for the free exchange of material to limit redundancy in the use of personnel and so a maximum amount of war activity could be covered. Exceptional work was done by newsreel and armed forces combat cameramen throughout the war. The casualty rate among them was high. In combat situations where troops could dig into foxholes, those who had to move about aboveground—platoon leaders, medics, cinematographers and still photographers—suffered most.

Documentary was needed to deal with the background as well as the foreground of war. Those first months were marked by a worrisome complacency; the British didn't yet realize their danger. Evidence of naive overconfidence is offered in a feature film Alexander Korda produced for the government on a voluntary basis entitled *The Lion has Wings* (1939). Directed by Michael Powell and starring Merle Oberon and Ralph Richardson, it combines newsreel footage with fictional material. Its climax occurs when a German air attack on London is thwarted by the height of the balloon barrage. (*Things to Come,* 1936, also produced by Korda, from H.G. Wells's science-fiction novel, had been closer to what enemy attacks on London would actually be like. It shows hundreds of large, dark planes thundering over the city and raining destruction upon it.)

In September of 1939 the Ministry of Information was established to take overall charge of the creation and dissemination of propaganda. Its Films Division, after initial inactivity, was headed by Kenneth Clark, art historian and director of the National Gallery (and later host of the widely distributed television series *Civilization*). The film advisers to the Chamberlain government were distrustful of the documentary people because of their leftward tendencies. Instead of the documentarians, filmmakers from the entertainment film industry were called on. The documentary group vented their frustration by grousing to each other and writing letters to *The Times*. Without any real authorization, let alone connection with Post Office activity, the GPO Film Unit had, on its own, made *The First Days* (1939) shortly after war broke out. Harry Watt, Humphrey Jennings, and Pat Jackson collaborated on it.

In January 1940 Prime Minister Chamberlain appointed Lord John Reith as Minister of Information. Lord Reith, first and long-lasting head of the British Broadcasting Corporation, was a dour Scot who seemed to feel God had entrusted him with responsibility for uplifting the British people. When Winston Churchill became prime minister in May, he transferred Reith to the post of Minister of Transport and named Brendan Bracken, his close associate, head of the MOI. Bracken in turn appointed Jack Beddington head of the Films Division. Beddington, a public relations officer who had been instrumental in the establishment of the Shell Film Unit, understood the aims of the documentary movement and had a feeling for the film medium. His first act, on becoming head of Films Division, was to request a paper from Film Centre explaining how to use films in time of war. Grierson alumni Edgar Anstey, Arthur Elton, and Basil Wright wrote it.

Throughout the spring of 1940 the government documentaries were aimed chiefly toward what was called the "spiritual arming of the people." A series of short story films begun under Clark were completed. Some of these were by distinguished feature directors. One example is *Men of the Lightship* (1940), directed by David MacDonald. It is what might now be called a docudrama. A true story reenacted by actors, it concerns a lightship attacked by German bombers. Its crew must row thirty miles through heavy fog to reach the shore. Attempting to land on a lonely part of the East Coast, their boat is overturned and only one man survives. *Channel Incident* (1940), produced and directed by Anthony Asquith, is a reenactment of an event in the evacuation of Allied forces from Dunkirk.

Produced at about the same time was an MOI series of shorts made in collaboration with the French to demonstrate solidarity. In regard to their French allies, a strategic problem existed for the British. If they sent large numbers of troops to France and France fell, Britain would be left unprotected. The Germans took advantage of this dilemma in their propaganda directed at the French. "Where ARE your British Allies?" they asked, or announced that "Britain will fight to the last drop of French blood."

After the summer of 1940, when France had fallen, the greater part of Western Europe had been overrun by the Germans. Britain was now a besieged island constantly under the threat of air attack. The documentarians reacted to these changed circumstances and became the interpreter of the British mood in war.

Another series of short factual films followed—half newsreel, half pictorial comment, and highly charged with the spirit of the time. *The Front Line* (1940) recorded life in the Channel port of Dover under air raid and bombardment by long-range German guns. *London Can Take It* (1940) pictured life in London during the great night raids of the Battle of Britain. Directed by Harry Watt and Humphrey Jennings, its commentary was written and read by American correspondent Quentin Reynolds. Cool images of actuality and hot prose of Reynolds's journalism are the basis of its style. He could say things about the British under fire which they couldn't modestly say about themselves.

London Can Take It (U.K., 1940, Harry Watt and Humphrey Jennings). National Film Archive/Stills Library.

With Beddington, the documentary old guard had entered the war filmmaking effort. *Squadron 992* (1940), produced by Alberto Cavalcanti and directed by Harry Watt, was made by the GPO Film Unit for the Air Force. About the training of a balloon barrage unit which then moves up into Scotland, it ends with a simulated German air raid on the bridge over the Firth of Forth. There is less attention to how it is done than in many documentaries, and more to mood and imagery including lovely shots of the bridge, countryside, and sea. The humor is noteworthy—including mild kidding of the Scots. (Watt was Scottish). We see at a distance one of the soldiers knocking on a door. A woman answers, listens to him, and shouts back over her shoulder "Willie, there's a man here who wants to put a balloon in our garden."

Squadron 992 (U.K., 1940, Harry Watt). Museum of Modern Art/Film Stills Archive.

As the war got fully underway, hundreds of training and orientation, scientific and medical films were produced for military and civilian audiences. There were films which enabled gunners to test the accuracy of their aim, or which taught airmen the use of their controls. Short films, "trailers" they would be called in the film industry, warned civilians to economize on fuel and water (*The Burning Question*, 1945, on fuel economy), to collect salvage (*Salvage with a Smile*, 1940, waste paper for cartridges, household waste for pig food), and the like. Each month the MOI presented a fifteen-minute film on the progress of the struggle: the fall and rehabilitation of Naples (*Naples Is a Battlefield*, 1944), or the devastation created in Walcheren by the flooding of the dykes (*Broken Dykes*, 1945), for example. The scientific and medical films included a film dealing with the National Blood Transfusion Service (*Blood Transfusion*, 1942), an MOI film for doctors on the diagnosis and treatment of a skin disease caused by parasites (*Scabies*, 1943), and another on a new antibiotic drug (*Penicillin*, 1944).

In addition to these more directly utilitarian films, three major types of British wartime documentaries emerged between 1941 and 1945. They were the (1) semidocumentary indoctrinational features, (2) a continuation of the peacetime social documentary with new subjects and forms, and (3) the records of battle.

INDOCTRINATION

Alberto Cavalcanti, who had succeeded Grierson, was producer in charge of the GPO Film Unit. In the summer of 1940 he was succeeded by Ian Dalrymple. Shortly thereafter the name of the unit was changed to Crown Film Unit and it became responsible to the Ministry of Information rather than an appendage of the General Post Office. Under Cavalcanti and Dalrymple (and subsequently J.B. Holmes and Basil Wright) the aesthetic aspects of documentary were nurtured. Harry Watt would continue to develop the narrative line he had begun with *Night Mail* (1936), *The Saving of Bill Blewitt* (1937), and *North Sea* (1938). Humphrey Jennings would add impressionist poetic elements (evident early in *Spare Time*, 1939), becoming a sort of film laureate of wartime Britain.

Evidently the Ministry of Information decided that the best sort of support and inspiration for the population at large could come from showing British men and women going about their wartime tasks with resolution, efficiency, and quiet heroism. In taking this approach, a main line of British indoctrination films moved toward Flaherty, and also toward fiction features, in depicting the drama of survival inherent in war. It was Harry Watt in *Target for Tonight* (1941) who created the prototype for the feature-length semidocumentary indoctrination films that would come from Crown and be made by commercial studios as well, Ealing particularly.

Target for Tonight concerns a Royal Air Force bombing mission into Germany to destroy an oil refinery and storage and distribution center at Freihausen. It follows a Wellington bomber and its crew. The bomber is hit by flack over the target, one of its crew is wounded, and it limps back to base on one engine. The action is a composite representation of how such a raid would actually be carried out. It is acted by real airmen and has the real setting of airfield and airplanes. It comes alive through our direct dramatic involvement with the crew members in a way associated with story films. The deft characterization, the dialogue that seems to fit the men and the situation, and the bits of wry humor are all engaging. An airman says to the young Scottish navigator, "Listen, Jock, who was it who didn't know whether he was over Hanover or Hampton Court?" Jock, not amused, explains indignantly to the others, "That's a joke." In giving these airmen a chance to be themselves, Watt was the first to depict the human undercurrents of war at a depth documentary had not previously attempted.

Following *Target for Tonight* out of Crown, a sort of companion piece to it was *Coastal Command* (1942), running 73 minutes. Directed by J.B. Holmes, with a score by Vaughan Williams, its theme is cooperation between shore-based RAF aircraft and the Navy in defending convoys at sea. In this case our identification is with the crew of a Sunderland Flying Boat.

Fires Were Started (1943), directed by Humphrey Jennings, is about the work of the Auxiliary Fire Service during the devastating German fire raids

Target for Tonight (U.K., 1941, Harry Watt). National Film Archive/Stills Library.

Fires Were Started (U.K., 1943, Humphrey Jennings). National Film Archive/Stills Library.

on London. By using the device of a new recruit, Jennings can let us see through his eyes and learn not only about the functioning of this fire fighting service but about the diverse and likable personalities brought together in it. When the raid begins we are able to follow the tactics of the fire fighters without aid of commentary through their actions and conversations, the phone calls from headquarters, the maps with pins stuck in them, the lists of equipment chalked on a board. Among other things, *Fires Were Started* is a model of teaching without didacticism.

But where its true greatness lies is in the way it informs, persuades, and moves all at the same time. In this film Jennings goes beyond other of the semidocumentaries in differentiating and developing the characters of his real/nonactor firemen. *Fires Were Started* together with two of his shorts—*Listen to Britain* (1942), an impressionist audiovisual poem about the country at war, and *A Diary for Timothy* (1945), a fusion of the impressionist/symphonic approach with (in this case multiple) narrative—comprise Jennings' masterpieces. His qualities as a filmmaker involve especially his formal experimentation, the intricate patterns of interwoven sights and sounds in his work. The individual images Jennings selected are rich in symbolic expressiveness, evoking peace as well as war, in combination and contrast. English tradition and English spirit saturate Jennings' films. He celebrates cultural heritage with a warmth that encourages us to share his feelings.

Listen to Britain (U.K., 1942, Humphrey Jennings). Museum of Modern Art/Film Stills Archive.

Western Approaches (1944, titled *The Raider* in the U.S.) was directed by Pat Jackson, who had assisted Harry Watt earlier (as had Humphrey Jennings before him). It is an account of the convoys of merchant vessels that left Halifax to transport supplies to Britain, and of the submarine warfare in the North Atlantic that they faced. It narrows down to the story of twenty-four men, survivors of a torpedoed freighter, who spend fourteen days adrift. Their lifeboat is used as bait by a lurking U-boat to attract an Allied ship.

This is the largest in scale, the most ambitious, and the most difficult technically of the British wartime semidocumentaries. Along with the documentary essentials of nonactors, location shooting, and description of process (how convoys and submarine attack and defense function), there is a high degree of skillfully handled artifice. The use of tightly scripted dialogue, sync-sound recording on location, and shooting with the cumbersome Technicolor camera on the high sea are all impressive. With its carefully plotted suspense and familiar characterizations, documentary here moves very close to fiction.

The semidocumentaries from the Crown Film Unit (*Merchant Seaman,* 1941, and *Close Quarters,* 1943, are others) were paralleled by semidocumentary features from the commercial studios. *In Which We Serve* (1942), co-directed by Noël Coward and David Lean and based on the experiences of an actual British destroyer commanded by Lord Louis Mountbatten and its crew, was the first of these. It was followed by some twenty or so others including *The Foreman Went to France, One of Our Aircraft Is Missing, Next of*

Western Approaches (*The Raider* in the U.S.; U.K., 1944, Pat Jackson). National Film Archive/Stills Library.

Kin in 1942; *San Demetrio London, Nine Men* (which Watt directed after he and Cavalcanti left Crown to work at Ealing); *We Dive at Dawn, Millions Like Us* in 1943; and *The Way Ahead* in 1944.

Two indoctrinational intentions of the British wartime semidocumentaries are apt to strike a viewer. One is their emphasis on togetherness. Over and over again the people are shown, civilians as well as military, working together to get the job done. Though microcosms of English society are frequently offered—with various identifiable regional and class accents, and a Scot or perhaps a Canadian thrown in—no tensions between regions or between classes are shown. In fact, such differences, very real in Britain, are minimized. Everyone is doing his or her work; all are working equally to win the war.

The other distinctive characteristic is the lack of violence shown on the screen and the lack of hatred expressed in either dialogue or narration. Rather than digging coal or working for an advertising agency or attending university, the job now is to destroy the unseen enemy and keep them from destroying us. If bombs fall from the night skies, it's as if they were an act of God, a natural disaster like an earthquake. The thing to do is to put out the fires, clean away the rubble, attend the wounded, and bury the dead.

While these two attitudes might be thought of as part of general wartime propaganda requirements, they seem very British to me; maybe even

In Which We Serve (U.K., 1942, Noël Coward and David Lean). Museum of Modern Art/ Film Stills Archive.

more specifically English. Nothing quite like them is apparent in the war-time films of Canada or the United States.

SOCIAL DOCUMENTARY

Notwithstanding the national peril, the social documentary survived. In fact, some interesting innovations of subject and form were added to it. In the wartime social documentary a common goal was put forward: not simply that the war should be won, but that it should be won to some purpose; that life should hold better opportunities for everyone after it. This attitude even appears in the Crown/Jennings indoctrinational *A Diary for Timothy*. When the Welsh miner is injured in an accident, the commentary, written by E.M. Forster and read by Michael Redgrave, adds: "It's pretty shocking that this sort of thing should happen every day though we've been cutting coal for five hundred years." As he is recuperating, the miner reminds his wife of the gains in health services made by labor since the end of the first World War. "Surely, if we can do that during that period," he says, "nothing can stop us after this war." If postwar opportunities was a frequent theme in British wartime documentaries, it was so because the working class felt that their great sacrifices and losses of World War I had not resulted in benefits for them.

World of Plenty (1943), Paul Rotha's compiled argument film, begins with the breakdown in international food distribution before the war—surpluses in some countries, starvation in others. The system of fair distribution by rationing enforced nationally during the war is then presented. It is suggested as a worldwide model for the future. Rotha always insisted (as did Grierson, less stridently) that documentaries had to deal with the economic underpinnings of any subject tackled. At the same time, economic abstractions are much harder to present in the language of motion pictures than are specific actualities. In attempting to solve this problem Rotha introduced a number of experimental elements. Diagrams, interviews, and trick optical effects were added to stock footage. The remarkable animated representations created by the Isotype Institute add clarity and drama to statistics of food production and distribution. Argumentative dialogue between an offscreen voice speaking for the audience to onscreen actors, and between onscreen actors, in roles of persons in various parts of the world speaking to each other, was especially original.

Children of the City (1944), produced by Rotha and directed by Budge Cooper, takes on the narrative aspects of the semidocumentary to deal with juvenile delinquency in a Scottish city. While the problem was not an exclu-

World of Plenty (U.K., 1943, Paul Rotha). Museum of Modern Art/Film Stills Archive.

Children of the City (U.K., 1944, Budge Cooper). Museum of Modern Art/Film Stills Archive.

sively wartime one, it had been exacerbated by the strains on families caused by fathers in military service and mothers working in war plants. *Children of the City* offers case studies of three boys who break into a pawnbroker's and are apprehended by the police as they are emptying the till. Not only the boys and their quite different family backgrounds but the social workers, the court officials, and the judicial and penal system within which they work are all observed.

As a final example there is *When We Build Again* (1945), about housing and planning. Sponsored by Cadbury Brothers, Ltd., makers of chocolates, it was produced by Donald Taylor and directed by Ralph Bond. Dylan Thomas wrote and read the poetic portions of the commentary. The film begins with a slight narrative of three returning servicemen (who are subsequently dropped). The music sounds like and is used in the manner of dramatic films. Inner city slums, suburbs, and new towns (like the greenbelt towns of *The City*) are surveyed. Interviews, statistics, visual demonstrations of existing housing, and models for the future are employed. "No private interest to stand in our way," intones the commentator, who calls people "the greatest capital—the future belongs to them." This film could be thought of as *Housing Problems* ten years later. It was made in the year of Labour's victory at the polls.

RECORDS OF BATTLE

Desert Victory (1943)—with production by the army Film Unit, direction by Roy Boulting, and music by William Alwyn—is about the British Eighth Army's campaign in North Africa against the German forces under the command of Field Marshall Erwin Rommel. Two creative problems are uppermost in this kind of filmmaking for the filmmakers working with miles of footage shot by combat cameramen. The first is to give clarity to the mass of confusing, technical detail. The second is to give it dramatic form. These problems are the same as those faced by Esfir Shub in *The Fall of the Romanov Dynasty* (1927), discussed in Chapter Three. In *Desert Victory,* the first problem was solved by the use of animated maps to establish the overall patterns and movement of the campaign, and by a carefully planned narration. As for the second, all of the nonartistic material with the irregularity of history inherent in it was given a beginning, middle, and end—like the chronicle plays of Shakespeare. In addition, the irrelevancies of the sponsor's requirements—to show each branch of the armed forces, the civilian workers, the presence of U.S. aid, and so on—were fitted into the whole without warping it out of shape.

 Desert Victory starts at the lowest point of the campaign. The British, who had retreated across the Sahara, pursued by the seemingly invincible Afrika Korps, are halted just sixty miles from Alexandria, deep inside Egypt. Then there is the fierce battle at El Alamein with the British emerging victorious. From there the film follows the triumphant 1300-mile pursuit of the German army to the final victory at Tripoli. To organize these events so they would appear both clear and dramatic, the filmmakers contrived an alternation of cause and effect. To personalize the mass action, and gain empathy, a number of closeups of individual soldiers (some of them obviously recreated, particularly in the night attack sequences) are inserted. Generals Alexander, Montgomery, and Wavell, and Prime Minister Churchill are introduced as well.

 In comparison with the indoctrinational semidocumentaries, which tended to make the violence of war part of a job of work to be done, *Desert Victory* is singularly bloodthirsty. Perhaps these filmmakers weren't inclined to conceal their elation over this first major British victory following the battering Britain had received in the desert fighting and from the air blitz. Perhaps because of its dramatic effectiveness, it received an American Oscar as the year's most distinctive achievement in documentary features.

 Tunisian Victory (1944), a British-American coproduction, was also directed by Roy Boulting. It carried the North African story from the American landings in November 1942 to the annihilation of the German forces at Cape Bon. *Burma Victory* (1945), Roy Boulting again, may have been prompted partly by a Hollywood feature, *Objective Burma* (1945), directed by

Raoul Walsh, that annoyed the British. In it Errol Flynn, as an American paratrooper, pretty much single-handedly mops up the Japanese enemy. *Burma Victory* succeeds in making clear the confusing phases of the Burma campaign, which was essentially a British operation, between 1942 and the end of the war with Japan.

The True Glory (1945) was produced jointly by the British Ministry of Information and the U.S. Office of War Information. It was directed by Englishman Carol Reed and American Garson Kanin, fiction film directors of considerable distinction. William Alwyn composed the music. It covers the period from the preparations for the D-day landings in Normandy through the fall of Berlin to the establishing of contact between the Western Allies and Russian troops at the Elbe River. Made from 5.5 million feet of combat footage shot by 500 American, British, and other Allied cameramen, it is a vast panorama, yet intensely human, even intimate at moments.

Emotional involvement is gained largely through the experimental use of commentary. The words are complementary to the images, sometimes in humorous or ironic counterpoint to them. Alternating with blank verse choruses are multiple voices representing soldiers involved with the particular action being shown. The general's version, spoken by Dwight D. Eisenhower himself, supreme commander of Allied forces in Europe, is irreverently interrupted by enlisted men who were there—New York cab driver, cockney Londoner, member of the French Maquis, and others. One marvelous moment occurs when a black American M.P. directing military traffic

Desert Victory (U.K., 1943, Roy Boulting). Museum of Modern Art/Film Stills Archive.

at a crossroads explains that the situation is tough, that the invasion forces are bottled up in the Caen Peninsula. "Then we heard that the Third Army was taking off," he says. "They'd pulled a rabbit out of a hat—and what a rabbit! A rabbit with pearl-handled revolvers." As he says this a tank bearing an erect General George S. Patton roars by.

The True Glory was the final triumphant record and hymn to Allied victory in Europe. The occasion permitted a kind of boasting and self-congratulation without it appearing to be so. Pride is expressed in the massiveness and efficiency of the military machine and in its democratic nature. The participation of many nations is indirectly reiterated without explicit statement being required. The Allied attitude toward war is presented as being purposeful and matter-of-fact, its violence accepted as part of a job to be done, as in the British semidocumentaries. Unlike the semidocumentaries, however, dislike and distrust of the German enemy are strongly stated. An American G.I., talking about guarding German prisoners of war, says: "I just kept 'em covered. . . . It wasn't my job to figure 'em out. . . . But, brother, I never gave 'em more than the Geneva convention, and that was all." Finally, though, it is the positive corollary of the G.I.'s attitude that

The True Glory (U.K. and U.S., 1945, Carol Reed and Garson Kanin). Museum of Modern Art/Film Stills Archive.

receives the strongest emphasis. What *The True Glory* is saying mostly is that this was a just and necessary war and that on the Allied side we can all feel proud of our part in winning it.

FILMS OF THE PERIOD

1940
London Can Take It (Harry Watt and Humphrey Jennings)
They Also Serve (Ruby Grierson)

1941
Merchant Seamen (J. B. Holmes)
Target for Tonight (Watt)

1942
Coastal Command (Holmes)
The Harvest Shall Come (Max Anderson)
Listen to Britain (Jennings)

1943
Desert Victory (Roy Boulting)
Fires Were Started (Jennings)
The Silent Village (Jennings)
World of Plenty (Paul Rotha)

1944
Children of the City (Budge Cooper)
Tunisian Victory (Boulting and Frank Capra)
Western Approaches (Pat Jackson)

1945
Burma Victory (Boulting)
A Diary for Timothy (Jennings)
The True Glory (Carol Reed and Garson Kanin)

BOOKS ON THE PERIOD

ALEXANDER, DONALD, *The Documentary Film*. London: British Film Institute, 1945. 9 pp.
THE ARTS ENQUIRY, *The Factual Film*. London: Oxford University Press, 1947. 259 pp.
HARDY, FORSYTH, "The British Documentary Film," *Twenty Years of British Film 1925–1945*, eds. Michael Balcon and others. London: The Falcon Press Limited, 1947. pp. 45–80.
HODGKINSON, ANTHONY W. AND RODNEY E. SHERATSKY. *Humphrey Jennings: More than a Maker of Films*. Hanover, N. H.: University Press of New England, 1982. 400 pp.
JENNINGS, MARY-LOU, ed., *Humphrey Jennings: Film-Maker/Painter/Poet*. London: British Film Institute, 1982. 75 pp.
LOVELL, ALAN AND JIM HILLIER, *Studies in Documentary*. New York: The Viking Press, Inc., 1972. 176 pp.
MANVELL, ROGER, *Films and the Second World War*. New York: Dell Publishing Co., Inc., 1974. 388 pp.
POWELL, DILYS, *Films Since 1939*. London: Longmans, Green and Co. Ltd., 1947. 40 pp.
SHERATSKY, RODNEY, guest ed., Spec. issue on *Humphrey Jennings: Artist of the Documentary*. *Film Library Quarterly*, 8.3,4 (1975). 64 pp.
SUSSEX, ELIZABETH, *The Rise and Fall of British Documentary: The Story of the Film Movement Founded by John Grierson*. Berkeley: University of California Press, 1975. 219 pp.
THORPE, FRANCES AND NICHOLAS PRONAY, *British Official Films in the Second World War: A Descriptive Catalogue*. London: Imperial War Museum, Inter-University Film Consortium, and University of Leeds, 1979. 320 pp.
WATT, HARRY, *Don't Look at the Camera*. London: Paul Elek, Ltd., 1974. 197 pp.

EIGHT
EXPANSION
Canada, 1939–1945

At the outbreak of World War II, Canada was something of a sleeping giant. In certain ways it was also a geographical and cultural anomaly which no orderly-minded nation planner would have perpetrated. Larger in area than the United States, with a sparse population stretched across a 200-mile-wide strip along its southern border, it represented physically a virtual extension of the United States up into the uninhabitable Arctic. Its prodigious breadth of forest and prairie, blocked at the western end by a fierce mountain range, took considerable conquering before the Atlantic was finally linked to the Pacific.

In addition to the formidable task of taming a wilderness, Canadians had always faced a struggle for national identity. At first it was the matter of establishing independence from Britain, greatly aided by the Balfour Declaration, which emerged from the Imperial Conference of 1926. It had declared the Dominions "autonomous communities ... united by a common allegiance to the Crown, and freely associated as members of the British Commonwealth of Nations." More recently, the gravitational pull of its powerful neighbor to the south was smothering Canada's distinctiveness. Economically and culturally, as well as geographically, Canada was something of an extension of the United States.

When war broke out in 1939 the film situation in Canada was considerably different from that in either Britain or the United States. In Canada there was no production of fiction feature films and theatrical distribution and exhibition were even more dominated by the Americans than in Britain. In fact, there was a negligible amount of Canadian film production of any sort. Britain had a firmly established documentary movement. If the United States' documentary efforts lacked the coherence and overall effectiveness of the British, it had distinguished documentary filmmakers and films it could point to with pride. War and documentary arrived together in Canada at the end of the thirties.

A pioneer Government Motion Picture Bureau in Ottawa extended back to 1914. But it provided largely "scenic and travel pictures" lacking the social relevance of the documentary. By the 1930s it had fallen badly out of touch with current realities and the filmmaking techniques and styles it employed were quite old-fashioned. Hollywood might occasionally make a nod to the romance of Canada in a musical (Jeanette MacDonald and Nelson Eddy in *Rose Marie*, 1936) or its epic scale in a spectacle (Cecil B. De Mille's *North West Mounted Police*, 1940). No image of productive, modern Canada appeared on screens anywhere; no adequate acknowledgment of its role as a rising world leader with vast natural resources, agricultural and industrial potential was made. No sure sense of national identity was being given to the Canadian people through film (or through other media, for that matter). Culturally, Canadians felt overshadowed by their southern neighbor, and they retained an inferiority complex about their former colonial status.

FOUNDING OF NATIONAL FILM BOARD

Representatives of the Canadian government in London had become interested in the success of British documentary—its dynamic presentation of government services, British people, and British problems. At about the same time, John Grierson was asked by the Film Committee of the Imperial Relations Trust, set up by the British government in 1937, to survey government film developments in Canada and other dominions. In 1938 he was invited to Canada, where he investigated, reported on, and made recommendations to the Canadian government regarding its use of film.

In his report, which "resembled other reports about as much as a machine gun resembled a plastic pistol,"[1] he recommended the creation of a new federal agency. It would produce films that would contribute to a greater sense of relationship among Canadians and present an accurate picture of Canada to the rest of the world. The acceptance of his recommendations followed; legislation establishing a National Film Board was passed by the Canadian Parliament in May 1939 and the search for the new Film Commissioner began. Though a Canadian was intended and sought, no Canadian with adequate qualifications could be found. Grierson was chosen, and accepted the offer in October 1939.

It is important to note that the Film Board was conceived in peacetime and for peacetime purposes. The legislation creating it decreed its principal mandate that of helping "Canadians in all parts of Canada to understand the ways of living and the problems of Canadians in other parts." This was the same function conceived at the Empire Marketing Board ten years earlier by Grierson and Stephen Tallents in their credo of showing one part of the Empire to the rest. The Film Board's position as an autonomous government agency with its own budget and representation in Parliament came out of Grierson's frustrations with the limitations of sponsorship by the EMB and, especially, the General Post Office, and made the NFB unique. The Board was also to concern itself with "distribution of Canadian films in other countries." The first six years of the National Film Board would, however, be devoted to Canada's war effort.

Grierson began in earnest to build the large and effective organization the National Film Board would become. In this he had the full support of Prime Minister Mackenzie King. Veteran colleagues from Britain were brought over. Stuart Legg, already in Ottawa making two films for the Canadian government, was joined by others including Raymond Spottiswoode, Stanley Hawes, Norman McLaren, and Evelyn Spice. Available documentary talent from other countries were hired as well: Irving Jacoby (producer and screenwriter) and Roger Barlow (cinematographer) among those from the United States; Joris Ivens and John Ferno from Holland; Boris Kaufman (Jean Vigo's cameraman) and Alexander Alexeiff (animator of the pinboard technique) from France. And the hiring of young Canadians began, not unlike the hiring of young Englishmen in the earlier EMB and GPO days, except now in much larger numbers. Julian Roffman (who already had film experience), Ross McLean (who became Assistant Film Commissioner), Donald Fraser, James Beveridge, Budge Crawley, Tom Daly, Michael Spencer, Guy Glover, and Sydney Newman were among the early recruits.

The production of hundreds and hundreds of films commenced. The first year closed in October 1940 with some forty pictures either in distribution, in production, or in script preparation; by the fiscal year of 1943–1944 the annual rate of release had increased to 200. Two monthly series modeled on "The March of Time" were distributed in the theaters and subsequently released to nontheatrical audiences. It was a newsreel war not a documentary war, Grierson said, requiring the crude immediacy of reportage rather than the considered refinement of art.

THEATRICAL SERIES

The first series was "Canada Carries on," intended primarily to depict Canada's part in the war to its own people and to others. Produced by Stuart Legg, it was distributed by Columbia Pictures. The first CCO release was *Atlantic Patrol* (April 1940). It was about the work of the Canadian navy in

John Grierson (right) looks over a poster for a 1944 National Film Board of Canada release. National Film Board.

protecting the huge convoys that sailed from Halifax to Britain from German submarine attack. *Churchill's Island* (June 1941), about Britain at war, won an Academy Award.

The Canadian series demonstrated an uncanny knack for latching onto what was about to happen. *Warclouds in the Pacific* (November 1941), appearing ten days before the Japanese attack on Pearl Harbor, contained some borrowed "March of Time" footage. Louis de Rochemont tried to hold up its release to prevent it from scooping the MOT. *Zero Hour* (June 1944) was another scoop: the first account of the Allied invasion of Normandy. NFB personnel had assembled footage on D-Day preparations in Britain. Then they prepared more than a dozen different endings covering possible

Zero Hour, "Canada Carries On" series (Canada, 1944, Stuart Legg). Museum of Modern Art/Film Stills Archive.

invasion points from Norway to the Mediterranean. When the invasion occurred, the appropriate ending was added and the film was released immediately.

If "Canada Carries On" paid "The March of Time" the compliment of imitation, the second, even more ambitious series began to compete with MOT in the world market, including the United States. Entitled "The World in Action," it appeared two years after CCO had begun. Stanley Hawes took over "Canada Carries On." "World in Action" became Stuart Legg's project; with some exceptions he wrote and directed every issue. United Artists distributed.

This Is Blitz (January 1942) was the first of the WIA. It used captured newsreel footage to reveal the devastation German aggression had caused. The second part dealt with Allied counter strategy. Many of the issues concerned noncombative but important wartime topics. Its treatment of economic/social/political subjects became one of its special distinctions. *Food— Weapon of Conquest* (March 1942) was the second WIA release. *Time* magazine called it "a blueprint of how to make an involved, dull, major aspect of World War II understandable and acceptable to moviegoers."[2] *Inside Fighting Russia* (April 1942) comprised mostly footage obtained from the Soviets. Since the Russians tended to be secretive, this represented quite a coup. It came about, Grierson said, when he recognized a Soviet official as one of the boys in the Soviet film *Road to Life* (1931), about homeless waifs during

Main title of "The World in Action" series (Canada, 1942–45, Stuart Legg). Photographed from the screen by Raymond Fielding.

the Revolution. *War for Men's Minds* (June 1943) concerned psychological warfare. (Grierson took secret delight in being called "the Goebbels of Canada," in reference to Nazi propaganda minister Joseph Goebbels, though he thought Hitler the true genius of propaganda.) The most ambitious and intellectual of the WIA films, *War for Men's Minds* was also the first of the Canadian films to look ahead to peace.

48 Hour Leave (Canada, 1945, James Beveridge and Sydney Newman). J. Fred MacDonald.

The two series were noteworthy for their departures from usual wartime propaganda emphases. There was very little hatred or violence in these films. "World in Action" emphasis shifted from matters of immediate wartime concern to those that would concern the postwar world. The international view and steady look ahead to peace were quite exceptional during wartime. The WIA particularly extended much beyond showing one part of Canada to the rest, and in that respect surpassed the documentary work in Great Britain.

Examples of internationalism would be *Labour Front* (October 1943) and, especially, *Global Air Routes* (April 1944). Grierson took satisfaction in turning the globe upside down, as he put it, in the NFB films: putting Canada at the center rather than the periphery of the world. *When Asia Speaks* (June 1944) was so accurate and farseeing in its analysis that it was still in active nontheatrical distribution long after the war. *Now—The Peace* (May 1945) dealt with the new United Nations organization.

NONTHEATRICAL FILMS

The great majority of those hundreds of films produced by the Film Board were for nontheatrical distribution rather than for the theaters. They dealt with a variety of subjects. These included intimate regional studies (for example, on the life of a Quebec priest or on Gran Manan Island), the building of the Alaska Highway, a pictorial analysis of the workings of credit unions, and animated charts on the meaning of unemployment insurance. There were also cultural shorts like the *Flight of the Dragon,* about the collection of Chinese art in the Royal Ontario Museum. *High Over the Borders* (written by Irving Jacoby and edited by John Ferno) concerned the facts and mysteries of bird migration in the Western Hemisphere. Gudrun Bjerring (later Parker) made a fifteen-minute film called *Before They Are Six,* intended particularly for mothers who ran a home and a lathe or a workbench in a wartime plant.

Canada's comprehensive system of nontheatrical distribution and exhibition was unequalled. It had an annual audience larger than the national population. The films, in fact, grew out of the needs of the audiences to a remarkable degree; "audience response" was the key term, uniquely important in the growth of the NFB. A network of nontheatrical showings was created by the Film Board—preceding television, of course—with rural circuits, national trade union circuits, and industrial circuits being established. One typical circuit program was: *Food as It Might Be,* on the postwar future of farming and food marketing; *Getting Out the Coal,* on coal mining; *Trees for Tomorrow,* on forest conservation; *Mites and Monsters,* a natural history topic; and *News Roundup,* a report on the latest war developments. Later the circuits were supplemented by regional film libraries, volunteer projection

services, and film councils doing the work locally with guidance and assistance from the Board.

Showings were held by the women's club or the library, for example,
or by the YMCA or at a grange meeting. Sixteen-millimeter prints were borrowed from regional libraries. Volunteer projection services provided
trained projectionists and trained others to operate projectors. The film
councils consisted of representatives from each of the local organizations
using films. They would meet, once a month perhaps, to discuss and plan
ways of improving the use of films. So, a kind of decentralized leadership
emerged and a feedback process started. It was not just the government
telling the Film Board what they wanted government films to be about and
what kinds of information on those subjects they needed.

SUMMARY

The essential point to be made about the National Film Board seems to be
that the kind of institution Grierson was able to construct in Canada was
an unrivaled information system, the largest and best coordinated government film operation in the world. By 1945, the end of the war, it was producing 300 films a year (this in contrast to 300 documentaries produced in
Great Britain in the ten years before the war). Most of the Film Board releases reached an audience of roughly four million. It had a staff of about
700 in production and distribution. All of this was achieved by a nation
with a population of only twelve million.

Looking back over the hundreds of films produced by the NFB during
wartime, it must be admitted that they had little staying power. Almost none
of them is distributed today, unlike a number of the British and American
wartime documentaries and even some made in those countries in the
1930s. This would not have mattered to Grierson at the time; the need for
direct and rapid communication was the main consideration. The "5½
films a week," as Grierson characterized Film Board output when it had
reached full speed, were often skillfully made, usually timely in subject matter (rather than timeless), quickly produced, and designed to reach as wide
an audience as the subject and purpose permitted. In artistic terms they
had a roughness along with their urgency. Those films were valued by their
audiences as well as by their producers for what they were—an almost television-like flow of information and coverage of important topics before television.

During the war a rift occurred between Grierson and his former British colleagues over the kinds of documentaries that needed to be made.
Grierson thought the British documentaries too soft and aestheticky. "Sure,
London can take it," he would say, in reference to the influential British
documentary by that title, "but can she dish it out?" paraphrasing dialogue

from one of his favorite gangster movies, *Little Caesar*. Grierson saw early British wartime propaganda as reflecting a country preparing to go down with quiet heroism into defeat. There is an anecdote about Grierson preventing the young Canadians from screening the print of *Listen to Britain* he had received so that they would not be distracted by its beauty from the more vigorous style he wanted them to develop. Some of the British, for their part, found the Canadian films illustrated lectures lacking in artistic sophistication, which infuriated Grierson. They may have been at least as effective as the more polished British production in reaching their intended audiences and achieving their purposes. It does seem to me indisputable that the Film Board played a part in giving Canada a sense of national identity and pride.

Perhaps, finally, the sheer establishment of the National Film Board— which went on to other kinds of achievements, including aesthetic excellence, while the documentary movements in Britain and America faltered— is the great legacy of the wartime documentary efforts in Canada. It stands as the largest and most impressive monument to Grierson's concepts and actions relating to the use of film by governments in communication with their citizens. It became a model for national film boards established in New Zealand, Australia, South Africa, India, and elsewhere. Grierson himself called the Film Board "a tidy operation, the tidiest [he] was involved with."[3]

NOTES

[1]John Grierson, *Grierson on Documentary*, ed. Forsyth Hardy (Berkeley: University of California Press, 1966), p. 25.

[2]"Cinema: The New Pictures," *Time* (June 15, 1942).

[3]John Grierson, Personal Interview (September 1966).

FILMS OF THE PERIOD

1939
The Case of Charlie Gordon (Stuart Legg)

1940
Atlantic Patrol ("Canada Carries On" series, Legg)
Hot Ice (Irving Jacoby)
Letter from Camp Bordon (CCO, Raymond Spottiswoode)

1941
Canadian Landscape (F. R. Crawley)
Churchill's Island (CCO, Legg)

Peoples of Canada (CCO, Gordon Sparling)
Strategy of Metals (CCO, Stanley Hawes)
Warclouds in the Pacific (CCO, Legg)

1942
Action Stations! (Joris Ivens)
Food—Weapon of Conquest ("The World in Action" series, Legg)
Geopolitik—Hitler's Plan for Empire (WIA, Legg)
13th Platoon (Julian Roffman)
West Wind (F. R. Crawley)

1943
High Over the Borders (Jacoby)
The War for Men's Minds (WIA, Legg)

1944
Look to the North (James Beveridge)
When Asia Speaks (WIA, Legg)
Zero Hour (CCO, Legg)

1945
Food—Secret of the Peace (WIA, Legg)
Listen to the Prairies (Gudrun Bjerring [Parker])
Maps in Action (Evelyn Lambart)
Music in the Wind (Jean Palardy)
Now—the Peace (WIA, Legg)

BOOKS ON THE PERIOD

BACKHOUSE, CHARLES, *Canadian Government Motion Picture Bureau 1917–1941*. Ottawa: Canadian Film Institute, 1974. 44 pp.

BEATTIE, ELEANOR, *A Handbook of Canadian Film*. Toronto: Peter Martin Associates Limited, 1973. 280 pp.

BEVERIDGE, JAMES, *John Grierson: Film Master*. New York: Macmillan Publishing Co., Inc., 1978. 361 pp.

BUCHANAN, DONALD WILLIAM, *Documentary and Educational Films in Canada 1935–1950: A Survey of Problems and Achievements*. Ottawa: Canadian Film Institute, 1952. 24 pp.

ELLIS, JACK C., *John Grierson: A Guide to References and Resources*. Boston: G. K. Hall, 1986. 262 pp.

EVANS, GARY, *John Grierson and the National Film Board: The Politics of Wartime Propaganda*. Toronto: University of Toronto Press, 1984. 329 pp.

FELDMAN, SETH AND JOYCE NELSON, eds., *Canadian Film Reader*. Toronto: Peter Martin Associates Limited, 1977. 405 pp.

THE JOHN GRIERSON PROJECT, McGill University, *John Grierson and the NFB*. Toronto: ECW Press, 1984. 171 pp.

HARDY, FORSYTH, *John Grierson: A Documentary Biography*. London: Faber and Faber Limited, 1979. 298 pp.

JAMES, C. RODNEY, *Film as a National Art: NFB of Canada and the Film Board Idea*. New York: Arno Press, 1977. 760 pp.

MANVELL, ROGER, *Films and the Second World War*. New York: Dell Publishing Co., Inc., 1974. 388 pp.

McKAY, MARJORIE, *History of the National Film Board of Canada*. Montreal: National Film Board, 1964. 147 pp.

MORRIS, PETER, ed., *The National Film Board of Canada: The War Years*. Ottawa: Canadian Film Institute, 1965. 32 pp.

NINE
EXPANSION
United States, 1941–1945

In the U.S., the first two years of the 1940s were really an extension of the 1930s. The extreme hardships of the Depression were gradually alleviated as the country backed into war, supplying Great Britain in its fight against Germany through the Lend-Lease Act and other forms of aid, some of them covert.

At President Roosevelt's request, Prime Minister Winston Churchill had agreed not to send official British wartime propaganda to the U.S. until we were in the war. Roosevelt was concerned that such a clear indication of his administration's pro–British and pro–war stance would disturb the illusion of neutrality and provide American isolationists with evidence to use against him. Since no such agreement had been made with Canada, John Grierson, head of its National Film Board, saw to it that British documentaries entered the United States along with those of Canada. Britain's and Canada's early wartime documentaries may well have contributed to moving us from sympathy to action on behalf of Britain.

Not until the Japanese attack on our naval base at Pearl Harbor on December 7, 1941, followed by Germany's declaration of war, did we join the widening world conflict. Our entry into war had as profound an effect on documentary film in this country as it had had on our new allies, Britain and Canada.

The war brought English-language documentary together in ways and to a degree not true of any other period in its history. The peoples of Britain, Canada, and the United States viewed each other's films about the war. We exchanged film materials—stock-shot library footage, combat footage, and captured enemy footage—to be made into compilation films reporting wartime events and giving historical backgrounds. We made films about each other to orient troops and civilians as to our differences as well as to our common ways and to the ways in which we depended upon each other for survival. The joint production ventures near the end of the war of the "victory series" discussed in Chapter Seven, culminating with *The True Glory,* were the final and most complete examples of this collaboration.

The centripetal force exerted by war not only brought together documentaries and documentarians of the three nations, it pulled together documentary and fiction within each country. Filmmakers of all sorts were working in common cause and sometimes on the same projects. Documentaries gained an unprecedented amount of theatrical screen time; fiction features were donated by the Hollywood industry for showing to troops at home and abroad.

The degree and kind of wartime pulling together in each country were different of course. Differences among the films of the three nations are examined in the final section of this chapter. The next four sections deal with the four major types of wartime films—training, indoctrination, records of battle, social documentary—made in the U.S.

TRAINING

The military training films (and civilian training films pertaining to war industries, civil defense, conservation of materials needed for war, and the like) were not documentaries, of course. But they are closely enough related as part of the general wartime film effort to warrant some attention in this history. As mentioned in Chapter Seven concerning British wartime documentary, hundreds of such "nuts and bolts" films were made, on every conceivable subject. A random sample might include the following: *Articles of War, Military Courtesy, Keep It Clean* (how and why to take care of a gun), *Resisting Enemy Interrogation, Clearing Enemy Mine Fields, Notes on Jungle Warfare,* and *Sex Hygiene.* In *Identification of the Japanese Zero* (1942) a young Ronald Reagan plays a flyer who mistakes a friend's B-40 for a Japanese Zero and tries to shoot it down. In the end he gets a chance to shoot down a real Zero. These training films were thought to be, and were tested to be, extremely effective pedagogically (see Hovland, Lumsdaine, and Sheffield, *Experiments On Mass Communication,* listed in *Books on the Period*). A story about the use of film at Fort Leonard Wood, Missouri, where Army engineers were trained, encapsulates this view. The second lieutenant who was to have instructed the platoon on how to construct a pontoon bridge failed to appear. The sergeant projected a film on the subject without the usual lecture and presentation of models and diagrams. The men were marched out to the river and constructed the bridge without error in less time than it had taken earlier trainees who had had the benefit of full instruction.

INDOCTRINATION

Rather than indoctrination or propaganda, the U.S. Armed Forces engaged in what it called "orientation." Central to the massive effort directed at the more than nine million Americans in uniform was the seven-part "Why We Fight" series.

The production of this series and of other large-scale information and education films was entrusted to Lt. Col. Frank Capra. One of the most popular Hollywood filmmakers of the 1930s (*Mr. Deeds Goes to Town, Mr. Smith Goes to Washington*), he had no prior documentary experience. (The same could be said of virtually all the Hollywood filmmakers involved with wartime documentaries.) Capra was assisted by Major Anatole Litvak, and Captains Anthony Veiller and William Hornbeck—Hollywood veterans all. Sgt. Richard Griffith, subsequently head of the film department of the Museum of Modern Art, did research. In addition to "Why We Fight," the Capra group made large-scale films designed to orient American troops to the foreigners—allies and enemies—with whom they were about to come into contact. Examples are *Know Your Ally—Britain* (1943), the script by novelist Eric Knight (*Lassie Come Home, This Above All*), *Here Is Germany* (1945), and *Know Your Enemy—Japan* (1946).

"Why We Fight" was based on the assumption that servicemen would be more willing and able fighters if they knew about the events leading up to, and reasons for, our participation in the war. The spirit of isolationism—still strong in this country right up to the Japanese attack on Pearl Harbor—had to be counteracted. In this attempt "Why We Fight" offered a gigantic historical treatise from a particular, "liberal" point of view—that is to say from the point of view of the New Deal Democratic administration, which became the predominant point of view in the country during the war. (The irony here is that Capra's personal politics were conservative Republican. But they rested on a kind of populism that united him with the common effort led by President Roosevelt.) History as the basis for orgainzation was frequent in American documentaries, from *The Plow That Broke the Plains* (1936) and *The River* (1937) on. It was not used in that way by the wartime filmmakers in Great Britain or Canada.

"Why We Fight" is most impressive in the scale of its conception and skill of its execution. Almost entirely compiled (from existing footage including newsreels, Allied and captured enemy records of battle, bits from

Hollywood features and Nazi propaganda films) through editing and commentary, it presents a vast and coherent panorama.

The first three films—*Prelude to War* (1942), *The Nazis Strike* (1942), and *Divide and Conquer* (1943)—cover the period 1918 to 1941. They document the rise of Japanese aggression in the Orient, the growing menace of Hitler in Europe, and—above all—the changing American foreign policy and public opinion between the end of World War I and our entry into World War II. *The Battle of Britain* (1943), *The Battle of Russia* (1943), and *The Battle of China* (1944) cover the efforts of our allies, who were in the war before we were and continued to fight alongside us. *War Comes to America* (1945) offered a recapitulation and even more detailed examination of changes in American attitudes over the past two decades and the conflicting impulses and ideologies that shaped them. Picking up and consolidating the themes of the first three films, it was made last but was intended to be shown first.

Though the seven films, short features in length, were designed for showing to military personnel, when their excellence and dramatic power were recognized by the War Department, some of them were made available for civilian audiences through theatrical exhibition. They were shown to all servicemen; viewing of all seven was compulsory before embarkation for overseas duty.

The chief artistic problem the makers of these films faced was one of giving structure to vast amounts of unstructured history. In this respect their work was like the work of Shakespeare in his chronicle plays. Dramatic form was given to each of the seven films, with exposition, mounting action, climax, and denouement. They can be broken down into acts, in fact. *Divide and Conquer,* for example, has five acts, like the classical tragedy. Act I contains exposition: Poland has been overrun by Germany; conquest of Britain is now its goal; German strategy is outlined; the theme of Hitler's lying treachery is sounded. The content of Act II is the successful German campaign against Denmark and Norway. Act III deals with the position of France, the Maginot Line, and French weakness. Act IV comprises the German conquest of Holland and Belgium. Act V is the fall of France. The various participant countries are given character; they become characters, like dramatis personae. In this respect, rather than the Shakespearean histories this film bears a curious resemblance to *Hamlet,* with Germany as Claudius, the murderous villain, France as Hamlet, DeGaulle and French North Africa as Horatio, and England as Fortinbras. Here, as in *Hamlet,* things are not what they seem, with the villain protesting friendship and the tragic hero constricted by an incapacity for action.

A considerabe variety of visual and audio resources are used in these compiled documentaries—very nearly the full range conceivable. Visuals in *The Nazis Strike,* for instance, include, in addition to newsreel footage, excerpts from the Nazi *Triumph of the Will, Hitlerjunge Quex,* and *Baptism of Fire,* bits of staged action (the victims of firing squads), still photos, drawings and maps, animated diagrams (the animation by Walt Disney Studio), newspaper headlines, and printed titles (Hitler's pronouncements). The sound track includes two narrators (Anthony Veiller for the factual, Walter Huston for the emotional), quoted dialogue (Churchill, and an impersonation of Hitler), music (by Dmitri Tiomkin, one of Hollywood's best), and sound effects.

Dramatic conflict is obtained by painstaking manipulation of combat footage. Editing conventions of matched action and screen direction are observed. German attackers always move from right to left. A synthetic assemblage of diverse shots is edited into a cause-effect order: German bombers in formation, bombs dropping from planes, explosions in villages, rubble. The result is almost as if all of this footage had been shot for these films under Capra's direction.

Maps and animated diagrams give scope to the live-action sequences, clarify and relate random material to formalized patterns consistent with the actual movement involved. In *Divide and Conquer* the sequence of refugees on the roads being strafed by German fighter planes is especially striking; one reads into the actual what has just been seen in animated representation. In another instance from the same film, the animated arrows

Divide and Conquer, "Why We Fight" series (U.S., 1943, Frank Capra and Anatole Litvak). Museum of Modern Art/Film Stills Archive.

representing the Panzer divisions thrust into an outlined Ardennes forest with speed and power. And the animation takes on symbolic and rhetorical meaning; in *Divide and Conquer*, yet again, swastika termites infest the base of a castle, and python-like arrows lock around the British Isles.

It must be admitted, however, that though "Why We Fight" may be greatly admired on technical and aesthetic grounds, there is some convincing evidence that it was not as effective indoctrination as hoped for and even thought to be. (See Hovland, Lumsdaine, and Sheffield, *Experiments on Mass Communication*, listed in *Books on the Period.*) The problem, the social scientists inferred from their testing, was with the historical approach. It seemed to have the desired effects only on those with the equivalent of some college education; it appeared to be too intellectual and over the heads of a majority of soldiers tested. As films, though, "Why We Fight" offers incontrovertible evidence of very great filmmaking skill and a remarkably full and varied use of film technique. It stands as a peak of achievement in the history of documentary and influenced subsequent historical compilation films, especially the many appearing on television which will be discussed in Chapter Twelve.

RECORDS OF BATTLE

As with the "Why We Fight" series, other of the most prestigious wartime documentaries were made for the Armed Forces by Hollywood veterans.

John Ford's fiction features of the thirties (for example, *Stagecoach, Young Mr. Lincoln*) gave him a status comparable to Capra's. Ford enlisted in the Navy. He filmed much of *The Battle of Midway* (1942) himself with a 16mm camera and was seriously wounded during the filming. It is early and unusual in using color; color would come into documentary for the first time during the war. *The Battle of Midway* won an Academy Award. Ford's *December 7th* (1943) is a largely recreated account of the Japanese attack on Pearl Harbor using miniatures, rear screen projection, process photography, and actors. It was shot by Gregg Toland (cinematographer of *Grapes of Wrath* and *Citizen Kane*). Though the emotionalism of these two films may strike audiences today as excessive, they accurately reflect the feelings of many people at the time they were made.

John Huston (whose prewar success was *The Maltese Falcon*) made some of the finest and most personal of the wartime documentaries. His subsequent filmmaking seemed to gain considerably from that experience.

Report From the Aleutians (1943) is the first and least outstanding of Huston's three major documentaries. The problem with it is not so much of his making as of the situation the film is about. On the desolate Aleutian Islands extending out of Alaska, American and Japanese forces feinted and parried. Bombing missions over Japanese-held Kiska Island comprised the

Report from the Aleutians (U.S., 1943, John Huston). Museum of Modern Art/Film Stills Archive.

principal U.S. military activity. The color filming (16mm Kodachrome) was done over a period of six months in the rain and almost constant fog of Adak. The commentary, written by Huston and spoken by his father, Walter, offers a sense that the dreary weather, the boredom, and the loneliness were as much the enemy as the Japanese.

Many think *The Battle of San Pietro* (1945) is the finest of the American wartime documentaries; I think it is among the finest films yet made about men in battle. It is an engrossing account of a full week of savage fighting between American and German forces for control of the Liri Valley in Italy. The taking of a small military objective becomes an indictment of modern warfare in general, with its incredible cost both in military and civilian casualities. The theme is further underscored as we see the bodies of soldiers being buried beneath dogtag markers. After the battle, the people of San Pietro return to their devastated village and must somehow find the strength to rebuild their shattered lives. The weary Americans will move on to "more rivers, and more mountains, and more towns ... more 'San Pietros,' greater or lesser—a thousand more."[1] The commentary was written and read by Huston.

Let There Be Light (1946), Huston's final wartime documentary, will be discussed later.

William Wyler (of *Wuthering Heights* and *The Little Foxes*) served in the Air Force. His *The Memphis Belle* (1944) is, in a way, an answer to the British *Target for Tonight*. It is interesting that Hollywood director Wyler used candid color footage of a real raid (one of his cameramen was killed while filming)

The Battle of San Pietro (U.S., 1945, John Huston). Museum of Modern Art/Film Stills Archive.

with voice-over narration, while documentarian Harry Watt used recreated action (some of it shot in a studio), scripted dialogue, and directed performances. The "Memphis Belle" is a Boeing B17 "flying fortress" on its last bombing mission over Germany before its veteran crew is sent home. The world we see and hear is that of the airmen—refracted images of sky and enemy fighters seen through plexiglass, the drone of engines and excited voices over the intercom. The film seems to come very close to the reality of their experience.

The title of Wyler's *Thunderbolt* (1945, in color) is what the P47 fighter-bomber was called. The film deals with the activities of the 57th Fighter Group in Italy destroying vital supply routes deep behind German lines. Much of it supports a statement made in the narration that "The airman never sees the face of the people, but only the face of the country." The sequences on the ground suggest something of the prevailing fear and boredom. Between missions, these young men attempt to distract themselves through various forms of recreation but can't altogether overcome the nagging regret that they are not home getting jobs and getting married.

In addition to documentaries identified with particular Hollywood directors were those made collaboratively by film crews (sometimes including Hollywood talent) of the various armed services. A distinguished group of these reported on the warfare in the Pacific. The examples mentioned here are still in active circulation.

The Battle for the Marianas (1944) concerns a joint Army, Navy, Marine, and Coast Guard assault on Saipan, Tinian, and Guam, the major islands

The Memphis Belle (U.S., 1944, William Wyler). Museum of Modern Art/Film Stills Archive.

Production still of the making of *Thunderbolt* (U.S., 1945, William Wyler). Museum of Modern Art/Film Stills Archive.

of the Mariana group. In *Attack—The Battle for New Britain* (1944) explanations of the strategy are accompanied by comments about life in the jungle. *To the Shores of Iwo Jima* (1945) is one of the fullest and most skillfully made accounts of a combined operation. *The Fleet That Came to Stay* (1945) documents the planning and staging of the Okinawa invasion as well as including much combat footage. *Fury in the Pacific* (1945) is unusual in the number and intensity of the shots of Japanese and Americans being killed in battle. Nine combat cameramen fell while filming. It was not released until after the war.

The Fighting Lady (1944) is about the final phase of the war in the Pacific (fought almost exclusively between American and Japanese forces). It is feature-length and in color. The title refers to an aircraft carrier. The action concerns defense against attacks of kamikaze pilots diving to their deaths, trying to take American warships with them. It was produced by Louis de Rochemont, who had left "The March of Time" for Navy service, and was distributed by Twentieth Century-Fox, which was currently distributing "The March of Time."

The Fighting Lady (U.S., 1944, Louis de Rochemont). Museum of Modern/Film Stills Archive.

SOCIAL DOCUMENTARY

In 1940, before our entry into the war, President Roosevelt appointed Nelson Rockefeller as Coordinator of Inter-American Affairs (CIAA). This new agency was occasioned largely by U.S. nervousness about the growing German presence in Latin America, through increased immigration and increased trade. The conception of the CIAA was not unlike that of the earlier British Empire Marketing Board—government public relations working to increase economic and political interdependency and mutual support. CIAA films were intended to play an important role somewhat similar to that of EMB films: to show aspects of life in the United States to the Latin American countries, and to show aspects of their life to us.

One film about Latin America made for the CIAA is *The Bridge* (1944), directed by Willard Van Dyke and Ben Maddow. It is about the economics of South America and the importance of air transport in connecting its countries with each other and with North America. Another example would be *High Plain* (1943), directed by Jules Bucher, about the Indians of the Bolivian plateau. The latter is one of many films about Latin America produced for CIAA by Julien Bryan and intended for showing in the U.S.

High Plain (U.S., 1943, Jules Bucher). Museum of Modern Art/Film Stills Archive.

Another cluster of films for the CIAA were produced by the Walt Disney Studio. They are clever and imaginative animated teaching and communication. (The Disney Studio also made instructional films for the Armed Forces. *Cold Front* and *Fog,* both 1943, part of a series produced for the Bureau of Aeronautics of the U.S. Navy, are two examples.) *The Grain that Built a Hemisphere* (1943) is a historical survey of the importance of maize/corn in the nutrition and economies of the American continents. *Water—Friend or Enemy* (1944) offers basic education in the importance of uncontaminated water and methods for obtaining it. The Disney films were distributed widely in both Spanish- and English-language versions.

Closest to a continuation of the prewar American social documentary among the CIAA films were those in the "Ohio Town" series produced by Julien Bryan in 1945. Made for showing in Latin America (in part to counteract Hollywood representations) they were also circulated widely in this country and in Europe. Bryan selected Mt. Vernon, Ohio, as representative of small-town U.S.A. Four of the five films were built around a person and his or her work—a doctor, a factory craftsman, a county agricultural agent, an elementary school teacher—the fifth gives an overview of the town.

In 1942, following our entry into the war, the Office of War Information (OWI) was set up. This office was equivalent to the British Ministry of Information and the Canadian Wartime Information Board. News commentator Elmer Davis was named head of OWI. Its function was to coordinate all government information released to the media and to develop its own means of informing the public. The Motion Picture Bureau of the OWI was headed by Robert Riskin, script writer for some of Frank Capra's most

The Grain that Built a Hemisphere (U.S., 1943, Walt Disney). Museum of Modern Art/ Film Stills Archive.

successful features (*It Happened One Night, Mr. Deeds Goes to Town, Meet John Doe*). It established liaison with the Hollywood studios, primarily to insure that entertainment films did not contain material harmful to morale or to our relationships with our allies. The Motion Picture Bureau also produced its own films. Philip Dunne, another Hollywood script writer (*Suez, The Rains Came, How Green Was My Valley*), was chief of production.

The purpose of the Domestic Branch of the Motion Picture Bureau was to make films for American civilian viewing, somewhat along the lines of the British Crown Film Unit or the Canadian National Film Board, presumably. The Overseas Branch was to make films for showing to our allies, neutral countries, and countries which had been under Axis occupation. It is characteristic of our suspiciousness about government information directed at us that the Domestic Branch never succeeded in getting a production program underway. The Overseas Branch, on the other hand, had a distinguished wartime record. Its films were made largely by documentary veterans. Though not as big and prestigious (or expensive) as the Armed Forces documentaries made by the Hollywood directors, the OWI films, taken together, offer a broad and sensitive picture of diverse aspects of life in the United States. Let me cite some examples.

Autobiography of a Jeep (1943, Joseph Krumgold) is a jaunty tribute to that item of American wartime technology. Following a showing of it in liberated France the audience is said to have burst into shouts of "Vive le jip! Vive le jip!"[2] *The Town* (1944, Josef von Sternberg) is about the contributions of many cultures to the United States as evidenced in the eclectic architecture, mixed populations, and many religions of Madison, Indiana. *Pacific Northwest* (1944, Willard Van Dyke) describes and interprets the Northwestern states, rarely settings for Hollywood entertainment (or other documentaries, for that matter). *Hymn of the Nations* (1944, Alexander Hammid), produced in honor of the liberation of Italy, is mostly a skillful and responsive film recording of Arturo Toscanini conducting the NBC Symphony Orchestra in Giuseppe Verdi's piece by that name. *The Cummington Story* (1945, Helen Grayson and Larry Madison; score by Aaron Copeland) is a moving reenactment of an actual experience of the tensions created and eventually overcome when war refugees moved into a Connecticut town. *The Library of Congress* (1945, Alexander Hammid) presents many of the aspects—science, painting, music, literature—of this great institution as symbolic of our regard for the non–materialistic things in life. *Tuesday in November* (1945, John Houseman; score by Virgil Thomson) is about our electoral system and election day in a small town. *Capital Story* (1945, Henwar Rodakiewicz) shows detective work of the U.S. Public Health Service in tracing a harmful ingredient in a shipbuilding process. *The Window Cleaner* (1945, Jules Bucher) offers a charming little sketch of life in the United States as seen from the point of view of a window washer on the Empire State Building in New York City. *A Better Tomorrow* (1945, Alexander Ham-

The Cummington Story (U.S., 1945, Helen Grayson and Larry Madison). Museum of Modern Art/Film Stills Archive.

mid) is a study of three progressive schools in the New York City system as representative of American public education.

Let There Be Light (1946, John Huston), though produced by the Army Pictorial Service, was intended mainly for civilian audiences. It serves as a painful and moving reflection on the mental and emotional casualities of war. What had been called "shell shock" in World War I became "battle fatigue" in World War II. Whatever called, the symptoms are equally debilitating. The film examines the rehabilitation of the psychosomatically disabled at Mason General Hospital in Brentwood, Long Island. The psychotherapy is observed with close attention to particular cases. A G.I. who lost his memory during a shellburst at Okinawa is hypnotized and begins to recall his fear and terror of battle. Another soldier who stutters is given sodium amytol. He begins to speak and then to shout, half sobbing: "I can TALK! Oh, God, listen! God, I can talk." By the end of the film it is clear that the inabilities of these men to walk, to speak, or to remember are not symptoms of abnormality. Rather, "in the fulfillment of their duties as soldiers, (they) were forced beyond the limit of human endurance."

Let There Be Light was not released until almost forty years after it was completed. The Army said they were concerned about invasion of privacy of the men shown. Huston said they were concerned about the human effects of war shown.

Frames from scenes in *Let There Be Light* (U.S., 1946, John Huston). Museum of Modern Art/Film Stills Archive.

COMPARISONS: GREAT BRITAIN, CANADA, UNITED STATES

In Britain, before the war, documentary had become a thoroughly established enterprise. It was not large in terms of amounts of money, numbers of filmmakers and films made, or total audience size, admittedly. But it had earned respect among opinion leaders and gained a central relationship to matters of public concern. The British entertainment film industry, on the other hand, rested more firmly on the distribution and exhibition of American films than on the production of British ones. As a result, it was the documentarians who obtained the choice assignments and made the finest of the British wartime documentaries. At the same time it must be acknowledged that the semidocumentaries—Britain's special wartime contribution—came both from the government Crown Film Unit and from the commercial studios. In fact, early in the war two of the leaders of British documentary, Alberto Cavalcanti and Harry Watt, left the government unit for Ealing Studios, where they worked on documentary-influenced fiction features.

In Canada, very little filmmaking of any sort had existed before the war. When the National Film Board was established, it became the main, virtually the only producer of Canadian wartime films. Its staff—consisting of a few documentary veterans from abroad and lots of Canadian tyros—made mainly documentary and related types of informational and instructional films.

In the United Sates, prewar documentary had been disorganized and lacking prestige compared to monolithic Hollywood with its proven success. As a result, it was the Hollywood filmmakers who got the big Armed Forces projects and made some of the most valuable and lasting of the wartime documentaries. (It seems curious that Hollywood filmmakers, experienced with story telling, did not follow the semidocumentary line. Instead, they stuck to vigorous propaganda or unalloyed records of battle—moved over into documentary, in other words.) The American documentary veterans, for the most part, worked on smaller-scale projects for the Coordinator of Inter-American Affairs and the Office of War Information. These were closer to a continuation of the peacetime documentary than were the other American wartime documentaries.

Let's conclude this chapter with a comparison of wartime films produced in the United States, Canada and Britain. Since the training films were generally alike, the comparison can be confined to indoctrination films, records of battle, and social documentary.

As one might expect, the greatest differences among documentaries of the three countries are evident in their **indoctrination films.** In Britain the most important of these took the forms of poetic shorts and semidocumentary features. One noteworthy characteristic of these films is the lack of attention given to the violence and destructiveness of war, even less to vilification and hatred of the enemy. Instead, two themes are repeated, subtly and insistently. One is that Britain will survive; or, as put in the final words of "Rule Britannia," which accompanies the conclusion of *Listen to Britain,* "England never, never, never shall be slave." The other is that we are all in this together, everyone is doing his or her job. The reason for the first of these two emphases is clear enough. Britain was facing German military might massed across a narrow Channel and destruction rained down nightly from the skies. Survival was a matter of real and immediate, of general and personal concern. The second emphasis relates to class divisions persisting in England. Many of the working class had come to feel that their sacrifices in earlier wars had benefitted the already priviledged more than themselves. This time everyone is shown working with everyone else for everyone's postwar world.

Canadian indoctrination films took the form of the two "March-of-Time"-like series of shorts: "Canada Carries On" and "The World in Action." These offer information about and interpretation of aspects of the world at war, showing their meaning for Canadians and Canada's relationship to them. There are two emphases here as well. One is that we Canadians are doing our part (in a distinctive Canadian way). The other is that Canada is an important part of the world. These themes would seem to follow from Canada's uncertainty about its national character and its sense of geographical isolation, from its newness as a nation and lack of recognition as a world power. The divisive issue of differences between French-speaking Canada (which did not fully support the war effort) and English-speaking Canada (which did) was avoided. Canadians are Canadians are Canadians in these films.

In the United States the main form of indoctrination films was the large (short feature in length) historical compilation. The "Why We Fight" series was the centerpiece. The emphases in them are, first, that our enemies (Germany, Japan, Italy) are unethical, sometimes even inhuman. (Audiences today are shocked by the racism, chauvinism, and incitement to hatred evident in these films.) Second, that it is in our own self-interest to join our allies in helping to destroy these enemies. If we don't, eventually they will invade and conquer us. These thrusts seem a reaction against the earlier, majority attitudes of neutrality (the war seen as a foreign war with one side much the same as the other) and isolationism (the war seen as a long way off and ourselves as protected by two oceans).

British **records of battle** were mainly the large-scale (feature-length) "victory series," which chronicled successfully completed campaigns. The series began with *Desert Victory* (North Africa) and ended with *The True Glory* (Europe).

Canadians made few "shot and shell" films, as Grierson called the records of combat. Strategy rather than tactics was the principal concern—the goals and progress of the war, the general problems that had to be resolved. Canadian films about warfare were mostly informational and analytical rather than descriptive and emotional.

The Americans made a large number of battle films, and became especially accomplished with this kind of documentary. They are, of course, full of violence and the attitudes expressed are extremely chauvinistic, frequently racist (especially in regard to the Japanese). We were more distant from the war than were the British; more of us were involved in it than were the Canadians (where general conscription, a draft, was never adopted). So, there was need for Americans to report back to Americans what war was like. Also, it is possible that the Hollywood genre of war dramas served as inspiration for this form—the finest of the battle records were made by Hollywood directors.

Finally, there were continuations of the **social documentary** of the 1930s. The British carried on with some nongovernment production. The work of Paul Rotha is noteworthy here; for example, *World of Plenty*, about international food distribution, and *Children of the City*, about juvenile delinquency. British government wartime documentaries frequently contain quite explicit references to what will be needed in the peace ahead, sometimes from what would seem a Labour Party (that is, socialist) point of view.

The Canadian films, virtually all government–produced, are exceptional in their selection of subjects having to do with peacetime needs and aspirations as well as with the wartime situation. Grierson said: "The aims of our society lie beyond war and in the love of peace. It would be a poor information service . . . which kept harping on war to the exclusion of everything, making our minds narrow and anemic."[3] He would also say, from time to time, that everything that was built at the Film Board in wartime was built for peacetime as well.

The American wartime documentaries—all government sponsored, all related to the war effort—continued peacetime subjects and themes only for a special reason. I am thinking of those films produced by the Coordinator of Inter-American Affairs and by the Office of War Information designed to show American ways of life to neutral peoples and those who had been freed from occupation by the Axis powers. Admittedly what was shown was idealized, but the CIAA and OWI films reflect how a lot of us like to think about ourselves. These films were made not only to counteract enemy propaganda but the pictures of American life offered by Hollywood movies, with their gangsters and millionaires, materialism and glamour.

By the end of the war, documentary in Britain, Canada, and the United States had reached a pinnacle. More money was being invested in documentary production, more personnel were making more documentary films than ever before. Vastly larger audiences were seeing documentaries and related types of realist and educational films in theaters and in greatly increased nontheatrical showings. The effect of this wartime expansion on immediate postwar film will be the subject of the next two chapters. In

Chapter Ten the very considerable influence of the wartime documentary on the postwar fiction feature will be examined. In Chapter Eleven the place documentary found for itself in the greatly enlarged nontheatrical film field will be considered.

NOTES

[1]National Archives Trust Fund Board, *World War II on Film* (catalogue) (Washington, D.C.: National AudioVisual Center, ca. 1984), p. 13.

[2]Richard Dyer MacCann, *The People's Films* (New York: Hastings House, Publishers, 1973), p. 144.

[3]John Grierson, *Grierson on Documentary,* ed. Forsyth Hardy (Berkeley: University of California Press, 1966), p. 225.

FILMS OF THE PERIOD

1943

The Autobiography of a Jeep (Irving Lerner)
The Battle of Britain ("Why We Fight" series, Anthony Veiller)
The Battle of Midway (John Ford)
Divide and Conquer ("Why We Fight" series, Frank Capra and Anatole Litvak)
High Plain (Jules Bucher)
The Nazis Strike ("Why We Fight" series, Capra and Litvak)
Prelude to War ("Why We Fight" series, Capra)
Report from the Aleutians (John Huston)
World at War (Samuel Spewack)

1944

Attack! The Battle for New Britain (War Department)
The Battle of China ("Why We Fight" series, Capra)
The Battle of Russia ("Why We Fight" series, Litvak)
The Bridge (Willard Van Dyke and Ben Maddow)
The Fighting Lady (Louis de Rochemont)
Hymn of the Nations (Alexander Hammid)
Memphis Belle (William Wyler)
The Negro Soldier (Capra and Stuart Heisler)
A Salute to France (Jean Renoir and Garson Kanin)

Steel Town (Van Dyke)
The Town (Josef von Sternberg)
Valley of the Tennessee (Hammid)
With the Marines at Tarawa (Marine Corps)

1945

El Agente agronomo (The County Agent, Julien Bryan)
The Battle of San Pietro (Huston)
A Better Tomorrow (Hammid)
Capital Story (Henwar Rodakiewicz)
The Cummington Story (Helen Grayson and Larry Madison)
Fury in the Pacific (Army, Navy, and Marine Corps)
The Library of Congress (Hammid)
Thunderbolt (Wyler)
To the Shores of Iwo Jima (Navy, Marine Corps, and Coast Guard)
Tuesday in November (John Houseman)
War Comes to America ("Why We Fight" series, Litvak)
The Window Cleaner (Bucher)

1946

Let There Be Light (Huston)

BOOKS ON THE PERIOD

BOHN, THOMAS WILLIAM, *An Historical and Descriptive Analysis of the "Why We Fight" Series.* New York: Arno Press, 1977.

CAPRA, FRANK, "Part III, The Great Struggle," *The Name Above the Title.* New York: Macmillan Co., 1971. pp. 325–67.

HOVLAND, CARL I., ARTHUR A. LUMSDAINE, AND FRED D. SHEFFIELD, *Experiments on Mass Communication*. Princeton, N.J.: Princeton University Press, 1949. Vol. 3 of *Studies in Social Psychology in World War II*. 345 pp.

Look, ed., *Movie Lot to Beachhead*. Garden City, N.Y.: Doubleday, Doran & Company, Inc., 1945. 292 pp.

MACCANN, RICHARD DYER, *The People's Films: A Political History of U.S. Government Motion Pictures*. New York: Hastings House Publishers, 1973. 256 pp.

MANVELL, ROGER, *Films and the Second World War*. New York: Dell Publishing Co., Inc., 1976. 388 pp.

SHALE, RICHARD, *Donald Duck Joins Up: The Disney Studio During World War II*. Ann Arbor, Mich.: UMI Research Press, 1982. 220 pp.

SHORT, K. R. M., ed., *Film and Radio Propaganda in World War II*. Knoxville: University of Tennessee Press, 1983. 350 pp.

TEN
EXTENSIONS
Influence of Wartime
Documentary on Postwar
Fiction Films, 1945–1952

In trying to define documentary, to distinguish it from fiction, certain amorphous, in-between bodies of films and individual pictures must be acknowledged. For example, the Soviet silent features such as *Potemkin, Mother,* and *Earth*—among the sources of documentary—combine the imagined and the actual. Films like Lorentz's *The Fight for Life* and Flaherty's *Louisiana Story* move from the documentary side over into fiction.

In Great Britain during World War II, as observed in Chapter Seven, there appeared the concept and the form called "semidocumentary." Not the most precise term of course, it seemed to signify half fact and half fiction. *Target for Tonight,* produced by the government Crown Film Unit and directed by Harry Watt, veteran of British documentary, was the prototype. It concerned a bombing raid over Germany. Though the raid is entirely simulated, it is representative—a sort of composite—and is enacted by real RAF airmen. *In Which We Serve,* co-directed by David Lean and Noël Coward, about a destroyer and its crew, was the first of the semidocumentaries produced by a commercial studio (Two Cities Films). Though experienced actors perform, the events and persons depicted are recreations of actuality. These two semidocumentary features were followed by some twenty or more from both the government unit and the studios. The traits they embodied would become common among postwar fiction films—to some extent in Britain, certainly in the United States, and especially in Italy. (Though Canadian fiction feature production didn't begin until the early sixties, it would then be in much the same vein).

GREAT BRITAIN

The British wartime semidocumentary seemed unable to find peacetime themes adequate to prolong itself. Harry Watt went on with an occasional success in the mixed mode (for example, *The Overlanders*, 1946, based on a harrowing wartime cattle drive across the Australian outback), as did Pat Jackson (for example, *White Corridors*, 1951, drawing upon the drama of hospitals). Crown Film Unit tried to continue the feature-length semidocumentaries as well, with *Children on Trial* (1946), concerning juvenile crime and punishment, *Life in Her Hands*, on nursing, *Out of True*, about mental hospitals, and *Four Men in Prison*, dealing with penology (the latter three 1950).

But these exceptions merely prove the rule: British semidocumentary became as rare soon after the war as it had been common during wartime. On the other hand, it might be argued that it didn't so much cease as go underground and come up looking and sounding like the Ealing comedy. Michael Balcon, head of Ealing Studios, had always been a friend of the documentary movement and favored fiction films that were distinctively British rather than imitatively American. When the documentarians began to cross over into feature filmmaking via the wartime semidocumentary, it was to Ealing that they came. Alberto Cavalcanti, former production head of the G.P.O. Film Unit, as well as Watt, one of its star directors, were among these. Three of the principal directors of the Ealing comedies—Charles Frend, Robert Hamer, and Charles Crichton—had been documentary editors. A fourth, Alexander Mackendrick, had begun his directing on documentaries during the war. The result of these biases and this personnel gave the string of comedies a distinctive flavor.

In the first of the cycle, *Hue and Cry* (1947), the lower-class milieu, location shooting, bumbling crooks and police, and fast pace established the Ealing manner. There followed, in fairly rapid succession, *Whiskey Galore* (1949, known as *Tight Little Island* in the U.S.), *Passport to Pimlico* (1949), *A Run for Your Money* (1949), *The Lavender Hill Mob* (1951), *The Man in the White Suit* (1951), and a number of others. Similar kinds of comedies were made at Group 3, a government-financed experiment in feature production headed by John Grierson, former leader of the documentary movement.

These British comedies have much in common with the documentary tradition; they simply turn documentary seriousness on its ear. The themes of the Ealing films are notably social, economic, political, or at least cultural (in the anthropologist's sense), designed to bring out a particular facet of national life. They deal with the Scots' fondness for a wee drop, strict Calvinism, dislike of the English (*Tight Little Island*), the bureaucratic entanglements in which the British found themselves after the war (*Passport to Pimlico*), the expected honesty and trustworthiness of the English middle class (*The Lavender Hill Mob*), the collusion among management and labor, government and opposition within the English system (*The Man in the White Suit*). Laughter is provoked only through the incongruities and exaggerations with which these subjects are treated; even so, the comic style is noteworthy for its deadpan seriousness, underplaying, and throwaway delivery of lines.

Casting called on nonglamorous, quintessentially British actors (rather than stars)—Alistair Sim (*Hue and Cry*), Stanley Holloway (*Passport to Pimlico*), Alec Guinness (*The Lavender Hill Mob, The Man in the White Suit*)—and used local citizens as extras. The humor in every case is heightened by realistic background and detail—of cockney London as well as of the Scottish Hebrides. The films were shot rather largely on location, and for *Tight Little Island* Mackendrick even set up processing equipment there so he could look at the rushes without undue delay, just as Flaherty had done for *Man of Aran* some fifteen years earlier. *Tight Little Island,* in fact, seems rather pointedly to be kidding the British documentary style in its opening postcard shots of the Hebrides (almost identical with those of G.P.O.s *The Islanders*) and voice-over commentary.

Whiskey Galore (Tight Little Island in the U.S.; U.K., 1949, Alexander Mackendrick).
National Film Archive/Stills Library.

UNITED STATES

If the British were able to hang onto some aspects of documentary in their comedies, the Americans were drawn toward a tradition of exposé which had need for a kind of fiction filmmaking that stayed close to actuality. The American postwar equivalents to British wartime semidocumentary began with *The House on 92nd Street* (1945), produced by Louis de Rochemont, former creative chief of "The March of Time."

Of three more or less distinct American subspecies of the fictional film with documentary tendencies, *The House on 92nd Street* fits into the one of films based on fact, on real persons or incidents. It recreates an actual FBI investigation that had uncoverd a German espionage ring centered in New York City. It also contains many documentary-like stylistic characteristics including even some blown-up 16mm footage taken surreptitiously by the FBI. *House on 92nd Street* was followed by *Boomerang* (1947, also produced by de Rochemont), based on events in the life of Homer Cummings, who became Attorney General of the United States under Franklin Roosevelt. Both films employ a Voice-of-Time style narration over their openings and subsequently to provide explanations and transitions. *Call Northside 777* (1948) is another example. It recounts the efforts of a crusading Chicago reporter that led to the exoneration of a prisoner who had already served ten years of a life sentence for the murder of a policeman.

Closely allied to the based-on-fact picture was "the inside story"; how a police department works, for example. In *The Naked City* (1948, produced by former newspaperman Mark Hellinger) the emphasis and most of the running time are given to the dogged, dull, day-to-day routine of a homicide squad trying to track down a murderer living somewhere among New York's millions. *Panic in the Streets* (1950) concerns the responsibility of government officials for protecting the citizenry from epidemic disease; it was shot mainly on location in New Orleans, and several minor characters, such as the dwarf newspaper vendor, were chosen on the spot. *The Frogmen* (1951) devoted at least two-thirds of its footage to clear and interesting exposition of how Navy underwater demolition teams are trained. Only the final scenes of a mission into a Japanese-held harbor seem within the more familiar mode of screen heroics. The same documentary emphasis on how a thing is done pervades the opening passages of *13 Rue Madeleine* (1946, de Rochemont again producer); it deals with the training and a mission of Office of Strategic Services agents.

Finally there were the "problem pictures." Sometimes these looked less real than the above two categories, but they did attempt to come to grips with real problems. It was in this line that the exposé tendency was strongest—films dealing with alcoholism (*The Lost Weekend*, 1945), prisons (*Brute Force*, 1947, Hellinger producer), and mental health (*The Snake Pit*, 1948, directed by Anatole Litvak, Capra's associate on the "Why We Fight"

Boomerang (U.S., 1947, Elia Kazan). National Film Archive/Stills Library.

series) are examples. A cycle concerning race relations began in 1947 with *Crossfire* and *Gentleman's Agreement,* both about anti-Semitism, and quickly moved to prejudice and discrimination directed against blacks. In 1949 alone there were *Home of the Brave* (produced by Stanley Kramer, who specialized in the problem picture), *Lost Boundaries* (de Rochemont once more), *Pinky, Intruder in the Dust* (from a William Faulkner novel; in my view the finest of the cycle), and others.

The trend in American film toward realism of treatment and/or social problems as subjects lasted from the immediate postwar years to the early 1950s. It ceased during an outbreak of political paranoia named after Senator Joseph McCarthy of Wisconsin. The impact of McCarthyism on American documentary will be dealt with in Chapter Eleven.

ITALY

Though the effects of wartime documentary on postwar fiction films was widespread, it was unquestionably Italy which assumed leadership in the new realism that resulted; neorealism as the Italians called it. The neorealist movement was stimulated by the removal of Fascist power after nearly a quarter of a century and the release of pent-up feelings of frustration and humiliation generated by Italy's ambiguous and shifting position in the war. It began with Roberto Rossellini's *Open City* (1945), set in Rome at the time when the Allied forces were approaching. It chronicles in cross section the activities of the partisans, the raids and reprisals of the German military and the Italian police, the painful tensions between the collaborators, the resisters, and the great majority of people who simply wanted enough bread and wine to sustain life and an end to the killing and misery of war.

The making of *Open City* is something of a marvel. Scraping together funds from various sources, Rossellini began filming secretly in 1943 while Rome was still under German occupation. Production conditions were incredibly primitive. Shooting was done on odds and ends of raw stock of various manufacturers. Studios were not available to him and nearly all the scenes were shot on the actual locations which they represent in the film. Even the electrical power was so erratic that maintaining consistent exposure was a constant problem. In spite of the financial and technical difficulties, the film emerged as a towering achievement that would inspire other Italian filmmakers to emulate its concepts and method of dealing with contemporary reality.

Of the three major directors of the neorealist period—Rossellini, Vittorio de Sica, Luchino Visconti—the first two better represent the techniques and commitments of the movement. At the same time it must be acknowledged that Visconti, with *La Terra Trema* (*The Earth Trembles*, 1948), offered one of the acknowledged masterpieces of neorealism. It is about a family of Sicilian fishermen driven into poverty by the dealers, who exert a monopolistic control over the prices and conditions under which the fish can be marketed. Sponsored initially by the Communist Party, shot entirely on location, the film uses nonactors exclusively.

Rossellini, for his part, quickly followed *Open City* with his other major film, fully within the general terms of the neorealist style and intentions, *Paisan* (1946). In six separate episodes it traces the Allied campaign up the long boot of Italy, exploring the changing relationships between the conquerors (principally American) and the conquered. Maps and newsreel footage connect the parts, suggesting that the dramatic vignettes are incidents happening within the larger historical context. Rossellini worked out the stories as he went along, with the aid of a group of writers which included Federico Fellini. The camera and editing techniques are as sparse and unprettified as the stories. Of *Paisan's* large cast only four members had had previous acting experience; the others were picked up by Rossellini as he found them on location.

Vittorio de Sica and his scriptwriter, Cesare Zavattini, continued this national saga with an examination of the immediate postwar years. Their *Shoeshine* (1946) concerns the Roman *ragazzi* who eked out a living by shining GIs' shoes, pimping, and dealing in black market American cigarettes, candy bars, and, in this instance, blankets. The two boys are apprehended, tried, convicted, and sent to a reformatory. In this film, though it ends in tragedy, there are no villains—simply a bad system. One is not sure why

Paisan (Italy, 1946, Roberto Rossellini). Museum of Modern Art/Film Stills Archive.

there aren't enough men and money to run the institution properly, except that there never are in institutions of this sort. Nor are we told what steps might be taken to obtain adequate resources. Though the neorealist films dealt with social problems, they tended to hold them up for examination in terms of their effects on individual lives rather than explain causes or propose solutions.

Zavattini's and de Sica's most successful collaboration, and among those films closest to the neorealist ideal, is *The Bicycle Thief* (1949). It deals with the simplest possible situation. An unemployed man, with his first chance to work for some time, has his bicycle stolen (which he needs in order to keep his job). In following the man's and his young son's search for the bicycle, various aspects of Italian society are sketched with social and political criticism implied. *The Bicycle Thief* was shot almost entirely outside the studio, in the streets and apartments and offices of Rome. The father in the film was in real life a machinist in the big Breda steelworks. The boy who plays his son was a Roman newsboy.

The working principles of the neorealist films—which Rossellini had first improvised partly by necessity and accident, partly out of conviction—in turn became loosely codified into a theory of cinema. The premises underpinning neorealism were most forcefully articulated by scriptwriter Zavattini, who became spokesman for, as well as one of the principal creators in, the movement.

Frequently Zavattini sounded exactly like a documentarian rather than a fiction filmmaker and many of his statements could fit quite comfortably into John Grierson's polemical writings on documentary. In a famous interview, translated and published in the October-December 1953 issue of the British journal *Sight and Sound,* Zavattini had the following things to say about the content and purposes of neorealism:

> The most important characteristic, and the most important innovation, of what is called neo-realism, it seems to me, is to have realised that the necessity of the 'story' was only an unconscious way of disguising a human defeat, and that the kind of imagination it involved was simply a technique of superimposing dead formulas over living social facts. Now it has been perceived that reality is hugely rich, that to be able to look directly at it is enough; and that the artist's task is not to make people moved or indignant at metaphorical situations, but to make them reflect (and, if you like, to be moved and indignant too) on what they and others are doing, on the real things, exactly as they are.[1]

Grierson had written about his own efforts as attempts to find "drama on the doorstep."

FORMS AND CONTENTS OF POSTWAR REALISM

It must be admitted that the effect of wartime documentaries and semidocumentaries on the postwar fiction films of Great Britain, the United States, Italy (and other countries) may not be as direct as the term influence, used in the title of this chapter, implies. True, in Britain some documentarians crossed over into features during and following the war; in the U.S., Hollywood filmmakers made documentaries during the war and returned to Hollywood filmmaking afterwards. Both sets of fiction filmmakers may have carried their documentary experience with them into the postwar years. Also, it is likely that the British and the Americans would have seen each other's wartime documentary work during the war. It is less likely that the Italian filmmakers would have seen the wartime films of either nation. On the other hand, they were coming from the experience of war, leftist political commitments, and a strong tradition of realism in the arts. Perhaps rather than derivation, analogy would be the more applicable concept in this case.

But, however caused, documentary characteristics, particularly traits like those of the British wartime semidocumentaries, did become common in fiction films after the war. In Britain they turned up in the whimsical form of the Ealing comedies. In the United States and especially in Italy these traits appeared in serious form close to documentary in content and purpose.

In this newly realistic style, films were based on a real incident, a composite of several, or a representative event—they had factual rather than fictional bases. For example, in the U.S. an actual case involving the breakup of a German espionage ring or, in Italy, a typical situation of two street urchins being arrested for black market activity. The problems dealt with had some degree of immediacy and broad concern. Themes were not necessarily universal and timeless, as those of the arts tend to be. These films were more tied to the here and now, like documentary: sociological as much as psychological in their approach. In the U.S., law enforcement, prison conditions, and race relations were a few of the subjects selected; in Italy, poverty, prostitution, and collaboration with and resistance to occupying military forces were among the prevalent concerns.

Works of this sort were split in the attention they gave to the social problem and to individual character and conflict. An effort was made to fuse the characters and the problem. Roles were created not so much for what the persons were like as for what they did—a United States Department of Health official, a state's attorney, a resistance leader—or did not do—an unemployed worker. Since the films were not about exclusively personal qualities, the personality of the protagonist could be of any sort—grouchy, or an unfaithful spouse—as long as the public function was performed. Various aspects of the problem are represented by individuals, but its social (anonymous) nature is kept to the fore.

To put much the same thing another way, in these semidocumentary-like films, there *is* a plot and there *are* characters, but they are less fully developed than in pure fiction, and are used quite directly to embody the theme and ideas. Conflict and resolution are apt to be drawn out of the larger situation rather than out of interpersonal relationships. The Department of Health official is responsible for the general public welfare; only when the threat of pneumonic plague is averted can he return to his neglected wife and child. A poor fishing family is in contention with the boat owners; when the owners win, the fishermen are forced to work the boats on the owners' terms. The family that had been resisting them is broken. In other words, in films of this sort the characters and their lives (plot incidents) are used deliberately to express an ideology.

Finally, in these films the filmmaking methods are drawn from both fiction and documentary. They tend to depend less on performance and dialogue than do conventional fiction films. Actors may appear in principal roles, but frequently nonactors are used in lesser roles and as extras, and even as leads in Italy. In any event there is usually an avoidance of stars. Considerable location shooting (exteriors) is combined with studio (interiors). Sometimes candid or newsreel footage is used. Frequently voice-over narration, montage, even maps suggest a broader scope and help bridge a less-tight plot. Lighting, costumes, makeup, and sets are actual, or naturalistic in style. The editing is less "smooth" than in the usual story picture, being dictated by the subject-matter requirements. The cutting pace is frequently more rapid, too, as it tends to be when ideas more than emotions are being dealt with, and when filmmakers (as in documentary) are working with people (nonactors) who cannot sustain performances. There tends to be a stress on source sounds and an avoidance of heavy musical scoring.

This sort of mixing and matching of documentary and fiction creative impulses and social purposes, forms and contents, is not confined to the immediate postwar period. Similar combinations had occurred earlier, in the Soviet films of the twenties, as mentioned at the outset of this chapter, and would occur later. The social-realist features appearing in Britain, in the late fifties and early sixties, along with the Angry Young Men, is another instance; they will be discussed in Chapter Thirteen. The politically radical and postmodernist mixture of film modes coming out of Europe following the French political upheaval in the spring of 1968 will be considered in Chapter Sixteen.

The extraordinary growth and change in documentary brought about by World War II did, however, have an unusually pervasive effect. Not only was the postwar fiction film affected. The nontheatrical, nonfiction documentary-proper became different, postwar compared to prewar, in a number of significant ways. These ways are the subject of Chapter Eleven.

NOTES

[1]Cesare Zavattini, "Some Ideas on the Cinema," *Sight and Sound,* 23 (October-December 1953), pp. 64–65.

FILMS OF THE PERIOD

Great Britain

1946
Children on Trial (Jack Lee)
The Overlanders (Harry Watt)
Theirs Is the Glory (Brian Desmond Hurst)

1947
Hue and Cry (Charles Crichton)

1949
The Blue Lamp (Basil Deardon)
Give Us This Day (Edward Dmytryk)
Passport to Pimlico (Henry Cornelius)
A Run for Your Money (Charles Frend)
Whiskey Galore/Tight Little Island (Alexander Mackendrick)

1950
Four Men in Prison (Max Anderson)
Life in Her Hands (Phil Leacock)
Out of True (Leacock)
Seven Days to Noon (John and Roy Boulting)

1951
The Lavender Hill Mob (Crichton)
The Man in the White Suit (Mackendrick)
Where No Vultures Fly/Ivory Hunter (Watt)
White Corridors (Pat Jackson)

1952
Mandy (Mackendrick)

Italy

1945
Open City (Roberto Rossellini)

1946
Paisan (Rossellini)
Shoeshine (Vittorio de Sica)

1947
Germany Year Zero (Rossellini)
Outcry (Aldo Vergano)
To Live in Peace (Luigi Zampa)
The Tragic Hunt (Giuseppe de Santis)

1948
The Bicycle Thief (de Sica)
La Terra Trema (Luchino Visconti)
Under the Sun of Rome (Renato Castellani)
Without Pity (Alberto Lattuada)

1949
Bitter Rice (de Santis)
In the Name of the Law (Pietro Germi)

1950
The Mill on the Po (Lattuada)
The Road of Hope (Germi)

1951
Bellissima (Visconti)
The Forbidden Christ (Curzio Malaparte)
Miracle in Milan (de Sica)

1952
The Overcoat (Lattuada)
Rome, Eleven O'Clock (de Santis)
Two Cents Worth of Hope (Castellani)
Umberto D (de Sica)

United States

1945
The House on 92nd Street (Henry Hathaway)
The Lost Weekend (Billy Wilder)
The Southerner (Jean Renoir)
Story of G. I. Joe (William Wellman)

1946
The Best Years of Our Lives (William Wyler)
A Walk in the Sun (Lewis Milestone)

1947
Boomerang (Elia Kazan)
Brute Force (Jules Dassin)
Crossfire (Edward Dmytryk)
Gentleman's Agreement (Kazan)

1948
Call Northside 777 (Hathaway)
The Naked City (Dassin)
The Search (Fred Zinnemann)
The Snake Pit (Anatole Litvak)

1949
All the King's Men (Robert Rossen)
Battleground (Wellman)
Home of the Brave (Mark Robson)
Intruder in the Dust (Clarence Brown)
Pinky (Kazan)

1950
The Men (Zinnemann)
No Way Out (Joseph L. Mankiewicz)
Panic in the Streets (Kazan)

1951
Fourteen Hours (Hathaway)

1952
My Son John (Leo McCarey)

BOOKS ON THE PERIOD

Great Britain

BARR, CHARLES, *Ealing Studios.* London: Cameron & Tayleur Ltd. in association with David & Charles Ltd., 1977. 198 pp.
PERRY, GEORGE, *Forever Ealing: A Celebration of the Great British Film Studio.* London: Pavilion, 1982. 200 pp.

Italy

ARMES, ROY, *Patterns of Realism: A Study of Italian Neo-Realist Cinema.* Cranbury, N. J.: A. S. Barnes & Co., Inc., 1971. 226 pp.
BONDANELLA, PETER, *Italian Cinema: From Neorealism to the Present.* New York: Frederick Ungar Publishing Co., Inc., 1983. 440 pp.

JARRATT, VERNON, *The Italian Cinema.* New York: Arno Press, 1972. 115 pp. (originally published in 1951)

MALERBA, LUIGI, ed., *Italian Cinema 1945–1951.* Rome: Carlo Bestetti, Edizioni d'Arte, 1951. 99 pp.

OVERBEY, DAVID, *Springtime in Italy: A Reader on Neo-Realism.* Hamden, Conn.: The Shoe String Press, 1979. 242 pp.

WLASCHIN, KEN, *Italian Cinema Since the War.* Cranbury, N. J.: A. S. Barnes & Co., Inc., 1971. 224 pp.

United States

HIGHAM, CHARLES AND JOEL GREENBERG, *Hollywood in the Forties.* Cranbury, N. J.: A. S. Barnes & Co., Inc., 1968. 192 pp.

MANVELL, ROGER, *New Cinema in the USA: The Feature Film Since 1946.* New York: E. P. Dutton & Co., Inc., 1968. 160 pp.

SHINDLER, COLIN, *Hollywood Goes to War: Films and American Society, 1939–52.* London: Routledge & Kegan Paul, Ltd., 1979. 152 pp.

THOMAS, TONY, *The Films of the Forties.* Secaucus, N. J.: Citadel Press, 1975. 278 pp.

ELEVEN
THE UNFULFILLED PROMISE
Postwar Documentary, 1945–1952

If, after the war, the fiction film took on some of the characteristics of documentary, as discussed in Chapter Ten, it is also true that postwar documentary drew toward the fiction film. For example *Benjy* (1951), a short produced for The Orthopaedic Foundation of Los Angeles and directed by Fred Zinnemann, used studio-style lighting and acted performances to tell an authentic story. It received the Academy Award for documentary. Mention has already been made of semidocumentary features produced by Crown Film Unit after the war—*Children on Trial, Life in Her Hands, Out of True,* and *Four Men in Prison.* A British short, produced for the Central Office of Information (successor to the Ministry of Information), *David: Story of a Welshman* (1951), used an even fuller range of fictional techniques. In the United States, the three big documentaries of the immediate postwar years (and there were only three big ones) were feature in length and narrative in structure. Two of them received theatrical distribution.

Robert Flaherty's *Louisiana Story* (1948) is about a Cajun family of father, mother, and young son, with a pet raccoon, who paddles his pirogue through the bayous. An oil drilling rig enters this primeval wilderness to tap the riches deep beneath the surface. Two worlds come together, natural and mechanical, and a tentative affection develops between the boy and the drillers. Some find this film the loveliest and most honest of the Flaherty films. It is, after all, called a story, thus disarming concerns about ethnographic accuracy.

The Quiet One (1949) was made initially as nontheatrical promotional film for the Wiltwyck School in upper New York state. It was scripted and edited by Helen Levitt, Janice Loeb, and Sidney Meyers. The latter directed. The narration was written by James Agee and read by Gary Merrill. The school offered a home and rehabilitation to emotionally disturbed adolescent boys, most of them black, from the streets of Harlem. The film is about one such case, that of "Donald," his painful past, the nature of his treatment, and the hopes for his recovery. The principled and courageous distribution team of Arthur Mayer and Sydney Burstyn acquired rights for theatrical distribution. (Mayer-Burstyn had distributed the first Italian neorealist films in the United States—*Open City, Paisan, The Bicycle Thief.*) *The Quiet One* was blown up from 16mm to 35mm and played with some success among art theaters in large cities. It has been widely shown nontheatrically ever since.

All My Babies (1952) began as an instructional film sponsored by the Georgia State Department of Health to demonstrate to midwives correct sanitary procedures to use in their deliveries. It was scripted and directed by George Stoney, himself a southerner, who became sympathetically involved with the rural black people the film is about and for. Though it is a

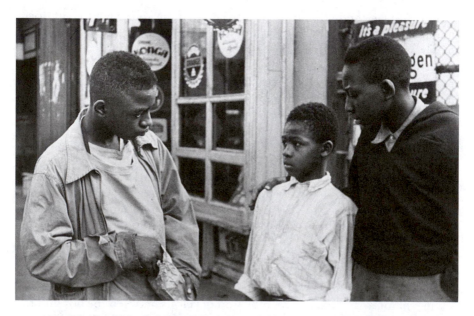

The Quiet One (U.S., 1949, Sidney Meyers). Museum of Modern Art/Film Stills Archive.

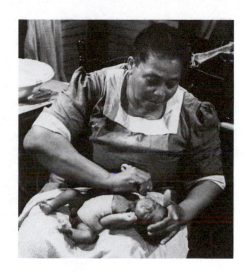

All My Babies (U.S., 1952, George Stoney). ©
1987 Robert Galbraith.

medical film and contains all the technical information required—some 118 points—it developed a length, a scope, and an emotional intensity that lift it into the realm of art. Its protagonist, Miss Mary, is not only a consummately skillful midwife, she is a magnificent person commanding affection and respect. The "Aunt Jemima" stereotype she might seem to represent is exploded before our eyes. The official sponsors at first didn't quite know what to make of this film; they were impressed (and surprised) when it was selected for showing at the Edinburgh International Film Festival. Because Miss Mary's skill in delivering babies was carefully recorded, the film is still shown in medical schools. The warm and wonderful feelings it contains— for birth, for people, for life—surely do the student doctors no harm.

But semidocumentary developments in the commercial entertainment and nontheatrical fields proved to be somewhat of a deflection from the purposes and forms of documentary developed during the thirties. Grierson had been distrustful of the blandishments of narrative form, and of box office returns as the main source for documentary financing. Efforts to hang onto the occasion provided by World War II to have documentary-like films playing in the theaters petered out by the early fifties.

The war years had marked a high point of documentary achievement: More filmmakers had made more nonfiction films for larger audiences than ever before. Given this vastly increased activity, with films being used in all sorts of new ways, it was assumed by most that the trend would continue onward and upward in the postwar years. Instead, what happened following wartime expansion was a severe cutback in the amount of money available for production, in the number of filmmakers employed, and in the quantity of films produced. Accompanying this contraction were losses in morale and leadership and uncertainties about postwar purposes and subjects.

PERSONNEL AND LEADERSHIP

Two acute problems of the immediate postwar years were more people wanting to make documentaries than there were documentaries to be made, and missing persons. Surfeit was accompanied by desertion.

In Britain some of the most talented of the documentary directors (for example Harry Watt and Pat Jackson) and principal producers (for example Alberto Cavalcanti and Ian Dalrymple) had moved from documentary units to commercial studios. Some of their fiction features may have been related to the documentary impulse. Watt's *The Overlanders* and Jackson's *White Corridors*, both mentioned in Chapter Ten, would qualify. So would Watt's *Where No Vultures Fly/Ivory Hunter* (1951, about an African game preserve). Nothing of Cavalcanti's postwar production could be said to be documentary-like, and of Dalrymple's only *The Wooden Horse* (1950, about the escape of three British servicemen from a prisoner-of-war camp).

In the U.S. during the war, not only had fiction film directors (among them John Huston, Anatole Litvak, William Wyler, Garson Kanin) been responsible for most of the major wartime documentaries, they had also been in positions of administrative leadership (among them Frank Capra and John Ford). When the war ended, these men returned to Hollywood. Some of them tended to make films more closely related to social problems and/or more realistic in style, perhaps as a result of their wartime experience. Ford's *They Were Expendable* (1945), Wyler's *The Best Years of Our Lives* (1946), Huston's *The Treasure of Sierra Madre* (1948), and Litvak's *The Snakepit* (1949) are examples. But neither they nor their films were any longer directly connected to documentary.

In Canada the situation was different. The National Film Board, which had almost a monopoly on Canadian film production, made no features. If there were no crossovers into fiction filmmaking, other sorts of difficulties arose. Canadian documentary was profoundly affected by Grierson's resignation from the Film Board and departure from Canada at the end of the war. The number of Film Board personnel was drastically reduced from the wartime high. As a result of this curtailment, some Canadian wartime filmmakers went into other fields; others moved to other countries.

Not only were there insufficient jobs available, the postwar filmmakers were different from those of the prewar years. The surfeit was made up mostly of young men and women who had received their training in filmmaking as a result of military service—"the R.A.F. types," as Stuart Legg called them. The wartime recruits had been thoroughly trained technically but ideologically only to the extent that they shared the universal desire to defeat the enemy. They lacked a common core of values and aspirations for peacetime filmmaking of the sort that had existed in Britain, and in the U.S. as well, even if the political schisms discussed in Chapter Six are taken into account. Since the peacetime demand for films was much less great than it had been in wartime, competition for opportunities to make films led filmmakers to offer their services cheaply and without professional standards.

Another, more complicated difficulty surfaced in the postwar years. Partly because of lessons learned during the war, a kind of split between the artist-filmmaker and the audio-visual educator was exacerbated and split the documentary impulse. Elaborate and sophisticated social-scientific testing of the effects of films on learning had been done on an unprecedentedly large scale during the war. The results of this testing—for instance, that reported by Hovland, Lumsdaine, and Sheffield in *Experiments on Mass Communication* discussed in Chapter Nine—seemed to define and limit what films could do in relation to audiences. Films seemed surprisingly successful at teaching troops to assemble a pontoon bridge or clean and maintain the breech of a coastal gun—the so-called nuts and bolts films. Films used to teach desired attitudes—the so-called orientation films—seemed much less certain in their effects. For all its brilliance, *The Battle of Britain*, of the "Why We Fight" series, did not seem to do much to move American servicemen towards a greater sympathy and appreciation for their British ally. In the postwar years, while the 16mm nontheatrical field expanded with educational and industrial applications drawn from the inspiration and models wartime use of film had provided, documentary languished.

The power of documentary and its uniqueness lay exactly in its fusion of social purpose with artistic form. It is worth remembering that the young tyros of British documentary had been well-educated in the liberal arts before Grierson drilled them in his social philosophy. After the war, especially in the United States, the social scientists (among educators) and the technicians (among industrial filmmakers) were predominant. Makers of classroom films worked from a formula: tell the audience what you're going to tell them; tell them; tell them what you have told them. It left little room for imagination, wit, or beauty. Makers of industrial films offered gorgeous color and perfect exposures and left it to the sponsor to determine what would be said. Neither the educational nor the industrial filmmaker was likely to make emotionally or intellectually stimulating films.

Having invoked an aspect of Grierson's earlier leadership, I think it worthwhile to consider his career during this period since it reflects some of the difficulties being discussed. Like others in Britain, the United States, and Canada, following the wartime experience, he was not only older but weary. He started losing battles, whereas he had tended to win them up to that point. There was no replacement for him—no other Grierson. His career from 1945 to 1952 follows the action, and connects Canada, the U.S., and Britain.

At the end of the war, Grierson apparently felt that documentary was ready to operate on an international level (rather than being confined to separate national developments). His thinking paralleled the emerging concept and institution of the United Nations. In 1945 he resigned as head of the National Film Board and established a private firm in New York City called The World Today. It was intended to produce and coordinate the production of films on international themes. Two factors ended this venture a little over a year after it began. Theatrical distribution could not be obtained and Grierson was denied a visa which would permit him to work in the United States. The former occurred when a deal with United Artists to distribute programs of shorts fell through. The latter occurred when Grierson was implicated in what were called the "Spy Trials" in Canada, though he was in no way guilty of any involvement in the Soviet espionage under investigation. The world was not ready for an international documentary movement, as Grierson seems to have hoped it was.

Following the abortive World Today, Grierson served as the first Director of the Department of Mass Communications and Public Information of the newly-formed United Nations Educational, Scientific, and Cultural Organization (UNESCO) during 1947 to 1948. Though he would seem to have been the ideal man for the job, and he did manage some solid achievements, he became frustrated with its paperwork nature. No agreement could be reached on what films should be made, no authority (that is to say, money) was granted to make them.

In 1948 Grierson returned to Great Britain to become controller of the Films Division of the Central Office of Information (COI), the peacetime form of the Ministry of Information (MOI). Though the shift in terminology may appear slight, a central office is a different entity from a ministry as far as political power, which is again to say money, and control over the making of films. As a result, Grierson was severely limited in what he could accomplish along the lines of social action or in advancing his internationalist view. The COI was confined to producing for other departments of government rather than on its own initiative (unlike the National Film Board, which he had established in Canada).

At the end of 1950, Grierson left the COI to become Executive Producer of Group 3, a government-funded experiment in the production of fiction feature films for the theaters. It was intended that these features would pay for themselves. More important, Group 3 was conceived as a training ground for novice writers, directors, actors, et al. to strengthen British theatrical film production. Grierson was able to move this undertaking along somewhat semidocumentary lines in the hiring of personnel with documentary experience and in the choice of subjects. Even so, it may be a sign of the reduced options of documentary that Grierson, who had earlier warned documentarians against the story and the false hopes of box office returns, here followed the theatrical route. Group 3's most notable success, and the film with which Grierson was most closely associated, was *The Brave Don't Cry* (1952), a recreation of the recent Knockshinnock mine disaster that had occurred near his birthplace in Scotland.

This period in Grierson's career saw the end of British documentary as a movement, at least as a Griersonian movement. Crown Film Unit—successor to the General Post Office Film Unit (1933 to 1940) and the Empire Marketing Board Film Unit (1930 to 1933)—was terminated in 1952. The grounds were that it cost too much and that if films were needed by the government, they could be made by private firms. Though this elimination of the central government documentary unit occurred while the Conservative Party was in office, it had been prepared for during a Labour government and during years that included those in which Grierson had been head of COI Films Division, of which Crown was part.

In the U.S., what collective leadership had existed on the political left or within the New Deal administration of Franklin Roosevelt had ended as war broke out. After the war, Pare Lorentz, head of the short-lived U.S. Film Service, lapsed into semiretirement. Others were making industrially-sponsored films and a comfortable living. Willard Van Dyke, for example, in *American Frontier* (1953), produced for the American Petroleum Institute, retained some of the themes and style of his earlier work, but a prevailing blandness replaced the originality and conviction of *The City* or *Valley Town*. [See the Appendix for an additional account by George Stoney, one of the filmmakers of the time.]

In Canada, the National Film Board carried on after the war but defensively and without inspiration. As Film Commissioner, Ross McLean, who had been assistant to Grierson from the early years on, patiently and determinedly warded off attacks on the Board from the political right and segments of the commercial film industry. The charges were that the Board was unjustifiably costly and extravagant, that it competed with private enterprise, that it harbored subversives, and that there was no need for it in peacetime. McLean's personality and the nature of his background in Canadian civil service equipped him well for his tenure. If he lacked Grierson's imagination and aggressiveness, he probably fought the battle of attrition more skillfully and successfully than Grierson would have done.

In summary of documentary personnel and leadership in the immediate postwar years, 1945 to 1952, it can be said that in Britain, the United States, and, to a lesser extent, Canada, the veterans were dispersed and disorganized with no clear leadership or rallying point; mostly they were scrambling for jobs in an overcrowded field. The younger documentarians, with only the war experience as background, had little commitment or sense of direction; they made any kind of film they could, to the sponsor's specifications, or they drifted into other fields.

SPONSORSHIP

The established institutional sources that have supported documentary are government, industry, and foundations and associations. During the war, governments were virtually the sole source of sponsorship. The wartime

Ministry of Information of the British **government** metamorphosed into the peacetime Central Office of Information. But the Labour Party, following its resounding election victory at war's end, failed to back documentary as fully as expected. This profoundly dampened the spirits of the documentary people, most of whom were on the political left and Labour supporters. One reason for this neglect seems to have been that Labour politicians were generally unimaginative in their thinking about government information services. When they thought about them at all, it was in terms of pamphlets and speeches. (The Conservative politicians, on the other hand, who had been in power in the thirties, mostly came from the upper classes. Having received educations that included the arts, and with some aristocratic attraction toward patronage, they had been more open to the sponsorship of films.) Second, the postwar years were ones of rigorous austerity; funds were lacking for many forms of government activity. When Grierson returned to Britain, he was unable to prevent the cutting down at the COI, which would come to include the elimination of Crown shortly after he left.

In the U.S., the Office of War Information was eliminated altogether and sustained government support for filmmaking existed only in the Department of Agriculture (with a long and honorable record of using films to communicate with farmers through the county agents scattered around the country), the Armed Forces (which, of course, had available an enormous stockpile of films of every conceivable sort), and the United States Information Agency (a branch of the Department of State which used films only overseas, for propaganda purposes).

Though the National Film Board of Canada was severely cut, it survived and adjusted to the more modest postwar needs of government and citizens. Financial support for it would gradually increase. By the mid-fifties it moved into a new sort of eminence with shorts that won the awards for documentary and animation at the major international film festivals. Documentary examples are: *Corral* (1953, Colin Low and Wolf Koenig), *Paul Tomkowicz, Street-Railway Switchman* (1954, Roman Kroitor), *City of Gold* (1957, Colin Low and Wolf Koenig), *Blood and Fire* (1958, Terence Macartney-Filgate), *The Back-Breaking Leaf* (1959, Filgate), *Lonely Boy* (1962, Roman Kroitor and Wolf Koenig).

Postwar **industrial** sponsorship in Britain was limited by the austerity of the economy. In the U.S., industry became a big sponsor of films for the first time. In all three countries businesses and industries were now justifying every dollar spent on films in terms of increased sales and obvious goodwill. There existed virtually no industrial sponsorship of films in the general public interest, such as those sponsored by the oil and gas industries in Britain in the thirties. After the war, company public relations officers, given the extensive use of films and the testing of their effectiveness during wartime, felt they knew very well what films should be like and could do. An increase in company profits rather than general public improvement was clearly their goal.

In Britain and in Canada, **foundations and associations** were less active sponsors of films than they were in the United States. There seem to have been fewer of them and they don't seem to have had as much money. But in the U.S., the large foundations and national associations were soon limited in what they would spend their money on by growing pressure from the political right. This postwar political reaction would come to be called "McCarthyism." Senator McCarthy headed congressional committees, and used whatever other power he could muster, to ferret out communists and communist sympathizers wherever he could find them. His work paralleled that of the House of Representatives Un-American Activities Committee, which was busy investigating communist influence in the film and broadcasting industries. McCarthy's investigations were into subversive influences in the Department of State and the Army. At the time of his death, he was about to start on the large foundations, most notably the Ford Foundation, which were accused of sheltering "reds" and radicals. As a result of this political climate, the foundations restricted their grants to existing and widely accepted institutions and activities. They did not sponsor films which might prove "controversial" or might be made by filmmakers with a "past" (involvement with organizations and causes on the left). The national associations concerned with education and various health problems like tuberculosis, cancer, or heart disease, stuck to small, well-defined promotional films or informational films used as "audio-visual aids."

The overall result of these restrictions on sponsorship was that there just weren't as many big and important film statements being paid for as there had been in the thirties and first half of the forties.

SUBJECTS

Documentary can be thought of as a Depression baby that came of age during wartime. It seems to be true that it has thrived on crisis and disaster, criticism and attack. Following the war, the great documentary causes of the thirties (unemployment and rural poverty, conservation of land and water, housing and urban planning) and early forties (the fight against fascism) were no longer relevant or popular. The situation in the immediate postwar era was greatly altered from that of prewar or wartime.

Internationalism

The first years of peace saw a great surge of international good intentions. The Axis powers—Germany, Italy, and Japan—had been defeated by the Allies—Great Britain, United States, Soviet Union, and China. A new United Nations organization had been established to sustain and extend this victory, to try to make one world out of this war-torn globe. In this spirit, documentarians saw that films were needed to interpret the meaning of the United Nations and its subsidiary organizations, and to show aspects of their services to the world at large. Also needed were films confronting particular postwar problems and the concerns of war-ravaged and the underdeveloped nations. For a brief period this international outlook prevailed.

In this country, the United States Information Agency worked in conjunction with American economic aid abroad (what was called the Marshall Plan, conceived by General George C. Marshall, who had become Secretary of State). One of its films, *The Pale Horseman* (1946), written and produced by Irving Jacoby, was a grim and forceful survey of world devastation, famine, and the threat of pestilence. It took the stance that it was in our own self-interest to combat this menace, whether through the United Nations Relief and Rehabilitation Administration (UNRRA) or other means. *Seeds of Destiny* (1946, David Miller) is similar in persuasive intent and compilation form. The Twentieth Century Fund, a foundation particularly concerned with economic matters, sponsored *Round Trip: U.S. in World Trade* (1947). Made by Raymond Spottiswoode and Stuart Legg out of The World Today, Inc., of New York (the firm established by Grierson), it too argued along lines of enlightened self-interest. Demonstrating that many of the products we use every day come from abroad, it argues that this does not represent a threat to our economy. On the contrary, American industry will be kept strong by matching these imports with exports.

The Pale Horseman (U.S., 1946, Irving Jacoby). Museum of Modern Art/Film Stills Archive.

The filmmakers also responded to increased curiosity about other parts of the world which had been aroused by a global war. *The Russians Nobody Knows* (1946) was shot for "The March of Time" by Julien Bryan (who had earlier shot *Inside Nazi Germany* and footage on the fall of Warsaw at the outbreak of WWII). In the postwar film about Russia, emphasis is placed on UNRRA aid to the war-crippled Soviet economy.

In Britain there was a similar United Nations emphasis. As successor to his *World of Plenty* (1943), Paul Rotha made *The World is Rich* (1947) for the Central Office of Information. Like the earlier film, it argues for more adequate international distribution of food and supports the work of the Food and Agriculture Organization (FAO). Rotha and Basil Wright made *World Without End* (1954) for UNESCO, showing how that organization helped solve food production and health problems in Mexico and Thailand respectively.

Following the war, Britain attempted to explain to its citizens (and the rest of the world) its changing conception of colonial stewardship. *Cypress Is an Island* (1946, Ralph Keene) is a film with such a purpose. It is about deforestation and goatherds rather than the conflicts between Greek and Turkish inhabitants that would erupt when Cypress achieved independence. *Daybreak in Udi* (1949, Terry Bishop), produced for the COI while Grierson was in charge of its Films Division, concerns the progress of community education in West Africa. It won an Academy Award.

Daybreak in Udi (U.K., 1949, Terry Bishop). National Film Archive/Stills Library.

In Canada during these early postwar years the National Film Board was struggling for its existence. One of the charges leveled at it was that it employed those with left-wing sympathies. In this climate, the internationalism that had characterized "The World in Action" disappeared from the NFB films.

In fact, in the world as a whole the spirit of internationalism dwindled by 1948 with the outbreak of a "cold war" (as opposed to the hot one just ended) between the United States and the Soviet Union. Though it centered on occupied Berlin, the cold war changed political attitudes and military strategies throughout the world. Also, the sponsorship and distribution of films by the United Nations and its subsidiary organizations proved inadequate to sustain development along international lines.

At UNESCO, Grierson and his successors did what they could, but lacked the means to support production. The United Nations Film Distribution Unit distributed what films were given to it. Later, when Thorold Dickinson became chief of the Film Service for the U.N. Office of Public Information from 1956 to 1960, he attempted to start a production program. *Power Among Men* (1959, Thorold Dickinson and J.C. Sheers) is a four-part feature about postwar problems and their solutions in Italy, Haiti, Canada, and Norway—the latter sequence about the peaceful use of atomic energy. *A Scary Time* (1960, Shirley Clarke) contrasts the real horrors of famine and disease with Halloween tricks-or-treats for UNICEF. The program was curtailed and Dickinson returned to England.

Other Postwar Subjects; New Types and Styles

No clear alternatives appeared to replace the fading prospects for international documentary. Increased prosperity caused the subjects and rhetoric of the Depression to seem inapplicable, even old-fashioned. Increased conservatism and a cold war caused the main lines of liberal and antifascist criticism to be suspect. Sponsors and filmmakers alike were unwilling to risk making a "statement" at a time when political positions were being subjected to investigation. Consequently, the documentary subjects were essentially noncontroversial; certainly they were not socio/economic/political by and large, as earlier documentaries had been. In their own way, they were for virtue and against vice.

Another change of postwar documentary was that it had to exist within the nontheatrical film field to a much greater extent. The theaters lost interest in showing documentaries once the drama of war ended. On the other hand, the nontheatrical film field was much larger as a result of the wartime stimulus. The documentaries that were made were geared to this field.

Grierson's discovery that more seats existed outside the theaters than within them was a valuable one. Still, major documentary achievements had reached large audiences in theaters with the possible social impact that that allowed—*Night Mail, The River, Target for Tonight, Divide and Conquer,* for example. Now the nontheatrical field was the main means for documentary distribution-exhibition, and nontheatrical films were mainly industrial and educational. Documentaries had to be largely sponsored by businesses and industries for their particular goals, or be fitted into educational curriculums so that sufficient numbers of 16mm prints could be sold and rented to pay the cost of production.

As a result of industrial and educational requirements, as they were seen at the time, documentary seemed to lose its identity, its sure sense of function and form. In a way, the new subject emphases represented a retreat from the job of documentary as earlier understood. No longer significant as an approach to public information, or in the forefront of public policy— as Basil Wright had conceived it—documentary was now following or at the fringes of national concerns. Subjects dealt with for the first time, or with a new frequency, were the arts, mental health, public health, and race relations.

In postwar Europe, especially in France and Belgium, films dealing with **the arts** first appeared. Distributed widely abroad, they attracted considerable attention and started two new genres of the nonfiction film.

Some of these used art-related works as visual documents to portray times and places not otherwise available to filmmakers. In *Paris 1900* (France, 1947, Nicole Védrès) photographs, early newsreels, drawings and paintings, newspaper front pages, and other artifacts were used for a historical essay. *1848* (France, 1948, Victoria Mercanton) takes its visual substance from engravings, etchings, and ink drawings of a contemporary Paris to revive that year out of a past century. *Images Médiévales* (France, 1950, William Novick) did the same with the Bibles created by fourteenth- and fifteenth-century monks, using the scenes of court and country life in these illuminated manuscripts as visual representation of the Middle Ages.

In a second kind of film, the arts themselves became the subject matter. Films were made about artworks, about their creators, and about the history of art. In France, Alain Resnais made *Van Gogh* (1948) and *Guernica* (1950), the latter about Pablo Picasso's great painting of the Spanish Civil War. In Belgium, Henri Storck made *The World of Paul Delvaux* (1946) with the painter himself and *Rubens* (1948) with art historian Paul Haesaerts. There were even two French films, by Roger Leenhardt, about the discoveries and inventions that led to the motion picture: *Animated Cartoons: The Toy That Grew Up* and *Biography of the Motion Picture Camera* (both 1946).

These films about the arts and those that used the arts to deal with other subjects became widely popular, perhaps owing to a general growth in art appreciation as prosperity and leisure increased. Sometimes they were shown as shorts in the "art theaters" specializing in European or other-

wise non–Hollywood feature films and in the film societies developing during these years. They were also shown in schools, libraries, and museums.

American, British and, to a lesser extent, Canadian documentary filmmakers turned to these forms. Many documentarians had been trained in
or were especially sympathetic to the arts. Even Robert Flaherty shot material for a study of *Guernica* (1949) and was involved in the promotion and
distribution of *The Titan—Story of Michelangelo* (a revised version released in
1950 of a film made in Italy by the Swiss director Curt Oertel between 1938
and 1940). The latter is a feature-length biography of Michelangelo using
only contemporary architecture, interior settings, and artworks as its visual
material. This sort of compilation would become a prominent form of television documentary, to be discussed in Chapter Twelve.

That this impulse towards the arts was a documentary impulse was
acknowledged by Englishman John Read, who called his films about artists
"documentaries." In his *Henry Moore* (1951), for example, we see and learn
about the artist's way of living and working, get a sense of the man and his
approach to art; examine him at work creating, and view some of his created
works. Willard Van Dyke, veteran American documentarian, made a similar
film about Edward Weston: *The Photographer* (1948). Read's *Artists Must Live*
(1953) explores the relationship between the artist and his or her patron.

More akin in subject and style to earlier documentary forms than
those concerning arts and artists were documentaries about **mental health.**
A profound difference between them and earlier documentaries, however,
was that the mental health documentaries dealt with men and women in
relation to themselves—their individual, interior lives—rather than with
their relationships to society and to social problems. *The Quiet One* (U.S.,

The Titan—Story of Michelangelo
(Switzerland, 1940, Curt Oertel). Museum of Modern Art/Film Stills Archive.

1948, Sidney Meyers), discussed at the outset of this chapter, is an outstanding example of this kind of film. It was produced under the auspices of the newly-formed Mental Health Film Board. If this film had been made in the thirties, it would have centered on the social, economic, and political causes for the unhappy lives we see. Here, the Harlem ghetto and broken families serve merely as background for the disturbances in Donald's psyche. In *Out of True* (U.K., 1950, Phil Leacock) a middle-class woman has a severe emotional breakdown and is helped back toward recovery by modern psychiatry.

But it was in Canada, at the National Film Board, that the most important pioneering work in the mental health documentary was done. The "Mental Mechanisms" series was made for the Mental Health division of the Department of National Health and Welfare. Directed by Robert Anderson, it made original progress in ways of presenting emotional disorders for study and understanding and provided models for subsequent films on mental health. On a case-by-case basis, Anderson dealt with various psychological malfunctionings. *The Feeling of Rejection* (1947), *The Feeling of Hostility* (1948), *Overdependency* (1949), and *Feelings of Depression* (1950) were among them.

Feelings of Depression, "Mental Mechanisms" series (Canada, 1950, Robert Anderson). John Caldwell.

Documentaries on matters of general **public health** became much more plentiful and effective than before. The most skillful and dedicated practitioner in this field was George Stoney, whose *All My Babies* (U.S., 1952), dealing with midwives and their work in rural Georgia, was discussed at the beginning of this chapter. Another film with which Stoney was involved, *Feeling All Right* (1949, his preliminary script; direction by Fred Lasse, cinematography by Gordon Weisenborn), dealt with the detection and treatment of syphillis in a semidocumentary narrative form. Sponsored by the Mississippi State Board of Health, it was set among the black population of Washington County. Among other noteworthy Stoney films about health problems is *Still Going Places* (1956, made for health professionals; the lay version is entitled *The Proud Years*), about the care and treatment of the aged. In Great Britain, *The Undefeated* (1950, Paul Dickson) was about the treatment of permanently disabled World War II veterans. It centered on a veteran who had lost his speech and the use of both legs at the battle of Arnhem. It won an Academy Award.

Films about **race relations** were much in evidence in the U.S. This subject was dealt with using a number of techniques in addition to documentary. In a theatrical short, *The House I Live In* (1945), made before the race cycle of Hollywood features discussed in Chapter Ten, Frank Sinatra sings the song of that title and speaks against anti–Semitism. A cluster of

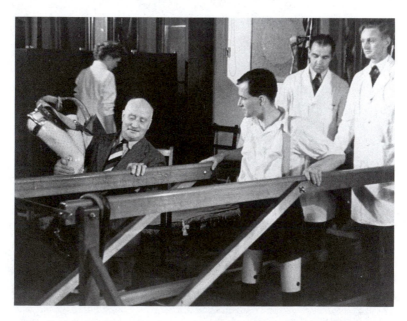

The Undefeated (U.K., 1950, Paul Dickson). National Film Archive/Stills Library.

animated race-relations films began with the very popular *Brotherhood of Man* (1946), sponsored by the UAW-CIO. It was an early effort of United Productions of American (UPA), the talented group that broke away from the Disney Studio and went on to create Mr. Magoo and Gerald McBoing Boing. It was followed by Philip Stapp's *Boundary Lines* (1947) and *Picture in Your Mind* (c. 1950) from Julien Bryan's International Film Foundation. Then there were dramatizations. *The High Wall* (c. 1948) presented a conflict among teenagers of different ethnic and class backgrounds and parental prejudices. Alas, neither the Hollywood features nor the "brotherhood films," as the nontheatrical shorts were called, seem to have contributed much to greater understanding and tolerance.

APPROACHES AND TECHNIQUES

Other observable differences of treatment between the documentaries of 1945 to 1952 and those that had preceded them apply more generally. The later films are more clearly aimed at nontheatrical application and more specialized audiences. They are educational mostly, since even industrially sponsored films were generally designed to be shown in classrooms. Films for adult education and discussion were also made—for parents with small children, say, or labor or management groups, or a cultural elite with one sort of interest or another. They were mainly films of reassurance rather than criticism or attack; they rarely dealt with social/economic/political problems. At the same time, they seem to have been intended to serve the community rather than to persuade or indoctrinate and to meet the needs of audiences for information and understanding of certain subjects. This was especially true of the work of the National Film Board of Canada.

As for their formal aspects, the postwar films are freer and more varied in their techniques than were the earlier documentaries. More nonactuality was employed—fictional and dramatic elements—and structurally they tended to be organized as narrative or as drama. There was an increased use of actors and performance and more location sound, especially sync sound. The latter was made possible by the availability of magnetic tape, which made recording outside the studio much more practicable than it had been with the optical system. The narrative structures and sync dialogue coincided with the tendency of these postwar documentaries to center more on individuals than had the films of the thirties. In the postwar years even large-scale problems—race relations, mental health—were dealt with in terms of how they affected individuals. In this respect the postwar documentaries not only resemble the British wartime semidocumentaries, they look ahead to the kind of documentary called cinéma vérité and direct cinema, to be dealt with in Chapter Fourteen.

FINAL OBSERVATIONS

The years treated in this chapter fall between the end of World War II, with the prominence documentary achieved, and the beginning of a United States blanketed by television. Between 1945 and 1952 documentaries were mostly industrial or classroom films.

Generally, the industrial documentaries were unenlightened and limited in scope. The oil industry provided the major exception. Perhaps this was because it had more money than other industries or because it had more public relations problems. In either case, it sponsored some noteworthy films during these years. In Britain the Petroleum Films Bureau sponsored *Forward a Century* (1951, J.B. Napier-Bell), a large-scale historical survey of technological and social advance. The film unit of British Shell Oil continued to produce brilliant informational and instructional shorts. In Australia, Shell sponsored *The Back of Beyond* (1954, John Heyer), an appealing semidocumentary feature about a mailman whose route took him into the far reaches of that vast subcontinent. In the U.S., Standard Oil of New Jersey sponsored Flaherty's *Louisiana Story* (1948), discussed earlier in this chapter.

Among classroom films, increased ambition and improving artistry were in evidence for awhile. Two examples about city planning were *The Baltimore Plan* and *The Living City*. Both were sponsored by the Twentieth Century Fund, directed by John Barnes, and released by Encyclopaedia Britannica Films in 1953. The latter was nominated for an Academy Award. But it turned out that such "prestige pictures didn't pay the rent," as they said at EBF at the time, as did those fitting more neatly into K-12 curriculums.

On the whole, the English-language documentary appeared shrunken and almost at its end by the early fifties. It had run out of sponsorship, out of audiences, and out of steam. Fortunately, before expiring altogether, it would be revived to full health (equaling that of wartime) by the new electronic means of distributing the moving image accompanied by sound that will be dealt with in Chapter Twelve.

FILMS OF THE PERIOD

1946
Cyprus Is an Island (U.K., Ralph Keene)
The Pale Horseman (U.S., Irving Jacoby)
Seeds of Destiny (U.S., David Miller)

1947
The Feeling of Rejection (Canada, Robert Anderson)

First Steps (U.S., Leo Seltzer)
Journey into Medicine (U.S., Willard Van Dyke and Jacoby)
Muscle Beach (U.S., Joseph Strick and Irving Lerner)
The Roosevelt Story (U.S., Julian Roffman and Ben Kerner)
The World Is Rich (U.K., Paul Rotha)

1948
Louisiana Story (U.S., Robert Flaherty)
Make Way for Youth (U.S., Robert Disraeli)
The Photographer (U.S., Van Dyke)

1949
Creation According to Genesis (U.S., Paul Burn-
ford)
Daybreak in Udi (U.K., Terry Bishop)
Feeling All Right (U.S., Fred Lasse)
Nomads of the Jungle, ("The Earth and Its
Peoples" series, U.S., Victor Jurgens)
One God—The Ways We Worship Him (U.S.,
Nicholas Farkas)
The Quiet One (U.S., Sidney Meyers)
A Time for Bach (U.S., Paul Falkenberg)
Waverly Steps (U.K., John Eldridge)

1950
The Titan–Story of Michelangelo (Switzerland,
Curt Oertel)
The Undefeated (U.K., Paul Dickson)

1951
Angry Boy (U.S., Alexander Hammid and Ja-
coby)
Benjy (U.S., Fred Zinnemann)
Forward a Century (U.K., J. B. Napier-Bell)
Steps of Age (U.S., Ben Maddow and Helen
Levitt)
Waters of Time (U.K., Basil Wright)

1952
All My Babies (U.S., George Stoney)
Notes on the Port of St. Francis (U.S., Frank Stauf-
facher)

BOOKS ON THE PERIOD

BEATTIE, ELEANOR, *A Handbook of Canadian Film*. Toronto: Peter Martin Associates Limited, 1973.
280 pp.
BEVERIDGE, JAMES, *John Grierson: Film Master*. New York: Macmillan Publishing Co., Inc., 1978.
361 pp.
BUCHANAN, DONALD WILLIAM, *Documentary and Educational Films in Canada 1935–1950: A Survey
of Problems and Achievements*. Ottawa: Canadian Film Institute, 1952. 24 pp.
ELLIS, JACK C., *John Grierson: A Guide to References and Resources*. Boston: G. K. Hall & Co., 1986.
262 pp.
FELDMAN, SETH and JOYCE NELSON, eds., *Canadian Film Reader*. Toronto: Peter Martin Associates
Limited, 1977. 405 pp.
Film Council of America, *Sixty Years of 16mm Film, 1923–1983*. Evanston, Ill.: Film Council of
America, 1954. 220 pp.
HARDY, FORSYTH, *John Grierson: A Documentary Biography*. London: Faber and Faber Limited,
1979. 298 pp.
JAMES, C. RODNEY, *Film as a National Art: NFB of Canada and the Film Board Idea*. New York: Arno
Press, 1977. 760 pp.
McKAY, MARJORIE, *History of the National Film Board of Canada*. Montreal: National Film Board,
1964. 147 pp.
ROTHA, PAUL, *Rotha on the Film*. London: Faber and Faber Ltd., 1958. 338 pp.
STARR, CECILE, *Ideas on Film*. New York: Funk & Wagnalls Company, 1951. 251 pp.
SUSSEX, ELIZABETH, *The Rise and Fall of British Documentary: The Story of the Film Movement Founded
by John Grierson*. Berkeley: University of California Press, 1975. 219 pp.
WALDRON, GLORIA, *The Information Film*. New York: Columbia University Press, 1949. 281 pp.

TWELVE
A NEW CHANNEL
Documentary for Television, 1951–

English-language documentary films began as a regular part of theatrical film exhibition from *Nanook of the North* in 1922 on. At the time of *Nanook* and before, the only way to see a movie was in a movie theater. The 35mm film stock standard for theatrical showings had a base of cellulose nitrate, which was highly flammable. It had to be projected from booths constructed in conformance with local ordinances. Exceptions, like the projection vans used by the Soviets and later by the British, were few.

In 1923, at the urging of educators, Eastman Kodak Company made available a film 16mm in width with a cellulose acetate base. Because it was noninflammable (it was called "safety stock") and the narrower width made lighter equipment possible, portable 16mm projectors could be set up in school rooms, church basements, union halls—anywhere, in fact.

With 16mm projectors manufactured and sold and prints of films available for rental and purchase, the nontheatrical field became a recognizable entity by the late 1930s. World War II caused an explosion in the use of films as means of informing and educating. Following the war the nontheatrical field, with industrially sponsored and classroom films predominating, expanded to the proportions it has maintained ever since. But, as discussed in Chapter Eleven, the expansion of the nontheatrical field did not work to the advantage of documentary. It didn't fit comfortably into the rather narrow requirements of industrial sales promotion or of formal education. Nor did it have the access to theaters it had had during wartime.

As documentary was sinking into the background, losing financial support and audiences, as well as earlier subject matter and purposes, a new channel for distribution and exhibition was opening up. This new channel would provide a substantial and sustained basis of support. Thanks to television, more documentaries and related types of public information programs have been shown to larger audiences than at any other time in history, except perhaps during the years of World War II.

HISTORICAL BACKGROUND

Telecasting had begun in an experimental and very limited way in both Great Britain and the United States before the war—Britain being ahead of the U.S. in this—but military requirements of wartime had stopped further development. After the war, regular television broadcasting began in Great Britain, then in the United States, then in Canada. Let me discuss briefly the arrival of television in Britain and Canada before turning to and concentrating on commercial network television in the United States, as this chapter will mostly do.

In 1946 the British Broadcasting Corporation began regular telecasting. But this quasi-governmental organization, supported by a tax on television sets, did not attract anything like the audience that would develop when commercial broadcasting was permitted to operate alongside BBC-TV in 1955. The Independent Television Authority (ITA, initially; now called Independent Television, ITV) ran programs produced by a number of commercial companies. Documentaries were included. For example, Granada Television Ltd. produced *World in Action,* a public affairs and documentary series the title for which was borrowed from the wartime National Film Board of Canada. Thames Television subsequently produced the outstanding documentary series about World War II, *The World at War.* Scottish Television produced John Grierson's television series devoted to documentary and experimental shorts, *This Wonderful World.* (Subsequently its title was changed to *John Grierson Presents.* For a brief period another documentary veteran, Paul Rotha, was head of the BBC-TV documentary department.)

The situation in Canada was anomolous. Though the Canadian Broadcasting Corporation (a government-related system) did not begin telecasting until 1953, most of Canada's population lived close enough to its southern border to receive United States television directly or via community antennae. Canada's bilingual culture was acknowledged by the CBC with a French-language as well as an English-language network. Curiously, the National Film Board continued to work separately from CBC-TV, with little exchange between them of produced materials or means of distribution-exhibition.

In the United States, 1946 was the year television was removed from the wartime freeze. In 1948 bigtime TV was born. A network out of New York linked the major cities; the most popular shows were Milton Berle's *Texaco Star Theatre* comedy and Ed Sullivan's *Toast of the Town* variety. By 1950, 100 stations telecast to four million sets. In 1951 coaxial cable and microwave relay connected the country coast to coast.

In the 1951–1952 season Edward R. Murrow's and Fred W. Friendly's *See It Now* (out of their radio series *Hear It Now*) appeared. (It was also the year "The March of Time" ended.) The 1952–1953 season contained *I Love Lucy* (starring Lucille Ball and Desi Arnaz) and *Victory at Sea* (supervised by historian Henry Salomon, Jr., and edited by Isaac Kleinerman). The situation comedy about a married couple (starring a married couple) and the twenty-six half-hour films about U.S. naval warfare in World War II (compiled from over six million feet of combat footage) are among the most successful and seminal television series ever aired. No doubt both are still playing somewhere in the world today.

While dramatic and other entertainment programs shown on television came from outside producing agencies, production of documentaries

Victory at Sea series (U.S., 1952–53, Henry Salomon, Jr., and Isaac Kleinerman). National Film Archive/Stills Library.

was carried on primarily by the networks and local stations themselves. Both the National Broadcasting Company (NBC) and the Columbia Broadcasting System (CBS) established units for this purpose, with personnel initially drawn largely from the ranks of the nontheatrical documentarians. American Broadcasting Corporation (ABC) documentary production was later and weaker, with a news emphasis. The main function of these units was the creation of special programs, frequently unsponsored, presented as prestige or public-service features.

In 1953 what is now the Public Broadcasting Service (PBS) began as National Educational Television (NET). This noncommercial network, supported by funds from the federal government, has initiated and distributed substantial quantities of documentaries and public affairs materials. Its budgets for documentaries tend to be smaller than those of the commercial networks, but it has made up for this by importing many significant documentary programs from abroad.

The number of documentaries shown on commercial and public television over the past five decades has, of course, been vast. What follows is a selective sketch of the series which were the longest lasting, contained some of the most memorable programs, and established the forms and contents most prevalent among documentaries made for television.

DOCUMENTARY SERIES

See It Now was the first regular documentary series. A sort of news magazine of feature stories in "The March of Time" tradition, it had a much quieter and more intimate tone suitable to the living room. Murrow and Friendly produced it for CBS; Murrow was the on-screen host and commentator. At first *See It Now*, like "March of Time" and the present-day *60 Minutes*, presented several different stories in each half-hour program. In 1953 the format changed to include only one story a week. Among the *See It Now* programs that stick in my memory are "Christmas in Korea" (1953), made during the Korean War, the several programs dealing with McCarthyism, including one in 1954 in which Senator McCarthy demanded the right to reply (consistent with an American broadcasting concept called "the fairness doctrine"), and a visit with nuclear physicist J. Robert Oppenheimer (1955).

Like "March of Time" too, *See It Now* contained consistent structural and stylistic characteristics—its format—which will be touched upon in a later section. A look at two programs may serve to give some sense of its distinctiveness.

"Argument in Indianapolis" (1953) presents opposing factions in that city when the American Civil Liberties Union, attempting to form a local chapter, is opposed by the American Legion post. One of the extraordinary things about this program is its balance in handling a controversial subject, necessary, I suppose, for it to be telecast at all. Depending on your sympathies, the American Legion members become fascist monsters or upholders of true Americanism; the American Civil Liberties group, pleasant, sensitive intellectuals or dangerous radicals and subversives. At any rate the faces, speech, and manner of the protagonists, are caught more or less candidly. A remarkable study is offered of diverse ideologies and personalities that exist in uneasy relationship to each other within this republic.

"Segregation in Schools" (1954) was made the week following the Supreme Court decision that declared that separate education for blacks and whites was neither equal nor constitutional. It reports on reactions to the decision in two Southern towns—Nachitoche, Louisiana, and Gastonia, North Carolina. What seems a curious stiffness and formality today—on the part of both black and white interviewees—with stand-up microphones visible and some statements read or rehearsed, may have to do with extremely strong feelings being controlled as well as a less flexible technology than is available today. When emotion does break through—actual expressed emotion of an elderly black woman, a black high school youth, an elderly white woman, and a black teacher—it is moving and becomes real in a way that helps us to understand more fully what is involved than do the prepared statements.

In 1955 Alcoa withdrew its sponsorship of *See It Now.* In 1958 *See It Now* was terminated, to be followed in 1959 by *CBS Reports,* which appeared irregularly as "specials" (media critic Gilbert Seldes quipped that it had become *See It Now and Then*) running an hour each.

Beginning of a *See It Now* series program on hurricanes (U.S., c. 1953, Edward R. Murrow and Fred W. Friendly). J. Fred MacDonald.

CBS Reports developed its own excellence. "The Population Explosion" (1959), while attempting to cover the problem generally, used India as the example. Spokespersons offering various solutions were presented. "Lippmann on Leadership" (1960) allowed the newspaper columnist and political philosopher to express his views. Murrow's last program for the series, "Harvest of Shame" (1960), was about the exploitation and hardships of migrant agricultural workers. It was aired on Thanksgiving Day. Murrow left CBS to become director of the United States Information Agency. Subsequent *CBS Reports* included "Biography of a Bookie Joint" (1961), a neat job of investigative journalism by Jay McMullen, "Hunger in America" (1969), and "The Selling of the Pentagon" (1971), the latter two by Peter Davis.

NBC's response to *See It Now* was the quite different *Project XX* series, which began in 1954. It grew out of the success of *Victory at Sea* and its production unit included many of the same creative personnel. Rather than a weekly series, however, *Project XX* offered occasional hour-long specials. Like *Victory at Sea* its programs were compilation films whose origins could be traced back to the "Why We Fight" series, which in turn could be traced back to "The March of Time." *Project XX's* programs were devoted to recreating aspects of the history of this century (thus *XX*) using existing footage—newsreel, documentary, and feature—and occasional reenactments. Among those that attracted most attention were "Nightmare in Red" (1955), which chronicled the rise of Soviet Communism, "The Twisted Cross" (1956), which did the same for German Nazism, and "The Real West" (1961). The latter, produced and directed by Donald Hyatt, used paintings

"The Real West," *Project XX* series (U.S., 1961, Donald Hyatt). J. Fred MacDonald.

and photographs—that is, still visual material—music, and words of the era to capture the spirit of a particular time and place. The commentary, written by Phil Reisman, Jr., and spoken by Gary Cooper, took on a contemporary flavor as well. Regarding the great cattle drives from Texas to the railroad towns of Kansas and Missouri: "The longhorns were as treacherous as the backlash of a bull whip. Later, the breed was white-faced and dimple-kneed, but spookier than a wing-busted bird in cat country."

NBC's series comparable to CBS's *See It Now* and *CBS Reports* was *White Paper,* begun in 1960. Executive producer was Irving Gitlin. For the most part, it stuck even closer to current or recent headlines. "The U-2 Affair" (1960) dealt with an incident that exposed United States aerial spying on the Soviet Union. Other programs also announced the currency of their topics in their titles: "Angola: Journey to a War" (1961), "The Death of Stalin" (1963), "Cuba: Bay of Pigs" (1964). A domestic local situation that had become national news was examined in "The Battle of Newburgh" (1962). At issue was the controversy that developed over the decision by the city manager of this New York town to rid the community of "welfare chiselers."

The Twentieth Century weekly series, which began on CBS in 1957, was sponsored by the Prudential Insurance Company and produced by Burton Benjamin and Isaac Kleinerman. Its programs were mostly half-hour, though a few were hour-long. Many of these were historical compilations such as "Trial at Nuremberg" (1958), "Paris in the Twenties" (1960), and "The Western Hero" (1963). The format of "From Kaiser to Fuehrer" (1959) is typical. Host Walter Cronkite introduces the program then retreats off-screen to voice-over commentary. It stems from *The Fall of the Romanov Dynasty* and "Why We Fight," of course. Clips from German films of the twenties are its main basis. In addition to newsreels, extensive use is made of

"The Battle of Newburgh," *White Paper* series (U.S., 1962, Arthur Zegart). J. Fred MacDonald.

"The Olympics," *The Twentieth Century* series (U.S., 1959, Burton Benjamin), with commentator Walter Cronkite, alongside the sponsor's symbol, introducing the program. J. Fred MacDonald.

Berlin: Symphony of a Great City and *Variety*, a fictional feature. The cutting pace is rapid and the editing skillful; a full orchestral score contributes much to continuity and dramatic effect.

Other *Twentieth Century* programs were on contemporary subjects and used freshly-shot material and interviews: "Ireland: The Tear and The Smile" (1961), "The Burma Surgeon Today" (1961), "So That Men are Free" (1962). Willard Van Dyke directed the latter (and a number of other *Twentieth Century* films including "Ireland," above, and "Sweden," 1961).

In 1966 *The Twentieth Century* became *The Twenty-First Century* before its final season of 1970–1971. The new title was intended to suggest a shift in emphasis to scientific development and the future.

ABC-TV distinguished itself with *Close-Up!*, a series using cinéma-vérité—more precisely the American version of it called direct cinema. This new technique, made possible by new technology, is the subject of Chapter Fourteen. The idea for the series came from *Primary* (1960) and *On the Pole* (1960), films produced by Robert Drew Associates (which included Richard Leacock, Donn Pennebaker, Terence Macartney-Filgate, and Albert and David Maysles) for Time-Life Broadcast. These undirected sync-sound records were of the Wisconsin presidential primary contest between Hubert Humphrey and John F. Kennedy and of the Indianapolis automobile race, following driver Eddie Sachs. They were shown on four stations owned by Time, Inc. ABC was sufficiently impressed to hire Drew Associates to produce four one-hour documentaries for the *Close-Up!* series: "Yanki No!" (1960), "X-Pilot" (1960), "The Children Were Watching" (1960), and "Adventures on the New Frontier" (1961). The first had to do with anti–Americanism in Latin America. The subject of the second is the final test flight of a new airplane and the personality of the test pilot. The third was shot in New Orleans during one week of a school integration crisis. It presents the attitudes of white segregationists and their effects on a black family whose daughter is supposed to be one of the first to attend a previously all-white school. Finally, "Adventures on the New Frontier" presents "a day in the life of" John F. Kennedy in the White House.

Drew Associates did not continue on *Close-Up!* but executive producer of that series, John Secondari, seems to have learned from them and produced valuable programs using direct cinema technique with his own personnel. Nicholas Webster was one of these, who produced and directed "Walk in My Shoes" (1961). It presents the anger, resentment, and feelings of frustration of black Americans largely from their point of view and in interview situations of one sort or another. Webster's "Meet Comrade Student" (1962) examines Soviet education after the launching of Sputnik which had caused Americans to feel left behind in scientific knowledge and training.

Frederick Wiseman, one of the most skilled and talented makers of direct cinema, has produced for public television. *High School* (1968), *Law and Order* (1969), *Hospital* (1970), and *Basic Training* (1971) were supported in varying proportions by the Public Broadcasting Service, WNET Channel 13 in New York City, and income from nontheatrical rentals of his films. After *Basic Training*, Wiseman contracted with WNET to do one documen-

"Walk in My Shoes," *Close-Up!* series (U.S., 1961, Nicholas Webster). J. Fred MacDonald.

High School (U.S., 1968, Frederick Wiseman). Zipporah Films, Inc.

tary each year to play on the PBS network. His subjects have been various American institutions, the titles generally baldly indicating which one. Wiseman's films will be discussed more fully in Chapter Seventeen.

The biggest television documentary success story to date is, of course, *60 Minutes,* CBS's news magazine that began in 1968. It has brought documentary-like content and production methods into commercial television just as "The March of Time" earlier introduced its own kind of nonfiction forms and subjects into movie theaters. Like "March of Time," *60 Minutes* has developed a format that fits the medium within which it is perceived. In this case, since the medium is television, its origins are directly traceable to *See It Now* and *CBS Reports.* In *60 Minutes* the American journalistic term "news story" is taken quite literally. The several stories of each program— some light, some serious—use a combination of aggressive investigative reporting, personable on-the-air reporters (Mike Wallace, Morley Safer, Harry Reasoner, Diane Sawyer), and tight narrative structures. It has been successful not only in comparison with other television news, public affairs, and documentary series, but has reached the Top Ten among television shows generally in terms of numbers of viewers attracted and amount of money earned. Its success has also earned it the compliment of imitation: ABC-TV's *20/20,* for example. The magazine format made up of short segments has mostly replaced conventional documentary forms on television. CBS even competes with itself in this format with *West 57th,* the title of which refers to the location of CBS News headquarters, and *48 Hours.*

Star reporters of the *60 Minutes* series (U.S., 1988, CBS News), from the left: Ed Bradley, Mike Wallace, Morley Safer, Diane Sawyer, and Harry Reasoner. CBS News.

COMPARISON OF TELEVISION DISTRIBUTION-EXHIBITION WITH THEATRICAL AND NONTHEATRICAL

Of the three systems available for the distribution and exhibition of documentary films—theatrical, nontheatrical, television—each offers advantages and disadvantages to the makers. Television has not replaced the other two channels; it merely adds a third channel to the existing ones.

Each has its own founding saint, constituting a kind of trinity: Flaherty (the father), Grierson (the son), and Edward R. Murrow (the holy ghost, I suppose, ghost being what a technical problem with early television images was called). Represented by these figures are three elements most documentaries and documentarians have in solution: (1) art, (2) education and propaganda, and (3) journalism. Documentary makers tend to concentrate on one more than the others. The theatrical—available from 1895 on with the first Lumière showings; Flaherty entering in 1922—best accommodates the artist. In comparison with the other two channels it offers big budgets, leisurely production schedules, and the refinements of a 35mm image projected by brilliant arc light/xenon lamp onto a large screen. Films distributed in this manner are reviewed in the press and are most likely to secure a place in film history. The nontheatrical—16mm from 1923 on; Grierson entering in 1929—is for the educator/propagandist who likes the classroom situation. This is a way to receive maximum attention from opinion leaders—those able and likely to influence public action. During and following World War II the nontheatrical channel became substantial. It now includes videotape as well as 16mm film, of course. Television—from 1948 on in the big cities; Murrow and *See It Now* entering in 1951—is best for the journalist/ reporter. It is the primary source of information and opinion in this country and much of the world and can reach a mass audience instantaneously, even scooping the daily newspaper. It has attracted many journalists and the journalistic *60 Minutes* is its biggest documentary success.

Though Flaherty, Grierson, and Murrow are no longer living, it seems to me that, given the social sense and creative strengths of each, if reincarnated each might choose the channel he originally worked in. Flaherty's last film, *Louisiana Story* (1948), was made for the theaters at a time when nontheatrical distribution was the usual route for documentary. Flaherty never made a film for nontheatrical (or television) distribution. Grierson's final work was as a teacher at McGill University in Montreal. During that period, as a consultant to the government in India, he advised that audio cassettes be used as the means of education and persuasion in regard to birth control. His idea was that a woman presenting herself as venerable and wise, talk informally in native dialect about intimate matters to Indian women. Inexpensive cassette players and tapes were to be provided free to the villages. With Grierson, it was not the medium but the educational job that interested him primarily: the possibility of changing opinion in a way that would change action. As for Murrow, his kind of journalistic documentary, out of newspapers and radio, is the main line of television documentary. Murrow would be drawn to it by the possibility of informing the largest number of people about the events with which he is concerned while they are taking place. *60 Minutes* may be said to go even a step further—creating events and making news.

The advantages of television as a source of financing and distribution for documentaries, in comparison with the other two channels, can be summed up succinctly. The leading attraction is the large demand for documentaries on television. Television is a source of sustained sponsorship greater than any ever known, and it returns the cost of production much more quickly than theatrical or nontheatrical distribution. It also reaches the largest audiences simultaneously—forty million individuals and small groups watching on a Thursday night in their homes—rather than audiences in theaters, students in classrooms, members in club rooms and grange halls, and so on over the course of several years.

The limitations of television for distribution-exhibition of documentaries (and other forms of art and entertainment) include its technological crudities. The image on the tube has much poorer definition—that is, it is lacking in sharpness and detail (American television has only 525 lines in contrast to other national systems; the British have 625 lines, for example)— than the projected 35mm or 16mm images. Television sound has a limited dynamic range (it lacks high and low frequencies) and the three-inch speaker standard on TV sets allows for little audio richness. (Developments in stereo television since the mid-1980s are beginning to correct this deficiency.)

Also, it has another kind of limitation. Television audiences tend to be more heterogeneous and less attentive than those in the other two viewing situations. Audiences in theaters have chosen the movie they are watching through the impression made by its promotion, the criticism it has received, and by the opinions of friends and neighbors who have already seen it. Nontheatrical audiences are generally engaged in some common undertaking involving the viewing and discussion of films. Less advance information is available to television audiences and a particular program is usually seen as one part in a flow of diverse television programming. Furthermore, there are the distractions of the television viewing situation—for example, ringing telephones or discussion of homework in an adjoining room. And, of course, there are the commercial breaks within the television programs themselves.

By and large it seems that the channel chosen by the documentary maker for distribution-exhibition should be determined by subject and purpose. If he or she wants to offer audiences a rich, aesthetic experience and to move them emotionally, the theatrical feature film is the form best suited to do that. If he or she wants primarily to educate, to instruct, and to provide information and understanding that will motivate and equip audiences for intelligent action, then the best form is the nontheatrical short. The short is designed to be shown to specific audiences prepared to receive that kind of education and to act on it with some effect. If the documentary maker wants to reach as many people as quickly as possible in order to inform them about and offer an interpretation of some matter that seems important to her or him, then the television program is the best form.

SPECIAL CHARACTERISTICS
OF TELEVISION DOCUMENTARY

Many of the new elements common to documentaries made for television can be traced to the new technological characteristics of this electronic means of distribution-exhibition and to the new relationship with the audience sitting—as individuals or members of small family groups—at home. Television emerged from the earlier forms of radio broadcasting and retained practices common to it.

In regard to the content of documentaries made for television, it seems to me that three types predominate, and that they correspond to emphases of the documentary series and specials discussed earlier. First is the documentary based on a newsworthy subject, something that is of current, widespread interest. This is television's major contribution to the evolution of documentary subjects and forms, a genre in which it has been uniquely effective. *See It Now* and *CBS Reports* offered noteworthy examples; among them: "Annie Lee Moss Before the McCarthy Committee" (1954) and "Protective Tariff vs. Free Trade" (1957) in the former; "The Business of Health: Medicine, Money and Politics" (1961) and "Storm Over the Supreme Court" (1963) in the latter. Second are the historical and often nostalgic subjects of the compilation series and programs—*Project XX* ("The Innocent Years," 1957; "The Story of Will Rogers," 1961) and much of *The Twentieth Century* ("The Olympics," 1959; "Turn of the Century," 1960). Lastly there is what could be called "human interest," the interest we all have in individuals, their personalities, and their problems. This sort of content is most manifest in the use of direct cinema, in the early *Close-Up!* ("The Miners' Lament," 1963; "A Vanishing Breed: Portrait of a Country Editor," 1963) and in the annual Fred Wiseman features (*Juvenile Court*, 1973; *Welfare*, 1975, for example).

The range of subjects of television documentaries may be wider as well as different from that of earlier documentaries. A kind of "entertainment documentary" has emerged—the nostalgia and human interest categories—in which the issues no longer are of national concern, or even social significance. Gilbert Seldes observed, in *The Great Audience* (New York: Viking Press, Inc., 1950), that the function of the mass media, the experience they offer, is more like that of gossip than like that of traditional art forms. Certainly television offers materials as diverse as those of a neighbor talking to us over the back fence—in our electronic global village as another media critic, Marshall McLuhan, suggested in *Understanding Media: Extensions of Man* (New York: McGraw Hill Book Company, 1964). Scandalous secrets are revealed (soap operas), amusing anecdotes told (situation comedies), conundrums posed (game shows), local events reported (news), and the like.

Another McLuhan concept was that television is a "cool" medium. Its lack of technological refinement of image and sound means the viewer has to complete the message rather than having it beamed at him with the visual and emotional intensity of movies or the auditory precision and richness of radio. The content of television documentaries seems less concentrated, less intense, slower paced, more redundant—in short, aesthetically and emotionally suited to a cool medium—than that of films made to be shown in theaters. In this view *The City* or *Listen to Britain* would be regarded as "hotter" than "Clinton and the Law" (1955) of *See It Now* or "The Death of Edward Nevin" (1980) of *60 Minutes.*

At the same time, television documentary tends to maintain a small-scale intimacy. In *The Twentieth Century,* for example, a program on "Gandhi" (1959) is as much about the man as about the size of his accomplishments; it seems quite unlike *The River* or films of the "Why We Fight" series. Television documentaries often center not only on individuals but on values (ethical, spiritual, psychological) rather than on material concerns (work, housing, poverty), as did earlier documentaries. (Perhaps this difference is due as much to changed postwar concerns as to the influence of television; whatever the cause, the difference is observable.)

Frequently in the television documentary the commentator is a star and appears on camera. In earlier documentaries the commentator was usually anonymous and unobtrusive; one heard his voice over the images and he never appeared on screen. At most he added a bit of emotional color. The few exceptions that occur to me seemed awkward at the time. In one of the "brotherhood films," *The House I Live In,* mentioned in Chapter Eleven, Frank Sinatra talked and sang directly to the audience. I felt embarrassed somehow (for him or for myself?), knowing that he was really not here and now, as he was pretending to be, but out in Hollywood several months ago. Television creates the illusion, and stresses it, that all of it is "live," though of course most of it is not. We know that images and sounds are constantly there in the set, just as electricity is in the wires and water in the pipes, ready to be turned on at any time. The star commentators—Ed Murrow, Walter Cronkite, Charles Kuralt, Chet Huntley, Dan Rather, et al.— feed into and emphasize this quality of liveness. The audience tuned in to see what Ed was offering on Friday night. He talked directly to us from the control room, his reporters available to come in over the monitors as he called on them. (Actually, given the technology available at the time, they were filmed beforehand with the film flown to New York, processed in the lab, and edited before being aired.) The scenes in *See It Now* were shot more as if they were being captured live and undirected than they were in earlier documentaries. Even when not using direct cinema technique, there is less

"Harvest of Shame," *CBS Reports* series (U.S., 1960, David Lowe). J. Fred MacDonald.

directorial control and less editing in the live-action documentaries for television than in the classic documentaries of the thirties and forties.

And perhaps out of courteous respect for us (the audience), the commentator's own point of view in what is said and in what is chosen to show us is generally withheld or balanced—or maybe just ambivalent, and therefore ambiguous. Exceptions to this rule have sometimes created a furor. "Harvest of Shame" (*CBS Reports,* 1960, Fred W. Friendly and Edward R. Murrow) drew outraged protests from the agriculture industry. "The Selling of the Pentagon" (CBS Special, 1971, Peter Davis) provoked a congressional committee to investigate the fairness of its presentation and threaten to subpoena the President of CBS, Frank Stanton, to force him to turn over out-takes (footage not used), sound recordings, and production notes from the program. "Sixteen in Webster Groves" (CBS Special, 1966, Arthur Barron) is an interesting special case. In a sequel, "Webster Groves Revisited," parents and other residents of this posh suburb of St. Louis were permitted to offer a counter-view to that presented by the teenagers in the first program.

In documentaries made for television there is an increased use of sync sound, especially talk; interviews are used much more extensively than they were prior to television. The sound track carries at least as much content as the visual track and the visuals tend to be less rich and interesting than in nontelevision documentaries. In the early days of television a former radio executive made the egregious blunder of proudly announcing at a sales meeting that more people were listening to television than ever before. As a result of this balance between words and images, the *auteurs* ("authors") of television documentaries are usually the producers, writers, and com-

"The Selling of the Pentagon," *CBS Special* (U.S., 1971, Peter Davis). John Caldwell.

mentators rather than the directors, as is more often the case in films made for theatrical exhibition. A redundancy develops in the documentary made for television that permits the viewer-listener to go to the refrigerator for a beer and still follow what's going on, or to vacuum the living room carpet keeping an eye on the tube without missing much.

As we've noted, television documentaries tend to appear in the context of a series. Before television this was true only in exceptional instances like "The March of Time" or "Why We Fight." Television documentaries also have to fit into quite precise air times, down to the second, allowing pauses for and building structures to accommodate the commercial breaks. The running times of earlier documentaries vary considerably and were determined, to considerable extent at least, by the form and content of each film: *The Spanish Earth* runs 55 minutes; *And So They Live*, 24; *London Can Take It*, 10; *Fires Were Started*, 65; *The Quiet One*, 66; *The Feeling of Rejection*, 21; and so on. The fixed times of television have resulted in some strains, with insufficient time available to deal adequately with a subject, or padding required to fill out the half-hour or hour even though less time was needed. In the series context and in the daily flow of television programming, it may be difficult for particular documentaries to offer the kind of aesthetic experience or to achieve the social impact on those they do reach (though they reach many more people quicker) to the extent that some documentaries shown in theaters and to nontheatrical audiences may have done. Gilbert Seldes, again, doubted that the mass media could do very much about educating people soundly or altering their opinions on the subjects with which they dealt. He thought the significance of the media in relation to their effects on social attitudes and behavior was essentially to call public attention to matters that seemed important to the media creators. Television has become virtually *the* mass medium, certainly as far as documentary is concerned. It is the best qualified of any medium of art and communication yet devised to quickly call large numbers of people's attention to various subjects. It has established its ability to do that—and sometimes has done it superbly.

Meanwhile, back in the theatrical and nontheatrical channels of documentary, there appeared in Britain in the mid-fifties the first revolt against the precepts of the Griersonian main line and the first alternatives to it. This demi-movement, called Free Cinema, is the subject of Chapter Thirteen.

FILMS OF THE PERIOD

1952–1953
Victory at Sea series (Henry Salomon and Isaac Kleinerman)

1953
"Argument in Indianapolis" (*See It Now* series, Edward R. Murrow and Fred W. Friendly)
"Christmas in Korea" (same as above)

1954

"Edward R. Murrow Talks on Senator McCarthy" (same as above)

"Segregation in Schools" (same as above)

1955

"Nightmare in Red" (*Project XX* series, Salomon and Kleinerman)

1956

"Out of Darkness" (*The Search* series, Albert Wasserman)

"The Twisted Cross" (*Project XX*, Salomon and Kleinerman)

1957

"The Innocent Years" (*Project XX,* Salomon)

1958

"From Kaiser to Fuehrer" (*The Twentieth Century* series, Burton Benjamin and Kleinerman)

"The Population Explosion" (*CBS Reports* series, Av Westin)

1960

"The Children Were Watching" (*Close-Up!* series, Richard Leacock)

"Harvest of Shame" (*CBS Reports*, Murrow, Friendly, and David Lowe)

"Paris in the Twenties" (*The Twentieth Century,* Benjamin and Kleinerman)

"The U-2 Affair" (*White Paper* series, Wasserman)

"Yanki No!" (*Close-Up!,* Leacock, Albert Maysles, and D. A. Pennebaker)

1961

"Angola: Journey to a War" (*White Paper,* Wasserman)

"Biography of a Bookie Joint" (*CBS Reports,* Jay McMullen)

"The Business of Health: Medicine, Money and Politics" (*CBS Reports,* Stephen Fleischman)

"Forty Million Shoes" (*Intertel* series, Douglas Leiterman)

"Ireland: The Tear and the Smile" (*The Twentieth Century,* Benjamin and Kleinerman)

"New York in the Twenties" (same as above)

"The Real West" (*Project XX,* Donald B. Hyatt)

"Vincent Van Gogh: A Self Portrait" (NBC-TV Special, Ray Garner)

"Walk in My Shoes" (*Close-Up!,* Nicholas Webster)

"The World of Billy Graham" (*The World of . . .* series, Eugene S. Jones)

1962

"The Battle of Newburgh" (*White Paper,* Wasserman)

"Fire Rescue" (*Dupont Show of the Week* series, John G. Fuller)

"Meet Comrade Student" (*Close-Up!,* Webster)

"Shakespeare: Soul of an Age" (NBC-TV Special, Guy Blanchard)

"So That Men Are Free" (*The Twentieth Century,* Willard Van Dyke)

"The World of Jacqueline Kennedy" (*The World of . . .* , Eugene S. Jones)

1963

"The Business of Gambling" (*White Paper,* Arthur Zegart)

"Crisis: Behind a Presidential Commitment" (For ABC-TV by Robert Drew Associates)

"The Death of Stalin" (*White Paper,* Len Giovannitti)

"Greece: The Golden Age" (*White Paper,* Lou Hazam)

"The Making of the President, 1960" (For ABC-TV by David Wolper Productions, Mel Stuart and Theodore H. White)

"Manhattan Battleground" (*Dupont Show of the Week,* William Jersey)

"The Miners' Lament" (*Close-Up!,* William Weston)

"The Plots Against Hitler" (*The Twentieth Century,* Benjamin and Kleinerman)

"Prisoner at Large" (*Dupont Show of the Week,* Jersey)

"That War in Korea" (*Project XX,* Hyatt)

"A Vanishing Breed: Portrait of a Country Editor" (*Close-Up!,* Sam Rosenberg)

"The Vatican" (*Close-Up!,* John Secondari)

1964

"Cuba: Bay of Pigs" (*White Paper,* Fred Freed)

"Cuba: The Missile Crisis" (*White Paper,* Freed)

"High Wire: The Great Wallendas" (*Dupont Show of the Week,* Wasserman and George Freeland)

"Orient Express" (NBC-TV Special, Thomas Priestly)

1966

"Sixteen in Webster Groves" (CBS-TV Special, Arthur Barron)

1967

"Morley Safer's Vietnam" (CBS-TV Special)

1971

"The Selling of the Pentagon" (CBS-TV Special, Peter Davis)

BOOKS ON THE PERIOD

BLUEM, A. WILLIAM, *Documentary in American Television.* New York: Hastings House, Publishers, 1965. 311 pp.

FRIENDLY, FRED W., *Due to Circumstances Beyond Our Control . . .* New York: Random House, Inc., 1967. 325 pp.

HAMMOND, CHARLES MONTGOMERY, JR., *The Image Decade: Television Documentary 1965–1975.* New York: Hastings House, Publishers, 1981. 256 pp.

KENDRICK, ALEXANDER, *Prime Time: The Life of Edward R. Murrow.* Boston: Little, Brown & Co., 1969. 548 pp.

MADSEN, AXEL, *60 Minutes: The Power & the Politics of America's Most Popular TV News Show.* New York: Dodd, Mead & Company, Inc., 1984. 280 pp.

MURROW, EDWARD R. and FRED W. FRIENDLY, *See It Now.* New York: Simon and Schuster, Inc., 1955. 210 pp.

SPERBER, A. M., *Murrow: His Life and Times.* New York: Freundlich Books, 1986. 795 pp.

SWALLOW, NORMAN, *Factual Television.* New York: Hastings House, Publishers, 1966. 228 pp.

THIRTEEN
BRITISH FREE CINEMA AND SOCIAL-REALIST FEATURES, 1956–1963

In the late forties and early fifties documentary had run down in Britain, as it had in the U.S. and, to a lesser extent, in Canada, following the wartime boom. Grierson and his old boys were locked into former subjects, purposes, and forms that no longer seemed as relevant to the needs of the society as they once had—not as urgent anyway, and certainly not as exciting. In part, they were suffering from their success. British documentary films of the thirties could be seen as having pointed the need for a more collectivized, socialized state. Now, that state had arrived.

Following the Labour Party's enormous postwar victory at the polls, it remained in office from 1945 to 1951. When the Conservative Party returned to power in 1951, it did little to reverse the social and economic changes effected by Labour. But beginning in the mid-fifties a sort of bloodless cultural revolution commenced, which affected British life generally and became manifest in film as well. With the advent of commercial television and a vitality in the political left that extended into the arts, new popular values ("vulgar" they were thought to be in some quarters) came to the fore.

Expressing these new values was a group of novelists, playwrights, and political essayists who were dubbed The Angry Young Men. What they were angry about was the conformity, the ugliness, the lack of individuality pres-

ent in what was being called a welfare state—the very sort of state that Labour and the earlier documentary films seemed to be seeking. Further, the
Angry Young Men protested that even within this welfare state the class
system continued to function, with the upper classes controlling government, business, education, and the media. These upper-class people
through these institutions—the establishment—were responsible for the
flattening of the working class, for keeping the common people not only
helpless but listless. Part of this agitation among young intellectuals and
artists—the initial public evidence of it, as a matter of fact—occurred in the
documentary film. It took the form of a short-lived and slight but highly
influential movement called Free Cinema. This was the first substantial reaction against the Griersonian main line since its beginning back in 1929.

CRITICAL BACKGROUND

The roots of Free Cinema lay in a critical position espoused by a group of
young people at Oxford University in the late forties. What they started as
Film Society Magazine in 1947 quickly became *Sequence*. The persons associated with *Sequence* would become extremely important in the British film
scene. Penelope Houston became longtime editor of *Sight and Sound,* a prestigious international film quarterly published by the British Film Institute.
Gavin Lambert was her assistant editor, then screenwriter and author of
some noteworthy short stories (*The Slide Area*) and a novel (*Inside Daisy Clover*)
about Hollywood. Tony Richardson, Karel Reisz (the only member of the
group not from Oxford; he was Cambridge, from which a high proportion
of the Grierson alumni had come), and Lindsay Anderson were three others. All three would become filmmakers of considerable distinction.

The editorial emphases of *Sequence* were clear-cut and contentious; it
was strongly against some things, strongly for others. The British entertainment film industry was denigrated for being dominated by the Americans
and failing to produce films having a national character. British documentary was scorned for its didacticism, dullness, and collective (as opposed to
personal) creation. Certain new European films and filmmakers were
lauded; for example *Farrebique* (France, 1946, Georges Rouquier), *People in
the City* (Sweden, 1947, Arne Sucksdorff), and *Blood of the Beasts* (France,
1949, Georges Franju). A poetic cinema in Britain was called for that would
also provide a national expression—a poetry of reality, and of the common
man. (This poetry was not to be confused with the poetry of ships, machinery, and trains prevalent in the Grierson documentaries, presumably.)

Lindsay Anderson was leader of this group. Like Grierson before him,
Anderson was the articulate spokesman and the first to begin making films.
Also like Grierson, Anderson searched for precedents for the sorts of films
he wanted to be made. He wrote seminal reevaluations of the work of Jean

Vigo, John Ford, and Humphrey Jennings, finding in their films evidence of the poetic and of the expression of their respective cultures. When *Sequence* ceased publication in 1952 (Anderson and Reisz edited the last issue), the former *Sequence* people made and wrote about Free Cinema. They were vigorous polemicists, as the Griersonians had been.

FREE CINEMA FILMS

Anderson, in addition to his work on *Sequence,* had been making sponsored shorts since 1948. His first significant documentaries were released in 1954. *Thursday's Children,* co-directed with Guy Brenton, celebrated the pupils and the loving, skillful teaching being done at the Royal School for Deaf and Dumb Children in Margate. *O Dreamland* castigated the dull and synthetic pleasures being offered the bemused masses at a seaside amusement park. Anderson himself described it as "a horrid little film." The cameramen on these two films would become principal technicians of the Free Cinema films: Walter Lassally (who subsequently became one of the world's great cinematographers) and John Fletcher (who would concentrate on sound and editing), respectively.

In 1955 Karel Reisz and Tony Richardson made *Momma Don't Allow,* about a lively London jazz club patronized by working-class teenagers. In the same year Lorenza Mazetti and Denis Horne made *Together,* which deals

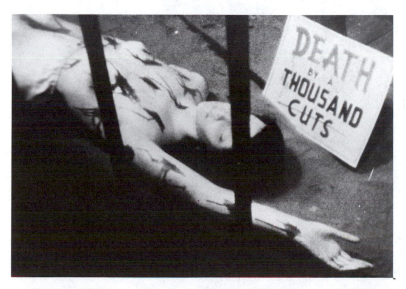

O Dreamland (U.K., 1954, Lindsay Anderson). Museum of Modern Art/Film Stills Archive.

with the emotionally impoverished lives led by two deaf-mute dock workers in London's East End. *Together* and its two makers were not really part of Free Cinema except as it along with *Momma Don't Allow* and *O Dreamland* comprised the first program shown under that heading in February 1956 at the National Film Theatre of the British Film Institute.

Of the subsequent Free Cinema films—there were only a dozen or so altogether—*Nice Time* (1957) was made by a couple of Swiss immigrants, Claude Goretta and Alain Tanner, who would return home to become fiction filmmakers. It is about the people in Picadilly Circus in London's West End (comparable to Times Square in New York City) on a Saturday night. Lonely and disconsolate by and large, they are shown seeking pleasure and diversion among the movie theaters, the refreshment stands, the prostitutes, and the milling crowds of others like themselves.

Every Day Except Christmas (1957), by Lindsay Anderson, is about the Covent Garden produce market (which no longer exists). It is an observation of the workers and their culture—the look, the feel, the activities of the place—from early evening, as the trucks come from the country with vegetables, fruits and flowers, until closing the following morning. *We Are the Lambeth Boys* (1959), by Karel Reisz, is about teddy boys—kids from a

Momma Don't Allow (U.K., 1955, Karel Reisz and Tony Richardson). Museum of Modern Art/Film Stills Archive.

Nice Time (U.K., 1957, Claude Goretta and Alain Tanner). National Film Archive/Stills Library.

Every Day Except Christmas (U.K., 1957, Lindsay Anderson). Museum of Modern Art/Film Stills Archive.

We Are the Lambeth Boys (U.K., 1959, Karel Reisz). Museum of Modern Art/Film Stills Archive.

tough part of London—at a social center and on an outing to a cricket match at a posh public school. It is a sympathetic and respectful view of these young people whom the popular press were presenting as gangs of dangerous delinquents.

What did these filmmakers mean by Free Cinema? Essentially, independent: free from serving the sponsor's purposes (as in traditional documentary); free from pandering to the demands of the box office (as in entertainment features). "Implicit in our attitude," they wrote in their program note for the first showing, "is a belief in freedom, in the importance of people and in the significance of the everyday."

Gavin Lambert, in an article in *Sight and Sound,* wrote of the three films shown at the first Free Cinema program. Likening their spirit to that of D.H. Lawrence's writings, he noted that they "sprang from non-conformism, from impatience with convention, sadness about urban life." Like Lawrence's work, too, they represented "a desire to regain contact with a more vital, individual force." Lambert wrote:

> In the broadest sense, they are films of protest; they are not conceived in sweeping terms ... but the camera-eye they turn on society ... is disenchanted, and occasionally ferocious and bitter.... If compassion is explicit in Lorenza Mazetti's film [*Together*], implicit in Lindsay Anderson's [*O Dreamland*], it is the most rigorous, difficult and austere kind of compassion: not for the moment or the particular situation, but a kind of permanent temperamental heartache for the world and the people apparently lost in it.

No doubt of it, this is the world in which we live. In seizing upon these aspects—the anonymity of urban life, the aimless lonely figures swallowed up in the greater loneliness of the crowd, the pleasures hideous and mechanical or imaginatively aspiring—these film-makers compel above all the shock of recognition.[1]

A collusion apparent here between critic and creators is reminiscent of the Grierson documentary people who wrote about their own films in *Documentary News Letter,* which they had established. Anderson, in his seminal essay "Stand Up! Stand Up!," also published in *Sight and Sound,* demanded that film criticism be socially committed.[2] Commitment, individuality, and poetry were key terms in the rhetoric of Free Cinema.

The subjects of the Free Cinema films continued to feature workers and the working class, as they had in the documentaries of the thirties. But rather than their work, Free Cinema was concerned with how workers spent their leisure time. The films address the values of the people, their pleasures or lack of them. Rather than material progress and improvements, they deal with matters of social psychology and of the spirit. The one Free Cinema film dealing with workers working, *Every Day Except Christmas,* shows what the people working in Covent Garden are like more than what they do and how they do it.

As for the purpose and approach, the Free Cinema films are nondidactic, aesthetic rather than informative; they appeal to emotions more than reason. The sluggish, unimaginative, and docile are censured (*O Dreamland, Nice Time*); the healthy, vigorous, and idiosyncratic are extolled (*Momma Don't Allow, Every Day Except Christmas, We Are the Lambeth Boys*). They have in common a vaguely anarchic, nihilistic, iconoclastic spirit. What they seem to be calling for is a total reordering of society—they are consistently anti–establishment—rather than trying to make the existing system work better. They are implicitly revolutionary rather than actively evolutionary, as Grierson saw his position to be. (He observed of them that they seemed to be strangely French.) If English precedents are required, I think they can be found in the writings of D.H. Lawrence, as Gavin Lambert suggested, and also in those of George Orwell.

The formal aspects of the Free Cinema films, especially their structural organizations, are closer to the work of Humphrey Jennings, much admired by Lindsay Anderson, than they are to the documentaries more directly in the Grierson main line. (Alan Lovell and Jim Hillier supply detail on this comparison and contrast in the three essays that comprise their *Studies in Documentary* [New York: The Viking Press, Inc., 1972].) The Free Cinema films are impressionistic. Though they employ a loose chronology, they follow feeling more than logic. Neither narrative continuity nor a topical outline will altogether account for the selection and ordering of their parts. Commentary is eschewed for the most part. (There is some in *Every Day* and

Lambeth but none in the other four examples cited.) Instead, the filmmakers' points are made through their choice and arrangement of sights and sounds. Juxtaposition of symbolic contrasts and counterpoint of the visible and audible abound. Considerable irony and humor result.

The production techniques and technology used grow out of the subjects and purposes of Free Cinema. The filmmakers confined themselves to what could be seen and heard on the location. The sights and sounds used are those that could be captured without direction (though bits of invented performance are inserted into *Momma Don't Allow,* as in *Rien que les heures* and *Berlin* much earlier). Quite a lot of Free Cinema is candid—the subjects are unaware they are being filmed—hence the preponderance of places where people gather publicly: amusement park, dance hall, Picadilly Circus, social center, Covent Garden. In the early examples cited the camera was hand-held, the images grainy and underexposed. Location sound, including the inferior quality of a public address system, constitutes the sound track. Between 1954 and 1958 there is increasing technical/technological refinement from nonsync sound (a so-called wild track being recorded and edited to the footage available), to simulated sync, to sync. The camerawork moves from candid to increasing awareness on the part of the subjects that a camera is present, to steadier and more carefully composed images. In adjectival terms it might be said that the visual-aural style progresses from ugly to casual. But throughout, the roughness of the impressionistic form and non-directed "grab" shooting are in contrast to the Grierson documentary.

The main reason Free Cinema ended seems to have been economic. Free cinema indeed, snorted Grierson, in the most expensive artistic medium yet devised by man! If the films were free from serving the sponsor (and those who could afford to sponsor films were not likely to pay for the dissent offered by Free Cinema), if their forms and contents did not need to be shaped for the box office (and the public was not much interested in poetry or commitment), how were the films funded? *O Dreamland* cost a few hundred pounds and was paid for by Anderson himself. The other three of the first four received grants from the British Film Institute Experimental Film Production Fund. The last two listed were sponsored by the Ford Motor Company, evidently with a sense of noblesse oblige similar to that which Grierson had cultivated in the thirties. But no more industrial sponsorship seemed to be available after *Every Day* and *Lambeth Boys.*

As for the arguments between the Free Cinema newcomers and the old-line documentarians, the former were just as much propagandists as the latter, despite their attacks on earlier documentaries as attempting to manipulate viewer opinion. Merely the ends were different—New Left vs. Old Left—as well as the techniques and styles used to achieve those ends. If Grierson was correct in anticipating that Free Cinema would cease for lack of economic base, he also foresaw that it would metamorphose into something else. It filtered into the fiction feature film in conjunction with the work of other Angry Young Men and Women of theater and literature.

POLITICAL AND CULTURAL CONTEXT

The year 1956 was a crucial one in the political and cultural life of Britain. It was the year of a last gasp of imperial arrogance in the foolish and failed invasion of Suez. As a result of that debacle the whole governmental system was discredited. To many on the Left, the Labour Party, which worked within the system, seemed as culpable as the ruling Conservatives. Nineteen fifty-six was also the year of the Khruschev attack on the cult of personality under Stalin, and of the Soviet invasion of Hungary, which caused many Marxist intellectuals to finally become disillusioned with Stalinist communism.

Partially in reaction to those events a politically sophisticated younger generation of dissidents arose around the universities—particularly Oxford, which most of the Free Cinema group attended. The label New Left was attached to them, and their publication was entitled *New Left Review* (originally *Universities and Left Review*). The New Left wanted to go beyond the old-line socialists, with their basis in dialectical materialism, trade unionism, nationalization of industry, and social welfare. They were concerned more with theory and a fundamental reorganization of society that would affect the total quality of people's lives. As an intellectual movement which also encompassed the arts, the New Left in Britain was more like the continental Left.

The artists in various media who arose out of the spirit of the time, many of them from the working classes, attacked the establishment and the rigidities and inequities of the class system. In 1956 John Osborne's play *Look Back in Anger,* directed by Tony Richardson, opened. (Both Richardson and Anderson have directed more plays than films for the simple reason that financing for theater is more readily available.) At about the same time Joan Littlewood's Theatre Workshop was started. Playwrights such as Arnold Wesker and Shelagh Delaney soon joined Osborne to create an outpouring of plays set among the lower classes that were articulate and sometimes strident in their social criticism. Novels of a similar tone began to appear as well, with John Braine's *Room at the Top* in 1957 followed by Alan Sillitoe's *Saturday Night and Sunday Morning,* Stan Barstow's *A Kind of Loving,* and David Storey's *This Sporting Life,* among others.

Though Free Cinema had in fact appeared slightly before the explosions in the other arts, it wasn't until it connected with the new drama and literature that its kind of expression moved over into the feature film and became economically viable. The Free Cinema movement as such virtually ceased with *We Are the Lambeth Boys* in 1959. Nonetheless, the attitudes and some of the rough-hewn style of Free Cinema were carried over into the new social-realist features which began just as the Free Cinema shorts ended.

SOCIAL-REALIST FEATURES

Room at the Top (1958), much more conventional than Free Cinema in both content and form, launched the new phase. Set in an industrial northern town, it deals with the compulsions and confusions of a cynical young arriviste determined to climb up out of his slum origins. Its romantic conflict is class-based. *Look Back in Anger* (1959) put some of the same matters, and others, in a clearer and less ambiguous way. Through the Jimmy Porter character's brilliant and paranoiac monologues, one could begin to understand what the anger was all about. At least it was clear what he was trying to tear down (the establishment, personified by his wife's parents) and what he was trying to preserve (the working-class virtues, represented by his friend Ma Tanner).

These two films, double-billed in the U.S., began the social-realist cycle that dealt with various aspects of working-class character and problems. As a body, the films tended to be set in the industrial regions north of London. Thus they contrasted with British entertainment films made up to that time, which, according to the Free Cinema group at least, had reflected almost exclusively the outlook of metropolitan southern English culture and the middle and upper classes. Here were efforts to include "the rich diversity of tradition and personality which is the whole of Britain" called for in one of Free Cinema's manifestoes.

Of the Free Cinema trio of Anderson, Reisz, and Richardson, it was Richardson who first entered the feature field with *Look Back in Anger*. Those three were joined by John Schlesinger, an Oxford classmate of Richardson's. Together they constituted the main directorial talent of the social-realist features of the early sixties. New in content—in their concern with working-class characters and criticism of the establishment—these films were essentially conventional in fiction film narrative technique. All of them were based on the writings of the so-called Angry Young Men (or Women, as the case might be). Richardson directed three more of those features in rapid succession. *The Entertainer* (1960), from another Osborne play and script, was seen as offering evidence of collapse within British society. *A Taste of Honey* (1961) was from a play by Shelagh Delaney, who worked on the screenplay as well. The remarkable location cinematography in Lancashire was by Walter Lassally, who became a prominent creative figure in the social-realist features as he had been in the Free Cinema shorts. *The Loneliness of the Long Distance Runner* (1962)—from a story by Alan Sillitoe, who also did the script—portrays the life, frustrated ambitions, and resentments of a lower-

The Loneliness of the Long Distance Runner (U.K., 1962, Tony Richardson). Museum of Modern Art/ Film Stills Archive.

class youth who wanders into crime and is sent to prison. The causes of his problems are portrayed as societal; sympathy as well as understanding is offered for his form of rebellion.

Karel Reisz directed only one of the social-realist features (Richardson produced it), but his *Saturday Night and Sunday Morning* (1960) is in many ways the most exemplary of their tendencies as a whole. The documentary intention dominates. Served equally by a story that grows out of the situation (rather than being imposed upon it) and by convincingly natural performances, it flies in the face of accepted demands of both box office and dramatic convention. From Sillitoe's popular novel (and he again did the script), it focuses on a working-class rebel. Though hostile to the system, the young lathe operator finally lacks the resources—the imagination and understanding—to break free from it. Proudly indigenous as the film is, one doesn't have to know England to sense that the rows of identically drab houses, the father glued to the telly, the job without meaning, and the inadequate release of a Saturday night drunk and tumble in the hay must be how it is for a large segment of the population (as it is elsewhere). If an epilogue were to be added to it, it could borrow from Dylan Thomas, as did the Free Cinema filmmakers for their first program: "This is the world. Have faith."

Lindsay Anderson, though acknowledged leader and spokesman of the Free Cinema group, was last to arrive at features. Curiously, his first, *This Sporting Life* (1963), if it marked a high point in the social-realist cycle,

Saturday Night and Sunday Morning (U.K., 1960, Karel Reisz). National Film Archive/
Stills Library.

also indicated a turning away from the sources that had given that demi-
movement its character and strength. From a novel and a script adaptation
by David Storey, it has the requisite general characteristics of northern industrial town and working-class background. Where it departs from the
other films is in its concentration on the tortured love affair between the
miner-turned-footballer and his widowed landlady, and in its flashback sequences of surrealist exaggeration. At the time of its release, Anderson was
complimented by British reviewers for having broken out of the confines
of the social-realist films—with their air of objectivity and use of the representative to make their criticism stick—into richer areas of individual feeling, the traditional concerns of great art. Perhaps what was by then being
referred to as the "kitchen sink" school of filmmaking was limited in certain
important ways and had run its course. Whatever the reasons, *This Sporting
Life* along with *Billy Liar* (directed by John Schlesinger in the same year)
proved to be the last films directly connected with the line that had begun
with *Room at the Top*.

The documentary influence has contributed to some of the most interesting and distinctive cycles of British fiction production: wartime semidocumentaries, postwar Ealing comedies, and social-realist features. It might be
argued that the quiet genius of British cinema has always pointed most
surely in the direction of realism and what John Grierson called the documentary idea. For awhile in the sixties, as the young men of Free Cinema
came together with the young men and women of theater and literature

who had been tackling similar themes, the veracity of documentary detail was warmed and strengthened by the addition of story and character. Perhaps those who made the social-realist features between 1958 and 1963 got some of the older documentarians' preoccupations and methods more widely and effectively before a larger public.

At the time Free Cinema ended and metamorphosed into the social-realist fiction features, another development began that would move documentary closer to the dividing line between art and life it has always tried to cross. Called cinéma vérité in France and direct cinema in America, this development is the subject of Chapter Fourteen.

NOTES

[1]Gavin Lambert, "Free Cinema," *Sight and Sound,* 25 (Spring 1956), pp. 173–77.
[2]Lindsay Anderson, "Stand Up! Stand Up!," *Sight and Sound,* 26 (Autumn 1956), pp. 63–69.

FILMS OF THE PERIOD

1954
O Dreamland (Lindsay Anderson)

1955
Momma Don't Allow (Karel Reisz and Tony Richardson)
Together (Lorenza Mazetti and Denis Horne)

1957
Every Day Except Christmas (Anderson)
Nice Time (Claude Goretta and Alain Tanner)

1958
Room at the Top (Jack Clayton)

1959
Look Back in Anger (Richardson)
We Are the Lambeth Boys (Reisz)

1960
The Entertainer (Richardson)
Saturday Night and Sunday Morning (Reisz)

1961
A Taste of Honey (Richardson)

1962
A Kind of Loving (John Schlesinger)
The Loneliness of the Long Distance Runner (Richardson)

1963
Billy Liar (Schlesinger)
The Leather Boys (Sidney Furie)
This Sporting Life (Anderson)

BOOKS ON THE PERIOD

GASTON, GEORG, *Karel Reisz.* Boston: Twayne Publishers, 1981.
LOVELL, ALAN and JIM HILLIER, *Studies in Documentary.* New York: The Viking Press, Inc., 1972. 176 pp.
ORBANZ, EVA, *Journey to a Legend and Back: The British Realistic Film.* Berlin: Verlag Volker Spiess, 1977. 213 pp.
SILET, CHARLES L.P., *Lindsay Anderson: A Guide to References and Resources.* Boston: G. K. Hall & Co., 1978. 155 pp.
SUSSEX ELIZABETH, *Lindsay Anderson.* New York: Frederick A. Praeger, Inc., Publishers, 1970. 96 pp.

FOURTEEN
DIRECT CINEMA AND CINÉMA VÉRITÉ, 1960–

In the late 1950s major breakthroughs occurred in the technology available to filmmakers. These occasioned what may be either something totally new under the artistic sun or merely new ways of doing old things. What they permitted was the synchronous recording of sight and sound outside the confines of sound stages and studio back lots. Virtually anything that could be seen and heard could now be captured on film almost anywhere.

These new technical possibilities did not dictate the uses to which they would be put, however. One of the uses was that of the Americans who called what they were doing direct cinema. Another was that of Frenchman Jean Rouch, who coined the term *cinéma vérité* (film truth) to apply to his own work. These two contrasting practices and theories will be dealt with in a later section of this chapter.

HISTORICAL BACKGROUND

Documentarians have always sought technological additions which would permit them to film more easily under difficult conditions and to convey more actuality to their audiences. The initial split between the creative impulses that led to documentary and those that led to fiction were caused at least partly by equipment. The films made by the Edison Company were shot with the Kinetograph. This electrically-powered camera was so large and heavy it was confined to a studio built to house it. Edison technicians recorded vaudeville and circus acts, and bits of stage plays, thus inaugurating the theatrical/fictional mode of filmmaking. Louis Lumière, on the other hand, designed a lightweight, hand-cranked camera, the Cinématographe, which permitted him to record life on the streets, thus establishing the documentary mode.

In the 1920s, when documentary proper began to develop, the cameras used were portable but still cumbersome, requiring tripods. The comparatively insensitive film—all of it black-and-white—needed lots of light. No sound was available until after 1927, except that provided in the theaters by pit orchestras, organs, or pianos. Flaherty's descriptive sort of documentary, which showed physical appearances and outdoor activities of unfamiliar peoples, was ideal for the limitations of that technology. Yet, though Flaherty was far from the studios, he used studio methods of directed action repeated for change of camera position and lens. His shots were edited together to match the action in the usual long shot-medium shot-closeup sequence.

In the 1930s, with the optical sound track added, the equipment became so bulky that synchronous recording of sight and sound on location was difficult to impossible. It was like Edison's camera all over again, and fiction filmmakers retreated into the studio. The standard documentary sound-film method became that of shooting silent, subsequently adding to the edited footage spoken words plus music plus sound effects. To have documentary "talkies," a "voice-over" commentary was obligatory. Though an artificial element, commentary did permit the addition of information and interpretation to visual surfaces, and the analysis of complex contemporary issues—the Grierson and Lorentz kind of documentary, in short.

Black-and-white images accompanied by post-sync sound remained the visual-auditory representation available to documentary makers throughout the thirties and forties. The so-called classic documentaries—*The Song of Ceylon, The Plow That Broke the Plains, Night Mail,* the "Why We Fight" series, and the rest—were all made within these limitations. Filmmakers kept trying to come closer to capturing the sound with the natural scene. This goal and the development of equipment to reach it were not confined to those with documentary interests (though the latter would win the race). Significant efforts were made by realistic fiction filmmakers as well.

The Italian neorealists, especially Roberto Rossellini, made remarkable strides in adding audible reality to their images. Their sound was still postsynchronized, however; the dialogue was all dubbed. Jean Renoir was another fiction filmmaker who disliked the confinement of the studio and the rigidity of the large and heavy Mitchell BNC camera, standard in studio shooting. (The Mitchell camera used in silent years had NC after it, for

Noiseless Camera. One can suspect its noiselessness if it had to become the Blimped Noiseless Camera with sound. A blimp is a casing containing acoustic insulation.) Renoir, in an amusing interview, likened the 35mm studio camera to a great metal idol to which humans are offered up sacrificially. Everything was done for the convenience of the camera. Actors had to move to chalk marks to be in focus, to turn their faces a certain way to catch the light. Renoir wanted instead that the machine (camera) be subservient to people (actors)—to follow them around, to attend them.[1]

Early efforts to achieve such a technology/technique were made by Morris Engle, a former still photographer. In three independent fiction features shot in New York City—*The Little Fugitive* (1953), *Lovers and Lollipops* (1955), *Weddings and Babies* (1958)—Engle moved towards an increasing flexibility of equipment. The latter film was the first 35mm fiction feature to be made with a portable camera with synchronous sound attachment.

Obviously the lighter equipment of 16mm offered advantages over 35mm. If desired, films shot on 16mm could be "blown up" to 35mm for theatrical exhibition. In 1956 Lionel Rogosin made *On the Bowery* and in 1958 *Come Back, Africa* in this way with some remarkable sync-sound actuality set within semidocumentary narratives. In 1960 John Cassavetes, in *Shadows*, allowed actors to improvise while their actions and words were recorded on portable 16mm equipment.

NEW TECHNOLOGY AND FIRST FILMS

From that point on the key technology that made direct cinema/cinéma vérité possible began to appear. As for the visual aspect, by substituting plastic for metal moving parts, 16mm shoulder-mounted cameras became even more lightweight and noiseless, no longer requiring blimps. The French Eclair NPR (Noiseless, Portable, Reflex), developed by André Coutant in 1961, and the German Arriflex SR (Silent Reflex) are cameras of this sort in standard use today. Cameras with reflex viewing (looking through the lens while shooting) plus zoom lenses permitted cinematographers to alter the field of view—from closeup to long shot, for example—without having to stop to change lenses or to focus. The French Angenieux 12 to 120mm is a zoom lens frequently used. Increasingly "fast" film stock (that is, very sensitive to light or needing little light) permitted shooting without adding illumination to that available, first in black-and-white and then in color. Eastman Kodak 16mm color negative has been in widespread use since the mid-1970s, replacing the reversal processes (Kodachrome and Ektachrome) because of its superior qualities. Added to faster film stock was a laboratory "intensification process" that could push the sensitivity of a film to over 1000 ASA. (ASA is an acronym for American Standards Association; the higher the number the faster the film. Current standard color negative has an ASA of 100.)

As for sound, $\frac{1}{4}$" magnetic tape sound recorders were developed which could be synchronized with cameras through the use of an inaudible sixty cycle pulse. The Nagra, developed by Swiss engineer Stefan Kudelski in 1958, is the tape recorder of this type in most common use. When crystal synchronization was added, there was no longer even the need for a cable between camera and recorder. Around 1960 vacuum tubes, which consumed a lot of energy, were replaced by transistors and the weight of sound recorders was reduced from 200 pounds to 20 pounds.

This new technology permitted filming action taking place in front of the camera and microphone without altering or interrupting it. The first successful films using it were made during 1958 to 1961 in Canada, the United States, and France.

In 1958 at the National Film Board two young French Canadians, Michel Brault and Gilles Groulx, using leftover film from another project, shot more or less secretly *Les Raquetteurs* (The Snowshoers). The event with which the film is ostensibly concerned—snowshow races in Sherbrooke, Quebec—seems mainly to be the occasion for a parade and a party. The film records these activities but concentrates on the people and their relations with each other. The filmmakers must have entered into the sociability and evidently were fully accepted by the townsfolk.

Les Raquetteurs raised some hackles in official Canada, however. Concern was expressed about the non–official way in which it was produced. More serious was the question about the motivation of the filmmakers. Though they appear to me to be in affectionate if amused sympathy with

Les Raquetteurs (The Snowshoers; Canada, 1958, Michel Brault and Gilles Gruix). National Film Board.

their subjects, some French Canadians were made uneasy by the unprettified view of robust conviviality presented. Such a portrayal, it was alleged,
helped perpetuate the false stereotype of the crude and dull-witted Ca-
nucks.

In 1960, in the U.S., *Primary,* already mentioned in Chapter Twelve,
was produced by Drew Associates. Executive producer was Robert Drew.
Most of the shooting was done by Albert Maysles and Richard Leacock;
Drew and Donn Pennebaker recorded the sound. All of the crew worked
on the editing; 18,000 feet (seven and one-half hours) of film were cut down
to 2,000 (fifty minutes).

The film deals with the 1960 Wisconsin primary election contest between senators Hubert Humphrey and John F. Kennedy. Not only does it
follow each candidate through his public appearances and activities, intercutting between them, as television news might do; it also enters into the
more private times when they are in their hotel rooms or in an automobile
riding to the next engagement. Of the many remarkable moments the film
contains, perhaps the most often mentioned is an uninterrupted shot which
follows Kennedy from outside a building into it, down a long corridor, up
some stairs, out onto a stage, ending with a view of the wildly applauding
audience. The novelty at the time was breathtaking. Of *Primary,* Leacock
said: "For the first time we were able to walk in and out of buildings, up
and down stairs, film in taxi cabs, all over the place, and get synchronous
sound."[2]

One could say that French cinéma vérité began in 1959 at a Robert

Producer and sound recordist Robert Drew (left) and cameraman Richard Leacock,
with their equipment, during the filming of *Primary* (U.S., 1960, Drew Associates). Drew
Associates/Direct Cinema Ltd.

Flaherty Seminar—an annual event started by Flaherty's widow, Frances, and brother, David. On that occasion anthropologist-filmmaker Jean Rouch saw *Les Raquetteurs* and met Michel Brault, who would become principal cameraman for *Chronicle of a Summer* (1961), directed by Rouch in collaboration with sociologist Edgar Morin. *Chronicle* was first shown in the U.S. at another Flaherty seminar, in 1963, along with Drew Associates' *The Chair* and Albert and David Maysles' *Showman* (both 1962).

Chronicle of a Summer broke from the Griersonian/Anglo-Saxon tradition in ways even more basic than did *Les Raquetteurs* or *Primary*. Its subject matter comprised a sampling of individual opinions, attitudes, and values of Parisians in the summer of 1960. What the film offers is a chance to understand something of the interviewees and of their culture, of their positions within it, and their feelings about it.

The filmmakers' purpose and approach seem, like Flaherty's, to be that of discovery and revelation. These natives play at least as large a part in the creation of the film as did Nanook or Moana. They are sophisticated (at least modern urban) and articulate, however. Their concerns, as well as those of the filmmakers, are about their feelings rather than about the work they do and how they do it. (In this respect *Primary* is more like Flaherty: It is about people working—what they do rather than what they think and feel.) In fact, work is viewed negatively—one has to be dishonest to make a living; one tries to earn enough money to be oneself; work is boring, repetitive, mechanical—and we see very little of it, only hear about it, for the most part.

Like Flaherty's films, the overall structure of *Chronicle* is a loose chronological narrative, as the title implies. From Morin, in conversation with Marilou, we learn that July 14, Bastille Day, was a month ago, and now it is August. It resembles an anthology of essays and short stories. Through it we get to know more about Parisians—Marceline, who survived a Nazi concentration camp; Angelo, a Renault factory worker; Marilou, an emotionally-troubled Italian working in Paris; or Landry, a black African student—than we do about Humphrey or Kennedy in *Primary*. We are told by the filmmakers that part one of the film is intended to deal with the "interior," personal lives of the subjects; part two is about the "exterior," more general world around them as they see it. (The Algerian war was still being waged.) Narrative links among the sequences are made through groupings of persons and topics of conversation, and there are some startling contrasts—a cut from newspaper headlines about the murder of whites in the Belgian Congo to a shot of a young woman water-skiing off St. Tropez. The approach is persistently reflexive: The people on camera and we in the audience are continually reminded that a film is being made, that we are watching a film. The penultimate scene is of the persons the film is about discussing themselves as they have appeared in the film they and we have just seen.

As for production method and technique, here the new sync-sound technology is used primarily for discussion and interview. There is even soliloquy as Marceline, strolling by herself in the Place de la Concorde and Les Halles market, recalls painful episodes from her past. Angelo, the Renault worker, gives a kind of improvised performance for the camera, pointedly ignoring its presence. He pretends to wake up in the morning, to get ready for work, to go off to work, to work, and later to return home—all this so that his actions might be recorded on film, as Nanook's were.

Throughout the film the cinematography of Michel Brault, Raoul Coutard, and A. Vignier, though different from Flaherty's in its spontaneity, is equal to his in skill and sureness. Their ability to move smoothly and seemingly effortlessly with their subjects is astonishing. Unlike Flaherty, however, the two directors are frequently on screen, engaged in conversation with their subjects. This is a film being made by Rouch and Morin, they seem to be telling us, and here we are so you can see how we are going about it.

The final scene is of Rouch and Morin talking to each other about their expectations in regard to the film and about their subjects' reactions to it. As they leave the Musée de l'Homme, where the screening has just taken place, Morin expresses his disappointment that not all the participants liked the persons and scenes he had liked. The final words on the sound track are those of Rouch saying to Morin "We're in for trouble" as the two separate.

Chronicle of a Summer (France, 1961, Jean Rouch [left] and Edgar Morin [right]). Museum of Modern Art/Film Stills Archive.

DIRECT CINEMA VS. CINÉMA VÉRITÉ

The American use of the new equipment, largely with an approach now called direct cinema, was pioneered by Drew Associates in the *Close-Up!* series on ABC-TV discussed in Chapter Twelve. Its tenets were articulated most forcefully by Robert Drew and, especially, by Richard ("Ricky") Leacock. The Drew-Leacock approach falls within the reportage tradition, coming from Drew's background in photo-journalism and Leacock's experience as a documentary cinematographer.

Their technique assumes the possibility of an objective observer. While acknowledging that subjectivity occurs in selecting persons and situations and aspects of them, once those choices are made the filmmakers do not direct or participate in or even influence (they contend) the scene in any way. They feel that the presence of the camera is soon taken for granted by the subjects—ignored mostly, sometimes forgotten altogether.

In their approach, the relationship between filmmakers and subject persons must be relaxed and trusting in order for the filmmaking to fit into ongoing action without affecting it. Leacock is especially adept in winning confidence from the people he is shooting; a warm and engaging person, he can be confident and unassuming with his camera and the people in front of it.

In the course of their work Drew Associates discovered that their method worked best if something important was happening to their subjects—if they were involved in an activity demanding their full attention and evoking a certain unalterable behavior. This was the case in *Primary*.

A young Richard Leacock shooting Flaherty's *Louisiana Story*. Museum of Modern Art/Film Stills Archive.

Humphrey and Kennedy were much more concerned with winning an election than with how they would appear on screen. They were attempting to charm and influence people in order to obtain their votes, and public appearance was a normal part of their lives which the presence of a camera would scarcely alter. *Mooney vs. Fowle* (1961, a.k.a. *Football*) builds up to and climaxes with a high school football game in Miami, Florida, between two rival teams. It concentrates on the players, coaches, immediate families—those most completely preoccupied with this contest. *The Chair* (1962) centers on the efforts of a Chicago attorney, Donald Page Moore, to obtain a stay of execution for his client, Paul Crump, five days before it is scheduled to take place. *Jane* (1962) concerns Jane Fonda in the production of a play, from the rehearsal period through the negative reviews following its Broadway opening and the decision to close the play.

As these examples suggest, Drew Associates also discovered that their method worked best if the situation they chose had its own drama (with beginning, middle, and end) which would come to a climax within a limited time. This conforms to certain characteristics noted by Aristotle as common to Greek drama. Stephen Mamber, in the best analysis of the films of Drew Associates (*Cinema Verite in America,* listed at the end of this chapter) identified this as the "crisis structure." When such a situation did not exist the films lacked point and force, Mamber felt. He gave as examples *Showman* (1962, by Albert and David Maysles), about movie mogul Joseph Levine,

The Chair (U.S., 1962, Drew Associates). Drew Associates/Direct Cinema Ltd.

and *Nehru* (1962, by Drew, Leacock, and Gregory Shuker), about the Prime Minister of India. Though these are interesting and significant figures, the days shown are cluttered and formless—nothing very dramatic happens and we don't really gain much in our understanding of either man or of why he behaves as he does.

The term cinéma vérité, which Jean Rouch first applied to *Chronicle of a Summer,* refers back to the Russian equivalent, *kino pravda,* used by Soviet filmmaker Dziga Vertov forty years earlier. Rouch has said that the film was an attempt to combine Vertov's theory and Flaherty's method.[3] While Rouch's approach to filmmaking grew out of his work as an anthropologist, it has similarities to that of other contemporary French documentarians, some of whom will be discussed in Chapter Fifteen. The term cinéma vérité is sometimes used generically for nondirected filmmaking (as in the title of Mamber's book, *Cinema Verite in America*), but now it is more often applied to the Rouch/French approach, to distinguish it from the Drew-Leacock/American direct cinema.

Rouch denies that the filmmaker can achieve objectivity or that the camera can be unobtrusive. Since it is, finally, the filmmaker rather than the subject who is making the film, Rouch feels that he or she must have a strong attitude toward the subjects, must plan what to draw from them.

In Rouch's films (and those of others following this approach) the subjects are not necessarily occupied with something more important to them than the camera. Virtually everything we see and hear in *Chronicle of a Summer* is occasioned by the making of the film. Rouch argues, and many instances can be seen in his films and those of others (Chris Marker's *Le Joli Mai* [The Lovely May, 1963], or Michel Brault's and Pierre Perrault's *Pour la suite du monde* [English title *Moontrap,* 1963], or the Maysle's *Grey Gardens* [1975] for example), that the camera acts as a stimulant. It causes people to think about themselves as they may not be used to doing, and to express their feelings in ways they ordinarily wouldn't do. Perhaps there is an appropriateness in this approach coming out of a Catholic culture; there is a strong element of the confessional in Rouch's films. It also bears some relationship to psychodrama and to group psychotherapy.

If Rouch's method is followed, people's lives can be changed through the filming experience. *Moi, un noir* (Me, a Black, 1958) involved a kind of "acting out" on the part of its protagonist, a young stevedore who called himself Edward G. Robinson, living in a slum in Abidjan on the Ivory Coast. One of the "gangsters" of *Moi, un noir* ended up in jail. In *La Pyramide humaine* (The Human Pyramid, 1961) Rouch approached a high school in Abidjan in which black and white students had been put together in the same classes. After observing that no real integration seemed to be taking place, he involved them in simulated social mixing for his film. This led to relationships being formed that would not have otherwise occurred (and which were worrisome to some of the parents) and several students were said to have flunked their exams because of their involvement with the film. In *Chronicle of a Summer,* Angelo, the worker in the Renault plant, was fired from his job partly because of his involvement with the film. Most of the people in *Chronicle* subsequently went to work in film, Rouch has said. One of them, Marceline (Loridan), became an assistant to documentary veteran Joris Ivens, and eventually his wife and co-producer. Rouch has conceded, in private at least, that the responsibility for personal changes that can result from this kind of fully participatory filmmaking has made him uncomfortable on occasion.

In 1963 in Lyon, France, a famous meeting devoted to cinéma vérité/ direct cinema was sponsored by Radio Television Française (the French national broadcasting system). Issari and Paul, in *What is Cinéma Vérité?*, offer an account of the most important aspects of this event and I am indebted to them for much of what follows.[4] Two of those present had contributed much to the technology that made the technique possible: André Coutant (Eclair camera) and Stefan Kudelski (Nagra recorder). While Coutant was displaying his camera he drew a pen from his pocket and said, "The camera is still not as simple to use as this, but we're working on it."[5] Filmmaker attendees included Jean Rouch, Mario Ruspoli, and Edgar Morin from France; Robert Drew, Richard Leacock, Albert and David Maysles from the United States; Michel Brault from Canada.

The greatest excitement was generated by a lively, on-going debate between Rouch and Leacock. According to Issari and Paul, both of them were hoping to find "the reality of life," "the truth in people" hidden under the superficial conventions of daily living. Rouch hoped to pierce the observable surface to reach this underlying truth by means of discussion, interview, and a fictional sort of improvisation. Leacock thought he could capture this same underlying truth by photographing people without intruding; that subjects would reveal what they really felt and were like when unselfconsciously relaxed or deeply involved in some activity. Rouch sought to unmask truth through a process of deliberately encouraged self-revelation. Leacock sought to expose this truth through capturing unguarded moments of self-revelation in the movement of real life. Rouch wanted to explain the *raison d'être* of life, Issari and Paul observe, whereas Leacock wanted to let life reveal itself.[6]

During the arguments anger developed and the two positions remained essentially unresolved; perhaps they are unresolvable. Leacock claimed that Rouch prevented people from being themselves, that he forced meanings from them according to a pattern he had arbitrarily set. Rouch blamed Leacock for being too uncritical, for accepting whatever came along as part of "the American way of life."[7] It could be said with equal justice that Rouch's view is especially French. Issari and Paul arrive at the following conclusion about the two filmmakers and their positions: "Their sharp exchanges of opinion at the Lyon conference may be explained by their different national and cultural backgrounds. The individual style of each is a reflection not only of his personality—and *cinéma vérité* [and direct cinema] probably reflects the personality of its author more faithfully than any other style of film making—but also the society of which he is a part."[8] Chapter Fifteen, which deals with French documentary of Rouch and others, will give a fuller sense of the cultural differences between the French and the Anglo-Saxon approaches.

EFFECTS ON DOCUMENTARY SUBJECTS AND STYLES

It seems quite proper that Ricky Leacock would be one of the pioneers of direct cinema/cinéma vérité. A scene in Flaherty's *Louisiana Story* (1948), for which he was cinematographer, made a profound impression on him and served as a foreshadowing of what was to come. The scene is the one in which the father tells a story about a man who had his jaw bitten off by an alligator. According to the recollection of some of those involved, this scene occurred while the crew were setting up to shoot a scripted scene. Camera and recorder were on merely for testing but Flaherty let them run to preserve the telling of the story. He was so taken by it that it appears in the film, though its nondirected verisimilitude is quite different from the style of the rest.

Leacock wished portable synchronous sound equipment were available that would permit recording actuality in this way generally—without script, without direction, with scarcely any editing. This was truly the thing itself, for its own sake, which is what Frances Flaherty said her husband was after.

The technology that developed has pulled documentary filmmakers back to Flaherty—Rouch and cinéma vérité as much as Leacock and direct cinema. It permits continuous takes even longer than those characteristic of Flaherty. Reflex viewing through a zoom lens requires no pause for lens changes or refocusing. A camera loaded with ten minutes of 16mm film can simply keep running until the film runs out. Of course, the act of cutting the 18,000 feet of film that passed through the camera down to the 2,000 feet that appears in a final version, as for *Primary*, suggests that a selective point of view is operating. Still, sync sound prevents the breaking up and manipulation of shots as freely as is possible with footage shot silent and sound added later. While whole scenes can be eliminated—as Flaherty evidently did in shortening *Moana*—within scenes the filmmaker is bound closely to the real time and real space of the events. It is hard to cut into a continuous sound track without the cut being noticeable; sound locks images into place.

This new technique, whatever form it takes, whether Leacockian or Rouchian, is a shooter's cinema rather than a cutter's, unlike that of either the Grierson documentaries or those of Free Cinema. Most cv/direct film-makers are their own cinematographers. Major selections are made at the time of shooting—"cutting" is done in the camera—rather than in subsequent editing. Frederick Wiseman (*High School*, 1968, *Law and Order*, 1969) and Allan King (*Warrendale*, 1967, *A Married Couple*, 1970) are exceptions. Wiseman has worked consistently with the same fine cameraman, William Brayne, and controls these choices to considerable extent by being his own mike operator. (Robert Drew also served as sound recordist on occasion.) King has not worked consistently in cv/direct.

This technique not only permits, but encourages coming in close, in selecting and concentrating on individuals (like Flaherty, unlike Grierson). In a film about Paul Anka, *Lonely Boy* (1961), made by Wolf Koenig and Roman Kroitor for the National Film Board of Canada, there is a scene in which Anka is singing before a huge audience at Freedomland amusement park in Detroit. The camera, panning a crowd of teenage girls screaming in adulation, passes one face that seems to be dissolving in emotion. Just after the camera passes her it stops, pans back, zooms in, and refocuses on a closeup of her face. You can almost hear the cameraman saying to himself as this image first registers on his consciousness, "Wow, look at that!" In *Welfare* (1975), a subject that would have been dealt with by earlier documentarians with attention to institutions and processes, Wiseman attends to individuals and their relationships in a particular New York City office—those applying for financial aid and those dispensing it.

Warrendale (Canada, 1967, Allan King). Museum of Modern Art/Film Stills Archive.

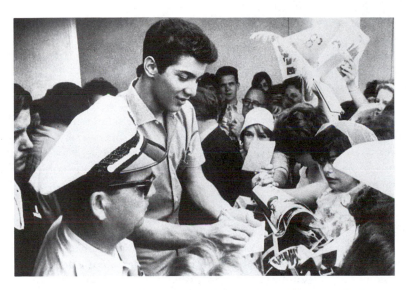

Lonely Boy (Canada, 1961, Wolf Koenig and Roman Kroiter). Museum of Modern Art/ Film Stills Archive.

Some of the human complexity of those being zoomed in on can now be suggested. They can tell us what they think and feel as well as show us what they do. Now we have a seeing and hearing machine that could film Nanook straight through while he is catching a seal, with Nanook's shouts to his family coming to join him and the thumping and bumping on the ice accompanying the images. Even more important, this new technology/ technique permits the filming of a sophisticated, urban Nanook in some psychological depth. In *The Chair* there is a moving scene in which the attorney breaks into tears and expresses his incredulity after he receives a phone call from a stranger offering support for him in his efforts to save his client's life.

An even greater innovation is the way in which the action is determined and who determines it. In *Nanook* (and virtually all documentaries dealing with individuals up through the 1950s), Flaherty observed what Nanook did. Subsequently—days, weeks, months later—he had him redo it for the camera. Flaherty might ask Nanook to do it a slightly different way, to do it again for another take or a shot from a different camera distance and angle. These shots would then be cut together to create an illusion of continuous action. In short, though Flaherty did not use written scripts, he "scripted" in his mind and "directed" Nanook according to that "script" in a way not fundamentally different from the creation of fiction films. In *The Chair* Donald Page Moore was essentially "directing" himself in action that could not have been scripted or even anticipated. No one had ever phoned him in that way before; neither he nor the filmmakers knew how he would react to the call.

Some people born since 1960 think earlier documentaries should not be called documentary at all, that they are patently fabricated and false. A counter proposition might be that the current predominance of cv/direct has brought losses as well as gains. It does seem possible to say that if cinéma vérité (and related forms) is not necessarily the cinema of truth, it does keep one from lying so much. But lying in this context may merely mean being as selective or as subjective as filmmakers or any creators may need to be. It seems to me that cv/direct is less efficient or effective for some subjects and purposes than other techniques. It is not as good for propaganda or poetry, for example, which require forms that are carefully selected and fully shaped. Both *Night Mail* and *O Dreamland* have a clarity and force in representing their makers' points of view and conveying them with heightened feeling. In the Wiseman films—which are very long, two hours or more currently—the accumulation of detail, rather than steadily adding to what we know about the subject, at some point may return the viewer to the uncertainties and confusions of life itself. On occasion Wiseman may even get an audience response opposite from the one he had hoped for and expected—what sociologists would call a boomerang effect.

Less shaping, less personal statement may mean less art—in the traditional sense at least. On the other hand, the cv/direct pull towards individuals, towards continuous recording of their words and actions, is a pull towards narrative—towards telling the sorts of stories that are true, the kinds of stories that Flaherty tried to tell. Cv/direct is closer to narrative forms, in any case, than to the descriptive, expository, argumentative, or poetic forms that documentary earlier concentrated on and developed in unique ways.

The technological bias of zoom lens and directional microphone that pulls cv/direct in on the individual has made it an attractive technique for television. Notable successes of early television included intimate realistic dramas about ordinary lives (*Marty, Bachelor's Party, A Catered Affair*), game shows (*You Bet Your Life, What's My Line*) and talk shows (*Tonight,* which began with Steve Allen and became a smash hit with Jack Paar) in which real people played themselves. If television is the cool medium McLuhan thought it to be, with its message completed by the viewer-listener, if it favors personalities and gossip, as Seldes thought, these characteristics are shared by cv/direct. Perhaps it is no accident that cv/direct arrived after television and that its first substantial successes, Drew Associates' in the *Close-Up!* series, were designed for exhibition on the tube. The rough-edged sights and sounds of cv/direct may be better suited for television than for the refinements of theater projection. (At about the same time cv/direct was developing, and in response to the competition of television, wide screens and stereophonic sound offered a theatrical equivalent of life more fully caught, of less editing, and resultant ambiguity. For all its formal polish and care in the making, Michelangelo Antonioni's *L'Avventura* [1960] resembles cv/ direct in the looseness and irregularity of the narrative structure.)

As has already been suggested, with the arrival of cv/direct the sharp distinctions between documentary and fiction (on which the first three-quarters of this book are based) have blurred. It may be that histories of documentary should stop at about 1960, just as histories of colonial America stop at 1776. The cv/direct technique, which marks the main line of documentary of the last quarter century, may be different in kind rather than degree from anything that went before it. Offering a close relationship to life as it is being lived, it is preponderantly, almost automatically, narrative in form. Cv/direct films show something happening, followed by something else that happens, followed by the next thing that happens, and so on. People in cv/direct are shown acting and reacting to each other in ways analogous to the behavior of characters in fiction and drama. *Eddie* (1961, Richard Leacock, Albert Maysles, D.A. Pennebaker [the original version entitled *On the Pole*]) is about a race car driver before, during, and after a race (which he did not win). So is the fiction feature *Red Line 7000* (1966, Howard Hawks). *David* (1961, Gregory Shuker, D.A. Pennebaker, William Ray) is about an attractive jazz musician who has sequestered himself in Synanon, a sanatorium on the beach in Venice, California, in an attempt to rid himself of his addiction to drugs. *The Man With the Golden Arm* (1956, Otto Preminger, from a novel by Nelson Algren) is about a similar topic and person. Vérité/direct films have suggested techniques and styles used by John Cassavetes in *Faces* (1968), Jean-Luc Godard in *Tout va bien* (1972), and fiction films coming from the Third World (*Blood of the Condor,* Bolivia, 1969, Jorge Sanjines; *The Jackal of Nahueltero,* Chile, 1969, Miguel Littín). Chapter Sixteen will deal with such mixtures of modes in films from the sixties on.

AESTHETIC AND ETHICAL CONSIDERATIONS

Aesthetically, one of the central issues of direct cinema and cinéma vérité is the one just raised. In their narrative structures, the forms of these films are analogous to those of fiction. The stories they are telling may be truer (or may not be, for that matter), but they are in many ways stories all the same. A second crucial matter is the extent to which cv/direct filmmakers can express a personal point of view through this increased amount of uncontrolled actuality. Ethically, the central questions involve the honesty and responsibility of the filmmakers towards their subject persons and audiences. These matters of form and authorial point of view, of art in relation to reality, of fact in relation to fiction, present intriguing perplexities.

Charlie Chan at the Opera (1936) seemed a known and classifiable aesthetic-ethical object when it was released. But what are we to make of *Gimme Shelter* (1970, Albert and David Maysles, Charlotte Zwerin), a record of an ill-fated rock music concert by the Rolling Stones at Altamont, California, in which a real murder becomes the climax of the film and is, at the same time, used as courtroom evidence?

Or, consider attaching camera and sound recorder onto a real family and filming the course of their relationship over weeks or months. With this new artistic possibility a whole new set of ethical problems are raised. In *A Married Couple* (1969), Allan King made such a record of two friends of his. He chose them at least partly because he sensed their marriage was undergoing stress.

The best-known instance of this sort to date is the twelve-part *An American Family* series produced and directed by Craig Gilbert and aired on public television in 1973. It raised a lot of questions and caused considerable controversy along ethical lines. Did the Loud family of husband, wife, and five teenagers behave differently than they would have done if the camera and mike hadn't been there? Were they performing for it? Did the filming exacerbate, perhaps even cause the strains and ruptures we witness? Did the filmmakers distort, through selection and arrangement, what actually occurred? What is "true" in it; what is "story"?

Along with these ethical considerations is an odd aesthetic aspect. At the time *An American Family* was aired, members of a documentary class I was teaching complained that the big scene—when Pat Loud announces to husband Bill that she has decided on divorce—was not well done. What they meant was that it was not sufficiently dramatic: the Louds didn't give good performances, they were too casual, and the episode did not build to a climax. I remember being startled by this reaction. In my opinion, this was viewing life as art; as art it was expected to follow the conventions of dramaturgy and performance one would find on *Days of Our Lives* and other afternoon serials.

The cv/direct technology/technique seems to offer an ultimate possibility of show and tell—of telling a real story as it is happening rather than sitting back and creating it out of remembered experience and imagination. At the same time it seems to me that cv/direct is closer to life than to art, that it can seem unselected, formless, dull—a mere record. "At such a point, cinema has disappeared," Louis Marcorelles observed.[9] Even at its best, cv/direct does not offer an aesthetic experience culminating in a final act like Shakespeare's *Hamlet,* with all the threads tied together, or Beethoven's *Ninth Symphony,* with its transcendental final movement. And what about the people whose lives have been invaded and used as material for the creation of this lifelike art object? Can we in fact trust the filmmakers' representations of them?

If the cv/direct filmmaker-artist is able to work directly from ongoing life, he or she shapes and refines the presentation of real people. Through selection and arrangement "characters" and "actions" are "created." This creation may be different from that in the traditional arts but it is still cre-

The Louds, subjects of *An American Family* series (U.S., 1973, Craig Gilbert). Museum of Modern Art/ Film Stills Archive.

ation of some sort. It could be the "writing with the camera" French film-maker-critic Alexandre Astruc called for with his phrase *caméra-stylo* (camera-pen). What Astruc sought was the possibility of creating the fiction in its making rather than merely supplying images and sounds for a fully realized and prefixed conception.[10] If we aren't yet able to write with the camera in this way, it does seem a potential that cinéma vérité/direct cinema has built within it.

Eventually mightn't little distinction be made between documentary and fictional/dramatic forms? Perhaps the Africans of A.D. 5289, looking back over the history of film, will regard what began to occur in the middle of the twentieth century as the beginning of *film art*. They may dismiss the first hundred years or so of the medium as dependent on earlier arts—stories taken from literature, actors from theater.

In documentary, if not in fiction, it is presently possible to create films as we go—with some of the freedom of action painting and jazz improvisation—without detailed scripts and resultant rigidities of preproduction planning. Perhaps this is full-circle to Flaherty. "Nonpreconception" isn't so much at issue as the possibility of recording and shaping actuality to fit a personal vision, as Flaherty in fact did. The technology now available simply brings film closer to life as it is being lived than Flaherty could do.

Perhaps what can now be offered is best identified as actuality drama, a term sometimes used to avoid the austerity and didacticism associated with documentary. In any case, it is the French rather than the Anglo-Saxons who have most fully addressed the complexities and subtleties of the relationships between film and life that the new technology has made closer and the new techniques have experimented with. Chapter Fifteen will step outside the English-language tradition to offer a cross-cultural comparison with some of the documentary work done in France in the recent past.

NOTES

[1]"Cinéma Vérité: A Survey Including Interviews with Richard Leacock, Jean Rouch, Jacques Rozier, William Klein, The Maysles Brothers," *Movie*, no. 8 (April 1963), pp. 12–27 (13–14).

[2]Ibid. (p. 16).

[3]M. Ali Issari and Doris A. Paul, *What is Cinéma Vérité?* (Metuchen, N.J.: The Scarecrow Press, Inc., 1979), p. 72.

[4]Ibid., pp. 7–8.

[5]Ibid, pp. 156.

[6]Ibid., p. 108.

[7]Ibid., p. 109.

[8]Ibid., p. 172.

[9]Louis Marcorelles, "Le Cinema direct nord americain," *Image et Son*, no. 183 (April 1965), p. 54.

[10]Alexandre Astruc, "The Birth of a New Avant-Garde: La Caméra-Stylo," *The New Wave*, ed. Peter Graham (Garden City, N.Y.: Doubleday & Company Inc., 1968), pp. 17–23.

FILMS OF THE PERIOD

1958
Les Raquetteurs (The Snowshoers, Canada, Michel Brault and Gilles Groulx)

1960
On the Pole (U.S., Richard Leacock, D. A. Pennebaker, William Ray, Abbot Mills, Albert Maysles)
Primary (U.S., Leacock, Pennebaker, Terence Macartney-Filgate, Maysles)

1961
Chronicle of a Summer (France, Jean Rouch and Edgar Morin)
Football/Mooney vs. Fowle (U.S., James Lipscomb)
Les Inconnus de la terre (The Unknown of the Earth, France, Mario Ruspoli)
Regard sur la folie (A Look at Madness, France Ruspoli)

1962
The Chair (U.S., Gregory Shuker, Leacock, Pennebaker)

Jane (U.S., Pennebaker, Leacock, Hope Ryden, Shuker, Mills)
Lonely Boy (Canada, Roman Kroitor and Wolf Koenig)
Nehru (U.S., Shuker and Leacock)
On the Road to Button Bay (U.S., Stanley Flink, Mills, Ryden, Lipscomb, Leacock, Pennebaker)
Showman (U.S., Albert and David Maysles)

1963
Happy Mother's Day (U.S., Leacock and Joyce Chopra)
Le Joli Mai (The Lovely May, France, Chris Marker)
Pour la suite du monde/Moontrap (Canada, Michel Brault and Pierre Perrault)
A Stravinsky Portrait (U.S., Leacock)
What's Happening! The Beatles in the U.S.A. (U.S., Albert and David Maysles)

1966
Don't Look Back (U.S., Pennebaker)
A Time for Burning (U.S., William Jersey)

BOOKS ON THE PERIOD

ISSARI, M. ALI and DORIS A. PAUL, *What Is Cinéma Vérité?* Metuchen, N.J.: The Scarecrow Press, Inc., 1979, 208 pp.

LEVIN, G. ROY, *Documentary Explorations.* Garden City, N.Y.: Doubleday & Company, Inc., 1971. 420 pp.

MAMBER, STEPHEN, *Cinema Verite in America: Studies in Uncontrolled Documentary.* Cambridge, Mass.: The MIT Press, 1974, 288 pp.

MARCORELLES, LOUIS, *Living Cinema.* London: George Allen & Unwin Ltd., 1973. 155 pp.

ROSENTHAL, ALAN, *The New Documentary in Action: A Casebook in Film Making.* Berkeley: University of California Press, 1972. 287 pp.

FIFTEEN
A CROSS-CULTURAL COMPARISON
Three *Auteurs* of French Documentary, 1961–

Though this book is devoted essentially to the English-language documentary, there is good reason to look at French documentary in relation to the sorts of aesthetic and ethical issues raised by cinéma vérité and direct cinema that were dealt with in Chapter Fourteen. In France, documentary film has remained closer to fiction film than in Great Britain, the United States, or Canada. For example, before turning to fiction features, Georges Franju and Alain Resnais had made a significant body of documentary shorts. The former's include *Blood of the Beasts* (1949), *Hôtel des Invalides* (1951), *Le Grand Méliès* (1952); the latter's *Guernica* (1950), *Les Statues meurent aussi* (The Statues also Weep, co-directed with Chris Marker, 1953), and *Night and Fog* (1955).

The French New Wave, which began in the late 1950s and included the first features of François Truffaut (*The 400 Blows,* 1959), Alain Resnais (*Hiroshima, mon amour,* 1959), and Jean-Luc Godard (*Breathless,* 1960), grew out of what in this country would be called the auteur theory. It was first articulated by Truffaut in an article in the influential critical journal *Cahiers du Cinéma.* Simply put *la politique des auteurs* argued that filmmakers (directors) should be regarded as auteurs (authors) of their work, as artists whose films can be studied with the same seriousness as can the paintings of Paul Cezanne, the novels of Gustave Flaubert, or the plays of Molière.

In this chapter, selected work of three French documentary auteurs will be examined as examples of new approaches and methods that made documentary different from that discussed prior to Chapter Fourteen. The filmmakers are Jean Rouch, Chris Marker, and Louis Malle. In a concluding section, common characteristics of their films will be summarized and contrasted to the main characteristics of the Anglo-Saxon line.

JEAN ROUCH

Trained as an anthropologist, Rouch became especially interested in the migration of native peoples on the west coast of Africa. He came to film as a tool for use in his anthropological work. Later he made documentaries in France, and at times has made fiction films, without giving up his anthropological concerns. In combining anthropology and film, Rouch has inaugurated new ways of approaching anthropological study. At the same time, his anthropological outlook has led to major innovations in filmmaking. In his anthropological filmmaking, Rouch involves himself fully with his subjects in the production of the films. He also explores fictional improvisation as a means of evoking cultural and psychological expression on the part of his subjects. What follows is a discussion of two of his works which represent his special approach and contributions to documentary.

Chronicle of a Summer (1961), on which Rouch collaborated with sociologist Edgar Morin, has been dealt with in part in Chapter Fourteen. The sorts of effects it might have on the social attitudes of audiences and the nature of the aesthetic experience it offers remain to be considered.

The kinds of effects Rouch and Morin hoped their film would have are not made clear. Curiously, given their forthrightness in other respects, their attitudes and values regarding the matters being talked about in the film remain muted; the questions they ask are devoid of emotion, like those of a psychotherapist. What seems true of all the interviewees is that they have learned to complain about their society. They have also learned to accept it. The absence of apparent anger or indignation on the part of Rouch or Morin, who are, after all, the masters of these ceremonies, places the film on the side of acceptance too. The makers of *Chronicle* appear to be saying, implicitly, that what they are showing is life as they found it among this particular group of Parisians in the summer of 1960.

In Griersonian terms the view *Chronicle* offers is a deeply pessimistic one. The existing social/political/economic system seems inadequate to allow the people being interviewed the kinds of lives they want to live. No way is put forward to alter this situation. All that one can infer is that the whole system would have to be torn down and rebuilt in order to achieve one more attune to the personal and emotional needs of individuals like those in the film. After seeing *Chronicle,* Grierson's observation that Free

Cinema seemed curiously French, mentioned in Chapter Thirteen, becomes understandable. Free Cinema seemed to only allow for a similar sort of radical solution to existing social problems. In a perceptive essay on *Chronicle of a Summer,* Ellen Freyer acknowledges that the Grierson kind of documentary, "A documentary whose aim is to change social conditions, confronts us with the social realities." She then suggests that *Chronicle* has a different purpose, and asks "Shouldn't a documentary attempting to change emotional and cultural conditions confront us with the emotional realities?"[1]

As an aesthetic experience, *Chronicle of a Summer* seemed unique when it appeared. It is most exceptional in the way it brings together something-like-art with something-like-life. As an artwork viewed in traditional ways, it is lacking in coherence; it gives no sense of completion. Do its parts in fact make a whole? Or are the parts themselves the experience being offered? Two contrasting views of the aesthetic-ethical problems it presents are voiced by those who appear in the film following their screening of it. One faction says that what's bad about it is that the people in it are "acting." (Marceline's introspection is singled out as an example.) The other faction says that it is wrong to expose people as it does, that the persons are stripped bare. (The scene in which Marilou breaks down might be an example.) Overplaying and artificiality on the one hand vs. real and natural on the other. These complaints regarding cinéma vérité or direct cinema—that it is boring or indecent—recur frequently in both public reaction and critics' responses.

The other Rouch film I would like to examine in some detail is *Jaguar* (1967). This was chosen because: it is in current distribution in this country (as is *Chronicle*); it is one of the African films; and, perhaps most of all, because it involves the combination of fictional improvisation with actuality that is among the most adventuresome aspects of Rouch's work.

In the opening narration Rouch tells us that along the Niger River, far inland, it is the custom for young men to journey to the West Coast, ostensibly to earn enough money in the cities so they can return home and marry. We see·shots of the flat countryside covered with long brown grass and of the lush riverside. Apparently, three young men have agreed to make the trip, with Rouch accompanying them to film it. Lam is a cowherd; Illo a fisherman; Damouré a public scribe, horse rider, and ladies man. The film chronicles their journey.

It conforms with remarkable closeness to the quest Vladimir Propp identified, in *The Morphology of the Folktale* (Austin: University of Texas Press, 1968), as common to Russian fairy tales (and presumably those of other cultures) and to traditional epics, sagas, and legends. Before the trio start off they receive instructions from a "magician" and perform a religious ceremony. "We ask the spirits to show us the way," one of them says.

On their trek across unfamiliar territory they encounter strange and exotic peoples and customs. When they reach the coast, the ocean is introduced with quiet drama following their long journey across mostly arid and uninteresting terrain. They split up and go off separately to Ghana (formerly the Gold Coast, English-speaking), the Ivory Coast, and Dahomey (both French-speaking). They work at various jobs in cities (Accra especially) and surrounding areas as longshoreman, forester, clerk in market stalls, and miner in the gold mines. They experience the city life available to them— including the open air markets, the bars, a race track—and witness political campaigning and an election day parade. The title of the film, *Jaguar,* refers not only to a jungle beast but is West African slang for someone (a cool cat, presumably) who has become savvy in the ways of the city. A song by that title is played over shots of Damouré sauntering about the streets smoking a cigarette.

My understanding of all this is that though at first they achieve some success in the cities, their curiosity and sense of wonder become vitiated and their actions desultory, confused, and meaningless. After about three months they return home. Illo gives away things he has brought back with him and catches a little hippopotamus along the river. Lam begins courting a girl and goes back to his herd. We see Damouré with a girl; a lance and umbrella are all he has to show for his trip. But they have tales to tell. Clearly the trip was successful as an adventure, and no doubt that was what was intended from the outset: a *rite de passage,* a last sowing of wild oats before settling down to traditional life in the bush. It concludes with a celebration of Lam's wedding, a proper ending for comedies.

Though this is an unprecedented film in many respects, comparisons with Flaherty are obvious. (Rouch claims Flaherty as one of his mentors.) It is concerned with a remote people and a traditional culture. Rouch, too, collaborates with his subjects in making the film. But he brings the natives into town and into contact with Europeans. Flaherty did not do this in either *Nanook* or *Moana* (except for the early scene at the trader's in the former) or, in a sense, in *Man of Aran.* In *Louisiana Story* "civilization" comes into the natural habitat. Also, Rouch's heroes are nonheroic, even antiheroic. Unlike Nanook harpooning a walrus or the Man of Aran a basking shark, the trio's junket is not designed for survival. It is instructive to them, and certainly to us as we see vestiges of colonial cultures mixing with native ones in complex and strained ways. (Basil Wright's *Song of Ceylon* comes to mind in this respect.) The trip is scarcely necessary, however; a bit silly, perhaps. Rouch is being ironic at the end of the film when he calls them "Heroes of the modern world."

What's more, the form and style of *Jaguar* foreshadow the blending of fiction with documentary (which Flaherty did not acknowledge or perhaps even recognize in his films). Rouch and the three young men are telling their story. The making of the film is not intrusive in regard to their feelings; the cameraman (Rouch) is tagging along, not leading. People are allowed to appear looking into the camera, reminding us it is a film we are seeing.

Made up of brief fragments, some of *Jaguar* remains cryptic. I doubt it was planned that way. Rouch is quite casual about visual continuity; there are many jump cuts—that is, breaks in the action. The color quality varies considerably throughout. It has (for me) a charming suggestion of home movies; or, if you like, of an ingenious salvage job. (Shot in 1953, it was not edited until 1967.) In either case, narration becomes necessary to hold it together and to make its meaning clear. It is spoken by Rouch but, unlike *Chronicle,* he does not appear on camera.

The sound track sometimes becomes dominant; it is full of experiment and interest. In addition to Rouch's narration, the three young men comment on the images; they seem to be sitting together watching the footage for the first time. They ask and answer questions to each other: "See me over there? I'm lost." "Is that him, Yakuba [the lumber yard boss]?" If they seem to be telling their story, it is not altogether clear to whom they are telling it. To each other? To us? They are mostly concerned with the businesses, industries, and economics of the places they are in—how much things cost, who's the boss. It is difficult to determine the point of view of this film without a firm knowledge of French; from the English subtitles alone even the tense and person of the commentary are not certain.

None of the sound is synchronous, though it seems to have been recorded at the time of shooting; even the brief interviews with Lam and Illo near the beginning appear to be nonsync tape recording cut to the images to simulate sync. The background sound is wild track used selectively as sound effects. There is a partial musical track, like a fiction feature. Most of it is indigenous source music being heard or played or sung by the people in the scene. But there is a curious passage in the sequence about gold mining in which shots of gold ingots are accompanied by modern piano music which becomes very strong; the effect is quite European avant-garde. Another odd experimental bit is a scene in which Damouré, on his way to Accra, is standing in the back of the truck waving. It is overlaid with cheering crowd noise mockingly suggesting a conquering hero riding into town.

Unlike many documentaries, and like many works of fiction or drama, the overall purpose of *Jaguar*—Rouch's reasons for making it, what he is trying to say—remains ambiguous. Even the title seems to be ironic. These are not jaguars in any sense. They are unsophisticated, gentle, engaging country boys who have an innocent adventure in town. The filmmaker and they share that adventure with us. In some ways *Jaguar* is a simple story, but it is also a myth, with multiple meanings offering the possibility for a number of interpretations. We may see much more in the relationship between their attitudes and those of the "civilization" they are visiting than they do.

This may very well be the kind of story the people along the Niger tell of an evening. In letting us see and hear it, Rouch may be telling us a lot about them that couldn't be told better in any other way.

Jaguar (France, 1967, Jean Rouch). John Caldwell.

CHRIS MARKER

To become familiar with Jean Rouch and his views is easy. He has been frequently interviewed and photographed. Chris Marker, on the contrary, is elusive bordering on mysterious. Born in a suburb of Paris, he has allowed a legend to grow about his birth in a "far-off country." Marker is not his name; it is one of half-a-dozen aliases he has used. His real name is Christian François Bouche-Villeneuve. He chose "Marker," it is thought, in reference to the Magic Marker pen. A magic marker he is.

Marker began his career as a writer (publishing poems, a novel, and various essays and translations) and journalist (whose travels took him all over the world). His filmwork is close to the personal essay in form. He is the writer of all his films and cinematographer on many of them. Their verbal and visual wit almost conceal the philosophical speculation and erudition they contain. Their commentaries are a kind of stream of consciousness; their poetry is about himself as well as about the subjects—his reactions to what he and we are seeing and hearing.

If Rouch is the anthropologist looking at the natives (in Africa or Paris), Marker is the foreign correspondent and inquiring reporter. He is interested in transitional societies, in "Life in the process of becoming history," as he has put it. A member of the intellectual Left, he is politically committed but not doctrinaire. "Involved objectivity" is his own phrase for his approach. His films are not only set in specific places, they are about the cultures of those places. *Le Joli Mai* (Paris, 1963) and *The Koumiko Mystery* (Japan, 1965) will be discussed in some detail. Marker directed and wrote the commentary for the first, which is spoken by Simone Signoret (in the English version) and Yves Montand (in the French version). The music is by Michel Legrand. Marker wrote, directed, photographed, and edited the second.

Le Joli Mai (The Lovely May) is much like *Chronicle of a Summer.* The Algerian War figures in both films; it was still being fought in the former, had just ended in the latter. The first half of *Le Joli Mai,* in particular, is similar to *Chronicle.* Like Rouch and Morin, Marker interviews Parisians about their ambitions, their political views, their understandings of the society they live in. But his sample is more of a cross section—a streetcorner clothing salesman, a clerk, a house painter, a black student, a young couple wanting to get married, an Algerian worker—with more working-class representation. Like the people in *Chronicle,* Marker's interviewees find that work has no value. Its goal is money; what happiness money will bring is by no means certain. Marker insists to one interviewee who opts for material success that his view of life is "a trifle limited." "No interest in other things?," Marker asks.

This exchange is characteristic. Unlike Rouch and Morin, Marker's tone is frequently judgmental. He engages in argument with the interviewees and makes known his disappointment in some of their answers. His interviews are more in the form of a dialectic than of a psychotherapeutic session, as in Rouch and Morin. One representative instance of Marker at work takes place outside the Bourse stock exchange. As Marker interviews two fifteen-year-old apprentice stock brokers, an onlooker grumbles "They shouldn't be allowed to interview minors." Marker calls "Stop," and sets up a new sequence (letting us see the clapperboard) in which the grumbler is pressed for his point of view. In another instance, as a fatuous man is talking about success, the camera leaves his face to follow a spider crawling down his jacket and across his shirt. The only interviewee presented with full sympathy is a former priest turned Communist organizer. He is allowed to speak uninterrupted with few cuts and no commentary.

Le Joli Mai is even less clearly structured than *Chronicle,* even more dependent for its content on the personal views of Marker and of those being interviewed. In the second part of *Chronicle* Rouch and Morin attempted to involve their subjects in discussion of the events in the world around them. In the second half of *Le Joli Mai,* Marker breaks away from individuals and interviews altogether. Instead he deals with news events—a police charge which crushed eight people to death in the Métro, the half-million mourners at their funeral, violent responses to the acquittal of General Salan (former commander-in-chief of French forces in Algeria), massive railroad and Renault strikes—intercut with nightclub revelry. The events refer back to those interviewed in the first half who felt themselves "unfree" to alter or even to question the social system.

Though the similarities of *Chronicle of a Summer* and *Le Joli Mai* suggest they would not make a good double bill, such a pairing would be instructive. It would highlight the very personal nature, the oblique and fragmented probes of Marker's approach. I would expect the idiosyncratic charm of his presentation of Paris to carry audiences along even if it were seen second.

The Koumiko Mystery is set amidst the 1964 Tokyo Olympics, and begins with the games. It returns to them occasionally, to report on their progress, but never stays with them for long. Its real subject is a young Japanese woman named Kumiko Muroaka, her city (Tokyo), her country, and the Far East as a whole. If, in a sense, Kumiko is protagonist, there is also an antagonist of sorts. The Western world and its influences are seen again and again in images on television screens, in the tastes evident in department store windows.

Like *Le Joli Mai, The Koumiko Mystery* is in two parts. In the first we follow Kumiko through the city while she describes herself. "She will not

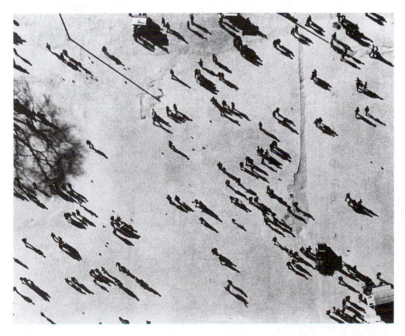

Le Joli Mai (The Lovely May; France, 1963, Chris Marker). Museum of Modern Art/Film Stills Archive.

make history," observes the commentator. "She is history, like you and me and the Pope." Kumiko examines and admires the narrow noses and big eyes of the occidental faces on the mannequins in Tokyo stores. When she mentions the moistness of the Japanese climate, we see, from overhead, people with brightly colored umbrellas crossing a rainy street while the Michel Legrand theme music from Jacques Demy's *The Umbrellas of Cherbourg* is heard.

The second part consists of Kumiko's recorded answers to questions Marker had left with her after his return to France. The questions—such as "What do you want from life?"—are overwhelming, and Kumiko's answers are suitably beside the point. She discusses her preferences in animals (as the camera observes toy animals—especially cats, evident in many Marker films); and she contrasts the veiled loveliness of Japanese children with the startling angelic beauty of Western children.

Toward the end of the film Tokyo sets about recovering from the onslaught of Olympic visitors. There is a sustained sequence showing lights on the Ginza, the entertainment district, through the night into the morning. We follow Kumiko, alone as a passenger on a monorail, then as she travels down a Tokyo street. Her final meditation, about violence, which she understands and does not fear, ends with her affirmation of faith in love and tenderness.

The Koumiko Mystery differs from previous Marker films, and from the tradition of cinéma-vérité generally, in being less concerned with developing the feel of an event or a moment in history than with exploring the slight histories of a few private and random feelings. Part of the film is photographed directly off black-and-white television screens. In this way the concerns and attitudes of the larger world are isolated. The rest of the film,

The Koumiko Mystery (France, 1965, Chris Marker). National Film Archive/Stills Library.

which is in color, is wholly personal. Marker is always willing to impose his own shaping intelligence and imagination on his material. In *The Koumiko Mystery* he will alternately transform a street full of people walking in the rain into a remembrance of the patterned artifice of a musical, or dissolve the controlled movements of Japanese duelers into darkly looming menace. The film's one constant factor is the articulate warmth, intelligence, and humor of the girl who is its subject.[2]

LOUIS MALLE

After attending the Jesuit College at Fontainebleau, Malle studied political science at the Sorbonne, then filmmaking at l'Institut des Hautes Études Cinématographiques. In 1952, when he was twenty, and still at IDHEC, he began work with Jacques Cousteau as an underwater cinematographer. This work continued on to *The Silent World* (1956), for which Malle received co-director credit. He then directed fiction features—*Ascenseur pour l' échafaud* (Escalator to the Scaffold/Frantic, 1957) and *The Lovers* (1958)—that placed him at the edge of the rising New Wave, which broke in 1959. Like François Truffaut, Alain Resnais, and Jean-Luc Godard, whose first features appeared at that time (*The 400 Blows, Hiroshima, mon amour,* and *Breathless,* respectively), Malle has been experimental and innovative. He has played with accepted conventions of the medium, constantly exploring, testing, and altering the relationship between film and reality, between the camera and what's in front of it.

Unlike other French filmmakers who had become important documentarians before turning to fiction, Malle has frequently returned to documentary. After *Zazi dans le Métro* (1960) and *Vie privée* (*A Very Private Affair,* 1961), he made *Vive le Tour!* (1962), a documentary about a bicycle race. In addition, his fiction films are often allied to documentary-like concerns. For example, *Le Feu follet* (*The Fire Within,* 1963), about the last forty-eight hours in the life of an alcoholic as he moves towards suicide, was based on an actual person and his actions. Following that Malle made a reportage on Thailand for French television, *Bon baisers de Bangkok* (1964). *My Dinner with Andre* (1982) offers a dialogue that is a dramatic creation, but the conversation, characters, and relationship of the two men are presented in ways closer to cinéma-vérité than to conventional filmmaking techniques. *Alamo Bay* (1985) is based on events on the Gulf coast of Texas between 1979 and 1981, when immigrant Vietnamese settled in the small fishing towns near Corpus Christi. It came out of Malle's interest in the "melting pot" concept and myth after he began work in the U.S. in the mid-seventies. (Interest in the same matter a half-century earlier had led Grierson to the conception of documentary.) *And the Pursuit of Happiness* (1986) is Malle's documentary treatment of this subject.

I remember being on a panel with Malle following a screening of his *Lacombe, Lucien* (1973), which stars a real-life provincial farm boy and is about the French under German occupation, as is Marcel Ophuls's celebrated documentary *The Sorrow and the Pity* (1971). When I asked Malle why he moved back and forth between fiction and documentary, he eliminated my function as the documentary specialist on the panel by saying he didn't see much difference between the two modes. He went on to say that for him the subjective and the objective are always intertwined in any statement and that (another startler) documentary is necessarily more subjective, fiction more objective. Malle's documentary films contain recurrent themes, perhaps more accurately concerns (present in his fiction films as well) that seem to preoccupy him.

One of these concerns is the camera as observer: what the camera can see, and what can and cannot be understood through it. (One part of Malle's seven-part "Phanton India" series [1969] is entitled *The Impossible Camera*.) Next is his concern with human life under pressure: how much his subjects can take; also, how much the viewer can take—how long can we watch, how close up? Malle is questioning the value of the endurance shown in his films: whether what one gets out of the effort is worth the time spent, worth the boredom, the discomfort, or the pain frequently present. But he also seems to admire the victory of mind over flesh; he may even be in awe of its achievement.

Malle is also concerned with who is the watcher and who is the watchee. In his documentaries people stare at the camera, even take pictures of the camera taking pictures of them. (The title of British documentarian Harry Watt's memoirs is *Don't Look at the Camera,* an instruction most documentary filmmakers give their subjects.) Malle's documentaries set up a separate reality he asks us to try to understand. We can attempt this through determined effort or through removing ourselves from our present reality. (It is the latter that is called for in "Phantom India.")

Malle is clearly and consistently interested in the underlying structure of things. In *The Indians and the Sacred* (part three of "Phantom India"), for example, he delves into the economics of the priesthood. Also, he attends to the privacy of the individual within the larger group. Critic Penelope Gilliat has characterized Malle's work as being "absorbed by ideas of solitude." Malle has said that he respects "people who really believe" (whatever it is they believe) and he presents them with respect.

Finally, it is evident from all of Malle's films, fiction and documentary, as well as from interview statements, that he is committed to an acceptance of the complexity of truth. This complexity seems to me equivalent to the ambiguity thought proper to works of art. Ambiguity is rare in English-language documentaries, in which clarity and singleness of purpose dominate—before the 1960s, anyway. As examples for a closer examination of the contents, purposes, and forms of Malle's documentaries I have chosen *Vive le Tour!* (1962) and *Human, Too Human* (1972).

Vive le Tour! is a nineteen-minute short about Le Tour de France, a grueling twenty-day bicycle race held each July. The film begins with visuals from the racers' point of view: a continuous extreme wide-angle take, with concomitant distortion, shot from a speeding car moving through a town. The music over it is a band march. This is followed by shots of spectators, then a parade with floats. The crowds watching include old people and children; many nuns and priests are evident. This is the beginning of the race.

Malle narrates in English over a French radio broadcast of the event. His word choice and tone of voice are youthful, fresh, amateurish, and interested. He explains how the race is conducted, the number of racers on each team, how they function in relation to each other, and the like—the process.

We see the racers sweating, two urinating alongside the road, another from his bike. They obtain and consume whatever liquids they can find along the way—"even water when there is nothing else"—to replace the nine pounds of sweat they lose each day. "My feet are burning," Malle offers as the observation of one of them; "Oh, my ass; it hurts so much," from another.

A funeral dirge is played over shots of cyclists falling. A Swiss racer, in a bad fall, has fractured his skull. At times the race was tainted by doping to hide the pain, Malle tells us, though the use of drugs is forbidden and the racers deny taking them. In one instance they attribute a bad reaction to drugs to contaminated sea food. There is a lot of footage on the falls, on exhaustion. One racer far behind the pack is followed. He's Italian, an "obscure racer with no other ambition than to help his leader." We watch as he pumps slower and slower. Probably unconscious, he wobbles to the side of the road, slowly topples and collapses in the ditch. This sequence ends with shots of ambulances.

Then it's back to the pack and their "moment of truth" climbing the Alps. Spectators push riders to help them up the steep inclines. Varied images are presented. Cheering crowds. A foggy mountain road. Racers stuffing newspapers under their shirts to protect them against the cold of high altitudes. Noises of bikes. Squeaking brakes in descent. Closeups of the sweating, grimacing faces of riders.

Vive le Tour! seems to be organized in three phases: the introduction—beginning of the race, seen at a superficial, media-coverage level, with lively carnival atmosphere; the second, more connected with the racers, more personal on Malle's part (but not so deeply involved as the third phase), with humorous bits of action and observation; the third phase, going into the mountains, a painful experience for the bikers (and for us), intent on their personal struggle. Intercut in this last phase are brief flash-forwards to the

Vive le Tour! (France, 1962, Louis Malle). New Yorker Films.

three prize winners holding their trophies, posed for photographs and adulation by the crowd. Music in the style of a romantic Parisian pop tune accompanies these final images.

On *Vive le Tour!* cinematography is by Malle, New Wave cameraman Ghislain Cloquet, and Jacques Ertaud. Editing is by Suzanne Baron, a regular and important collaborator of Malle's who has worked with other New Wave directors as well. The music was composed by Georges Delerue.

Human, Too Human is a seventy-seven-minute feature about the manufacturing and selling of automobiles. It was shot at the Citroën plant at Rennes, in northeast France, and at the Salon de l'Auto, in Paris. It is organized in equal thirds with seamless transitions between them. The first third deals with the overall process of manufacture. The second focuses on promotion and selling at a large auto show. The third, back at the factory, concentrates on the workers and the nature of the work they do. The complex and ambiguous opening sets the tone of the film.

In early morning light, evidently, we see countryside and highway, followed by a large parking lot, then, in long, slow pan, the exterior of a factory with workers entering—all of this from considerable distance. A tracking shot from below follows an overhead crane moving the length of a huge factory interior. Point of view shifts to closeups of the crane operator; then a reverse angle, from her point of view, of rolls of shiny sheet metal below. A sequence of other workers follows: one is flipping and inspecting rectangular sheets of steel; another is seen through a machine; another, at a distance, is shot in careful composition, his movements rhythmic. This latter

shot concludes with a slow zoom into a closeup of the worker. This sequence, the latter shot particularly, is like one from a fiction film made in
a studio; or, an even better analogy, like Leni Riefenstahl's celebration of
human grace in her vast documentary of the 1936 Olympic games, *Olympia*
(1938).

The opening sound track consists of noises of nature (sheep maybe, a
barking dog) and of highway (automobile engines). Outside the factory, music begins—austere, medieval sounding (a Gregorian chant?). It builds in
volume inside the factory and continues over the high-angle shot from the
moving crane. At the same time we hear the factory din, which also in-
creases in volume and finally drowns out the music. The clangor of a huge
press, through which we see the press operator, is nearly deafening.

But these are curiously handsome machines, materials, and processes.
The work being done seems mysterious, magical. Great power is involved
in this making, controlled power. The workers are attractive, sophisticated-
looking for the most part, and predominantly young. We see them through
their machines; they seem dominated by them. But then they also appear
to be beautifully in control of their tools and materials—athletic and energetic. They have the ability to make splendid things—strong, complicated
things. They engage in a kind of ensemble performance; the camera becomes part of the choreography.

This film does not permit one to compute the pros and cons of its
attitudes about this work and these workers into an inarguable sum. (I have
pages of notes which are attempts at this; *Human, Too Human* is a great film
for note taking!) Are we seeing exploited workers in an inhuman economy
that destroys them physically through mindless repetition of a single mechanical task? Or are we seeing members of a new race who somehow have
learned to soar above the routine and repetition of their tasks to make them
into a graceful and soothing ballet of a sort?

The reality being offered is mediated, to be sure. The images are con-
sciously chosen and strikingly composed. The artistry of the hand-held cinematography, by Etienne Becker, is exceptional: the light, the color, the fluid
grace are lovely; the sensitivity in response to the workers' motions goes
beyond skill. There is lots of camera movement (with constant alteration of
frame and focus) including a number of long tracking shots. Even recogniz-
ing that conscious creative choices are being made, I still don't know what
the camera is saying about the images.

The sound, after the opening, is all source sound and synchronous
mostly it seems, even when it needn't have been. (That is, when ambient
factory noise could have been recorded separately from the visuals.) There
is no narration or commentary; the only words we hear are bits of conversation at the auto show, mostly between company representatives and potential customers. In the factory we hear no conversation and see very little of
it taking place.

Human, Too Human (France, 1972, Louis Malle). New Yorker Films.

Human, Too Human ends on a freeze-frame of the woman flipping and inspecting the steel panels we saw near the beginning. The ambiguity that has been building throughout remains. What is this film saying about its subject? What does its title mean, anyway?

By anyone's definition this is a documentary, but it is not the Grierson sort. What we see seems a model of collective endeavor but what results from it is merely the making and selling of a luxury product. In one way or another *Human, Too Human* may be subverting the Grierson ethic. Nor is it like the work of Rouch as cinéma-vérité. The presence of the camera does not cause the action, or draw people out. It does not seem to interrupt or affect the work being done. On the other hand, it is not altogether unobtrusive. Some workers glance at it from time to time, their gazes impassive, guarded; ambiguous at least. Maybe, if aware of the camera, they still perform their prescribed tasks as they do every work day, as Leacock and direct cinema practitioners would like to have it. Perhaps the workers' minds and attentions are mostly on their work, the camera becoming merely a feature of their environment (like the woman with a clipboard who seems to be part of quality control), to be noticed only during the occasional inattention and looking around that accompanies their concentration. Is this essentially the same as the relationship between Kennedy or Humphrey and the camera in *Primary?*

Somehow, though, in *Human, Too Human* the fact that the aesthetic and philosophical basis is unstated, implicit, leads to bafflement and frustration more than it does in *Primary*. Could it be that we don't expect more from Drew Associates' journalistic approach than to see some interesting people

engaged in significant action? What is happening in Malle's film is unnews-
worthy in the extreme; it is uneventful, repetitious, and unstructured compared to the Drew Associates' films or even the institutional analyses of
Fred Wiseman. This allows us, forces us really, to ask why Malle is showing
us this material. Is there a hidden agenda? Is Malle quite sure in his own
mind what he is trying to say about these workers and their work and is
unable to communicate it? Or are we simply not grasping what he is saying?
Is this like those early Andy Warhole experiments in which the camera
merely offers for our contemplation a six-hour view of a naked sleeping
man (*Sleep*, 1963) and eight hours of the Empire State Building (*Empire*,
1964)?

When presented in this way actuality becomes strangely opaque and
unrevealing—or, again, ambiguous. The effect may not stem from an ambivalence on Malle's part (as in Wiseman's *Law and Order*, 1969, in which his
feelings about the Kansas City police at work become mixed). Malle's approach is seemingly one of openness, of unemotional response to what he
is observing. The deliberateness of this stance is much more apparent in
Human, Too Human than in "Phantom India," in which his commentary offers responses to what we are seeing. In spite of its apparent "reality," *Human, Too Human* is ultimately abstract. Though different in many ways, ultimately it presents audiences with difficulties in arriving at a sure sense of
what it's about, comparable to the "difficult" fiction films of Malle's New
Wave contemporaries like Jean-Luc Godard or Jacques Rivette.

Eventually I relax and enjoy *Human, Too Human* in a visceral way—the
hypnotic rhythm of these workers, the ritual of this work—and stop worry-
ing about its meaning. What they do seems so skillful I would like to be able
to do it; this is the same feeling I have watching Nanook construct an igloo.

The cultures Malle chooses tend to be "foreign" in one way or another
and he treats them as if there were underlying secrets and mysteries that an
outsider cannot see or know. This leaves us room to guess. Most English-
language documentarians attempt to answer the question of what a film is
about so clearly and emphatically that it will never be raised. This is not true
of the three French documentarians whose work we have just examined.

CONTEMPORARY FRENCH DOCUMENTARY
AND THE ANGLO-SAXON TRADITION

Though a limited sample, the six films discussed in this chapter are reason-
ably representative of contemporary French documentary. What I would
like to do in concluding this cross-cultural comparison is to see what characteristics they have in common and the ways in which they differ from the
documentary tradition of the English-speaking countries. They are not so
much distinguishable by their subjects—social attitudes of Parisians, Afri-

cans of a tribal culture in contact with a Westernized urban one, modern Japan, a bicycle race, the manufacture and selling of automobiles. Given available sponsorship, Grierson too might have made films about these subjects. But when we consider what interests the three French filmmakers in these subjects, the differences begin to emerge sharply.

First of all, the French approach is philosophical rather than sociological. Specifically, these films seem related to the branch of philosophy called phenomenology, in which the way of knowing is investigated along with what is known. Rather than didactic formulations, the French offer impressions and observations for contemplation. The Anglos tend to assume that reality is what we know it to be; "What to do about it?" is the relevant question. The French ask "What is reality?" They seem to expect us to reflect rather than to act, or even to understand exactly. (They do not suggest that exact understanding is possible.) When what seem to be social problems are dealt with in French documentary they are not presented as soluble. The situations are not seen as improvable (short of radical change, perhaps, if then). On the contrary, lacks and flaws are seen as being rooted in human nature and/or in the cultures humans have created.

Other differences occur in formal ways, in technique and style. In French documentaries the medium itself is put in the foreground, not rendered transparent as in the window-on-the-world approach to documentary. There is a playfulness with cinematic conventions in French documentaries; we are reminded frequently that we are watching a movie.

French documentaries contain ambiguities and offer complex symbolic meanings and feelings. They make use of counterpoint, paradox, and humor—rare in the Anglo-Saxon tradition.

The filmmakers intrude their viewpoints. They are striving to be uniquely personal in their work. This is contrary to the Grierson concept of the film unit made up of anonymous and selfless workers.

Finally, French documentaries are frequently devoted to a deconstruction of mythologies and ideologies rather than to an alteration or reinforcement of them, as is characteristic of the institutionally-sponsored English-language documentaries. (The French documentary economy is based on returns from theatrical and/or television showings and government awards for artistic quality. *Primes de qualité* for the production of short films made possible documentaries by Georges Franju, Alain Resnais, Chris Marker, and others.)

All in all, French documentaries are made more as aesthetic works (Grierson no doubt would have applied his term aestheticky) than are North American and British ones. They fall within modernist artistic creation generally. To be more specific, the characteristics one might note in the fiction films of the New Wave could be found in contemporary French documentary as well. This fusing of documentary with modernist film tendencies, especially from 1968 on, is the subject of the next chapter.

NOTES

[1]Ellen Freyer, "*Chronicle of a Summer*—Ten Years After," *The Documentary Tradition,* ed. Lewis Jacobs (New York: W. W. Norton & Company, Inc., 1979), pp. 437–43.
[2]Much of the description of *The Koumiko Mystery* is borrowed from a press release issued at the 1965 New York Film Festival.

FILMS OF THE PERIOD

Louis Malle

1962
Vive le Tour!

1964
Bon baisers de Bangkok (Good Kisses of Bangkok)

1969
Calcutta
"Phantom India" series

1972
Human, Too Human

1985
God's Country

1986
And the Pursuit of Happiness

Chris Marker

1953
Les Statues meurent aussi (The Statues also Weep, co-written and directed with Alain Resnais)

1955
Sunday in Peking

1958
Letter from Siberia

1960
Description of a Struggle

1961
Cuba Si!

1963
Le Joli Mai (The Lovely May)

1965
The Koumiko Mystery

1970
Cuba: Battle of the 10,000,000

1973
The Train Rolls On

1974
Loneliness of the Long Distance Runner

1977
Le Fond de l'air est rouge (The Bottom of the Air Is Red)

1982
Sans Soleil (Without Sun)

Jean Rouch

1955
Les Fils de l'eau (Water Currents)
Les Maîtres fous (The Mad Masters)

1958
Moi, un noir (Me, a Black)

1959
La Pyramide humaine (The Human Pyramid)

1961
Chronicle of a Summer (co-directed with Edgar Morin)

1963
Rose et Landry (Rose and Landry)

1965
The Lion Hunters

1967
Jaguar

BOOKS ON THE PERIOD

EATON, MICK, ed., *Anthropology—Reality—Cinema: The Films of Jean Rouch.* London: British Film
Institute, 1979. 77 pp.

ROLLET, RONALD T., guest ed., Spec. issue on *The Documentary Films of Louis Malle. Film Library
Quarterly.* 9.4 (1977). 64 pp.

SIXTEEN
BLURRING OF CONVENTIONAL DISTINCTIONS AMONG FICTION, DOCUMENTARY, AND EXPERIMENTAL, 1968–

In May of 1968 an uprising began in France at the University of Nanterres which spread to the Sorbonne and the Latin Quarter in Paris. The students established the seriousness of their protest against the government of President Charles de Gaulle and their solidarity with the working class. Students and workers were joined by professionals including many filmmakers. A general strike resulted. Ultimately, de Gaulle succeeded in defusing the situation, but ramifications from the uprising continued in France and spread to other countries. Nineteen-sixty-eight was a seminal year.

EUROPE

French filmmakers on the political Left formed cooperative production groups to make documentary and agit-prop films. Chris Marker had started SLON (Société pour le Lancement des Oeuvres Nouvelles/Society for the Launching of New Works) in late 1966. Given Marker's verbal agility and playfulness, he no doubt saw some significance in SLON being the Russian word for elephant. *Far from Vietnam* (1967) was its first production. A propaganda film against the war in Southeast Asia and the United States involvement in it, the documentary was made by six directors: Alain Resnais, Wil-

Three of its directors—left to right: Alain Resnais, Joris Ivens, Jean-Luc Godard—screen a rough-cut of *Far from Vietnam* (France, 1967, Chris Marker et al.). Museum of Modern Art/Film Stills Archive.

liam Klein, Joris Ivens, Agnes Varda, Claude Lelouch, and Jean-Luc Godard. Which segment each one contributed is deliberately obscured. Marker put the whole together. SLON then made films about French workers' problems and helped workers to make their own films. Among their many other projects was an homage to Alexander Medvedkin, *The Train Rolls On* (1973). Medvedkin was a pioneer Soviet filmmaker who had been in charge of film trains that moved about the country making films about local problems for local audiences.

Jean-Luc Godard established the Dziga Vertov Group in 1969, which made a number of documentaries and agit-prop mixtures of actuality and fiction, polemic and avant-garde. One example, *Pravda* (1969), uses the situation in Czechoslovakia as a basis to examine the "revisionism" moving established socialist states from left to right politically. Another, *See You at Mao* (also called *British Sounds*, 1969), deals with the working conditions of those on an auto assembly line in England and offers a feminist critique of leftist political attitudes about women.

These groups and other individuals were searching for means and methods for an alternative cinema that could function outside the capitalist system of financing and distribution. They were also searching for a new film aesthetic that would permit them to express their revolutionary attitudes in forms appropriate to them. Part of this search involved rejecting the traditional modes of narrative fiction, avant-garde experimentation, and documentary actuality. Or, rather, of mixing them in combinations that

would deny the viewer the accustomed emotional pleasures of the traditional modes and involve him or her in an active intellectual relationship
with the film.

Marker's films had played with cinematic conventions and audience
expectations long before 1968. *Far From Vietnam* includes newsreel footage,
a pair of traveling clowns, a mock book review interview, a historical compilation, a filmmaker speaking directly to the camera, a pop singer performing an antiwar ballad, and the speech of an American general photographed from a television set that moves in and out of kilter. Godard's
avowed purpose was to create cinematic structures that were as politically
effective as the statements within the films. He thus became aligned with
the concepts of distantiation associated with German Marxist playwright
Bertolt Brecht—rejecting narrative, denying audience identification with
characters, intentionally creating "displeasure" in the artistic experience.

Paralleling the political activity in France that climaxed in May 1968
were artistic developments that led to what would be called postmodernism.
Modernism, which had begun in the years between the turn of the century
and the outbreak of World War I, was a reaction against nineteenth-century
romantic literature and drama, and the eclecticism and decorativeness that
marked the visual arts. It was conceptual and analytical: Art became an
examination of art, each art trying to discover its own self-sufficient principles to differentiate itself from every other art. It was characterized by abstractionism, which took the forms of cubism, futurism, and the like. Film
became part of modernism in the avant-garde of the 1920s, and documentary took the form of the city symphonies (impressionism) discussed in
Chapter Four.

Though postmodernism is as yet lacking an agreed-upon definition,
the various understandings have in common a rejection of modernism. One
of the aspects of this reaction is the combining of various modes—just as
those experimenting with artistic forms for purposes of political discourse
were doing. In fact, Jean-Luc Godard became a leading figure in both political and aesthetic theory and experiment.

Godard has said that there are two kinds of cinema, Flaherty and
Eisenstein: There is documentary and there is theater; but that ultimately,
at the highest level, they are one and the same. Through documentary realism we arrive at the structure of theater, and through theatrical imagination
and fiction we arrive at the reality of life.[1] In *Sympathy for the Devil* (1968) and
elsewhere Godard mingled cinéma-vérité actuality with fictive elements. His
later films became defiantly expository and didactic. Voice-over commentaries, frequently deliberately overloaded, carried most of the content. In *Le
Gai Savoir* (1969), his first film after the May 1968 uprising, he abolished
narrative altogether (and alienated much of his audience) in an effort to
find a revolutionary form suitable to revolutionary content.

In developing a film form of mixed modes, Godard was joined by a

Sympathy for the Devil (a.k.a. *One Plus One;* U.K., 1968, Jean-Luc Godard). Museum of
Modern Art/Film Stills Archive.

number of filmmakers who shared his politics and aesthetics to one degree
or another. Among them was Vilgot Sjöman of Sweden. His *I Am Curious—
Yellow* (1967) and *I Am Curious—Blue* (1968) examine Swedish society in political and moral terms. (The colors in the titles are those of the Swedish flag.)
In *Yellow* Sjöman and a drama student named Lena Nyman play aspects of
themselves making the film, and offer a version of their relationship. The
film includes Yevgeny Yevtushenko, a Russian poet, reading his poetry to
a radical political organization. Lena interviews people on the streets of
Stockholm about the class system in Swedish society. Vilgot interviews Olof
Palme, then Minister of Transport in the Social Democratic government,
and subsequently Prime Minister, assassinated in 1986. There are other interviews, film of a protest march which Lena joins, and the like. This as-
sorted nonfiction material is interwoven with a story of Lena's relationships
with her father and with a car-salesman lover.

Political points are made in the story (sexual, anti-nuclear war, anti-
U.S. presence in Vietnam); the nonfiction material is partly contrived and
fantasized (someone presented as Martin Luther King, Jr., speaks to Lena
in voice-over). Politics and sex, the actual and the imagined, merge and affect each other—much as they do in life, seems to be implied.

But perhaps the filmmaker whose work has contributed most to the
expressive possibilities of mixed modes (alongside Godard), is Dušan Maka-

I Am Curious—Yellow (Sweden, 1967, Vilgot Sjöman). Museum of Modern Art/Film Stills Archive.

vejev of Yugoslavia. Beginning as a documentarian, he made some thirteen documentary shorts before his first feature, *Man Is Not a Bird* (1966). From that film on, Makavejev has employed the method of juxtaposing different modes of film communication in order to charge each piece with unexpected and deliberately ambiguous meanings.

The most significant Makavejev film combining modes is *WR: Mysteries of the Organism* (1971). Opening dedication titles tell us that "this film is in part a personal response to the life and teachings of Dr. Wilhelm Reich (1897–1957)." The psychologist Reich, early assistant to Sigmund Freud, argued the connection between sexual repression and political repression. (WR is also an acronym for World Revolution.) The opening titles include the observation that Reich had revealed "the deep roots of fear of freedom, fear of truth and fear of love in contemporary humans."

WR begins as a documentary about Reich shot in the U.S., replete with television-like interviews, earlier film footage of Reich, photos, newspaper headlines, background information provided in voice-over commentary, and the like. It ends as a fiction film shot in Yugoslavia centering around two young female roommates. One of them is engaged in more or less constant sexual activity with a Yugoslavian soldier, which seems to be mindless but apparently healthy enough. The other is theoretical and articulate about sexuality, politics, and the role of women in a socialist society. She becomes infatuated with a star of a visiting Russian ice follies whose name is Vladimir Ilyich (as was Lenin's). Rigid in his political and sexual views— "a genuine Red Fascist"—he murders her following intercourse.

The other sorts of filmic material interpolated into *WR* are even wider-ranging in type and more startling in placement than in Makavejev's earlier films. What he calls collage can be very funny, or sardonic, or savage; often the meaning of the juxtaposition is ambiguous or multi-layered. Archive material includes: a newsreel of a Chinese Communist celebration, with the assembled masses (holding their little red books) being regarded by Mao Tse-tung and other officials from a raised platform; horrendous medical footage of patients in a mental institution, one being subjected to electric shock treatment, another banging his head against a wall, a third crawling on all fours towards the camera; excerpts from a Soviet fiction feature (*The Vow*, 1947) deifying Joseph Stalin. Direct-cinema material not pertaining to Reich was shot mostly in New York City; much of it seems bizarre: a performer dressed as a combat marine equipped with a plastic replica of an M-16 rifle engages in guerrilla theater on the streets of Manhattan; an artist who paints subjects masturbating shows and discusses her work; a sculptor who makes plaster casts of sexual organs demonstrates her technique; a room full of patients writhe and groan on the floor while experiencing primal-scream psychotherapy. (What Makavejev thinks of all of this is not apparent.) Frequently the sound track, especially the music, is used in counterpoint to the images. It contains Communist hymns, the World War II (German) ballad "Lili Marlene," Smetana's "The Moldau," jaunty Serbian folk/pop tunes, a lugubrious U.S. pop/rock song the lyrics of which begin "Kill, kill, kill for peace."

WR is a difficult film to discuss; difficult even to recall except in vivid flashes. Though the introductory titles urge us to ENJOY, FEEL, LAUGH, the first time I saw the film I was startled and shocked, dreading what might come next. It *is* full of sex, full of politics, full of life (and death), of comedy and tragedy, of actuality and fiction—of ambiguity and contradictions.

But what at first viewing may seem random and unstructured, subsequently can be seen to have a clear thematic organization. It is dialectical rather than linear, however. Thesis is followed by antithesis rather than the rise of a narrative/dramatic line being followed by its fall. One sequence is in contrast to the next, sound alters the feeling and even the meaning of the visuals, and even the action within scenes is contradictory: what appears good (Stalin and the veneration of him by his people) may be awful; what is disturbing in appearance (unconventional psychotherapies and sexual behaviors) may in fact be good—liberating.

Makavejev has said that the whole film can be seen as a documentary—that the story and the many, diverse interpolations are merely extensions of the documentary about Reich and his theories. It was made in feature form, he has said, in order to reach a wider audience than would a documentary short. I would argue, however, and I think Makavejev might agree, that his conception of this subject matter—what he is saying—is embedded in this very special form and technique and could be communicated in no other way.

WR: Mysteries of the Organism (Yugoslavia, 1971, Dušan Makavejev). Museum of Modern Art/Film Stills Archive.

UNITED STATES

In this country it has not been the documentarians who have moved towards this sort of aesthetic experimentation; rather, it is experimental filmmakers who have used what might be thought of as documentary material (with an autobiographical core) as the basis for personal expression. Much of the work of Stan Brakhage, Bruce Conner, and Bruce Baillie seems to me to fit into this category.

Most of Brakhage's films describe his daily life: his wife and children, the house he lives in, the surrounding countryside, the death of his dog, and so on. He made *Gadflies* (1976), for example, about a reunion of a high school club he had belonged to. "The result," in the view of Fred Camper, then head of the film program at the School of the Art Institute of Chicago, where Brakhage has taught, "is a film which reflects some of the shifts of attention in a group meeting—from one person, one action, to another— as well as aspects of Brakhage's personal vision, characteristic of many of his films, which involve an unfixing or destabilizing of the existence of any specific object or situation."[2]

In the case of *The Governor* (1977), Camper observes that "Brakhage has seen through the figure of Colorado's present governor, Governor Lamm, a vision of the exercise of power—of the dominance of one individual over other individuals, over crowds, over rooms and buildings, over space itself. ... The formal style of the film can in fact be seen as representing the various forms of power which Lamm exercises."[3] So, documentary-like subjects and themes are absorbed into Brakhage's formal concerns, techniques, and styles.

Bruce Conner has worked mainly within the compilation form, constructing his films from bits and pieces of old newsreels, animated cartoons,

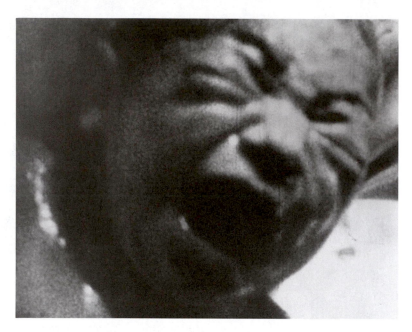

Window Water Baby Moving (U.S., 1959, Stan Brakhage).
Museum of Modern Art/Film Stills Archive.

Hollywood features, war documentaries, academy ("count-down") leader, home movies, and soft-core pornography. In *Report* (1967) he inserted kinescopes of television news coverage of the assassination of President John F. Kennedy on November 22, 1963, into a collage of documentary, feature, instructional, commercial, and experimental film clips in an impressionistic review of the sounds and images of that precise time. *Crossroads* (1976) is built entirely from declassified film records of early atomic bomb tests. Using films of many kinds to document a time also documents kinds of film that exist.

Bruce Baillie has connected even more directly documentary and experimental (and implicit autobiographical narrative) impulses, forms, and styles. Beginning in 1963 he embarked on a series of major films. Fred Camper, again, extends my observation about the duality of this work.

"The career of Bruce Baillie has two central aspects, which are also features of the whole American avant-garde film movement. First his films are generally intensely poetic, lyrical evocations of persons and places in which the subject matter is transformed by the subjective methods used to photograph it." *To Parsifal* (1963) and *Castro Street* (1966) come to mind especially. "Second, many of his films display a strong social awareness, describing attitudes critical towards, and alienated from, mainstream American society." *Mass for the Dakota Sioux* (1964) and *Quixote* (1967, revised version) are

Report (U.S., 1967, Bruce Conner). John Caldwell.

prominent examples. In many cases Baillie fuses these concerns within single films. *Quick Billy* (1970), as Camper points out, "contains thematic and stylistic elements of most of Baillie's previous films; its motifs include autobiography, 'portrait'–like representation of people and events, and an underlying theme, made explicit in the film's final section, of Western man's aggressiveness toward his surroundings."[4] Since *Quixote* is perhaps closest to documentary, I would like to provide more detail about it.

Baillie shot *Quixote* during a six-month tour of the United States. It includes a large number and variety of images of American life ranging from workmen to high school cheerleaders to Western Indians. The film opens with a closeup of an old man, a resident of the Rockies. He talks incoherently about some recent event, and the title appears in superimposition. The element of the hero's quest is introduced: Quixote/Baillie is searching for ideals in a land where ideals are quickly disappearing. The old man squints, looks up, and his voice is drowned out by the roar of an airplane. A Goldwater for President poster is examined closely by the camera, and Senator Goldwater's words are heard: " ... only the strong can rule—only the strong can keep the peace."

This idea is central to the film. Who are the strong? The strong are the man who herds the pigs near the end of the film, the man who pushes the horse into the trailer, the armed policemen who stand by the Negro march, the men in the stock exchange, the soldiers in Vietnam, the men who work the computers, and—potentially strong—the fiercely competing high school basketball players. Who are the weak? They are the penned animals, the Indians and their children, the cucumber pickers, and the victims of war.[5]

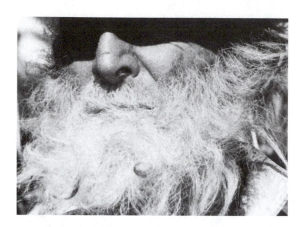

Quixote (U.S., 1967, Bruce Baillie).
Bruce Baillie.

Throughout his work Baillie celebrates nature, spaces, animals; he sympathizes with simpler, more traditional ways and cultures, the old, the weak. He castigates the strong, the synthetic, the mass-produced, the cluttered. He is against the despoilment of the physical environment, militarism and imperialism, mass entertainment, and racism. These topics were of special concern in the late 1960s and many documentaries were made about them. If Baillie is an experimental filmmaker, he is dealing with documentary material in forms that fall as easily into the documentary mode as the experimental.

Another kind of fusion in the work of American independent filmmakers within the past two decades has connected documentary with fiction and acted performances. An early and influential example is *David Holzman's Diary* (1968). It concerns a young man who begins filming his apartment, his girlfriend, the people in his neighborhood, and every aspect of his life with his portable sync-sound camera rig. Initially the film appears to be a direct-cinema documentary about such a situation. David Holzman is inspired by his conviction that the motion-picture camera is capable of recording and representing "truth." But his obsession with trying to capture everything as it really exists rather than leading him closer to reality removes him from it. As the film progresses the Eclair NPR camera and Nagra tape recorder replace David Holzman as protagonist. Further, when the credits appear at the end we discover that we have been subjected to a hoax. *David Holzman's Diary* was directed by James McBride aided by L. M. Kit Carson, who plays Holzman and wrote much of the dialogue; cinematography was by Michael Wadleigh. This is a fictional film about documentary filmmaking—about reality and illusion.

No Lies (Mitchell Block, 1973), shot in cinéma-vérité style, is a fictional film about rape. Pretending to be a documentary, it plays upon our expectations until we discover at the end that what we wish had not happened in fact has not happened.

David Holzman's Diary (U.S., 1968, Jim McBride). Museum of Modern Art/Film Stills Archive.

Another filmmaker who has worked in a similar vein is Michelle Citron. Her two most recent and well-known films, *Daughter Rite* (1978) and *What You Take for Granted* (1983), experiment with the traditional modes in the process of exploring issues of central concern to women. *Daughter Rite* is about the position of women in the nuclear family. It concentrates on the relationship between two daughters and their mother, and between each other. *What You Take for Granted* addresses the situation of women in jobs thought of traditionally as "man's work." They work as doctor, artist, carpenter, philosophy professor, cable splicer, and truck driver.

Both films are acted but the roles and the dialogue are drawn from extensive interviews—around forty in the first, fifty in the second. Citron has explained about the technique that

> the films are visually coded to look like documentaries. *Daughter Rite* is visually coded to look like cinéma vérité, complete with rack focusing, panning back and forth between people in conversation, not having the camera where the action is, and so forth. *What You Take for Granted* is done in a more didactic documentary style with talking head shots. But while the films are visually coded to be seen as documentaries they are always done with actors. In that sense they are fake.

Citron's strategy seems the reverse of that used by the makers of the British semidocumentaries of World War II discussed in Chapter Seven. In those films real R.A.F. airmen, say, performed roles scripted for them; here actors play roles the "real persons" suggested in interviews.

In both Citron films the documentary-style scenes alternate with other modes of cinema. In *Daughter Rite* the fake cinéma vérité is combined with sequences more along the lines of experimental film—a diary soundtrack is joined to slowed, looped, and rephotographed home movies. In *What You Take for Granted* the fake interview-didactic sequences alternate with a fictional narrative—a developing relationship between the truck driver and the doctor. Speaking to this point Citron has said:

> In both films the motivation for mixing modes involved a strategy for examining the issues. As far as I'm concerned, there is no one truth, no single perspective that will give you the truth. And I think that the only way you can even approximate or approach it is by having multiple perspectives. . . . The kind of information you get in one style is very different from the kind of information you get in another style, and that's inherent in the form itself.

The alternation forces a recognition of the way films construct reality for us; the films challenge assumptions about the "reality" of documentary in

Daughter Rite (U.S., 1978, Michelle Citron). Michelle Citron.

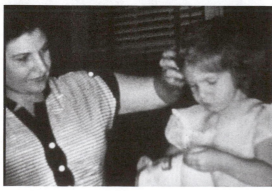

relation to narrative or experimental. Without weighing the value of the different approaches the juxtaposition emphasizes the relativity of meaning and experience available in any single film version or construction of an event.[6]

Another independent filmmaker, Jill Godmilow, has mixed the cinematic modes even more than Citron or McBride. The title of her *Far from Poland* (1984) suggests she was thinking of *Far from Vietnam* (1967, discussed at the outset of this chapter) while she was making it. The films are alike in at least two respects. Both confront a similar problem: filmmakers unable to visit the country their film is about. Both employ a similar solution: the use of whatever means are available to offer impressions of what the situation in that country might be like and of the filmmakers' attitudes about it.

When she started on the project it was Godmilow's intention to visit Poland to make a film about the Solidarity labor union established in 1980. She described herself as a person "steeped in the documentary traditions of the left" who was determined to show the world the road to salvation through the "miracle" of the Polish Solidarity movement.

When martial law was imposed in 1981 and Solidarity outlawed, Godmilow was denied a visa to shoot in Poland. Instead, she began to construct a film in New York City. Onto a small amount of uneventful footage shot by Solidarity film people she added dramatic reenactments of Solidarity texts, formally composed "vignettes," and swatches of soap opera, as she put it. An actress gives a convincing and moving performance as a fired Gdansk shipyard worker being interviewed.

The film begins with Godmilow in her apartment talking to the camera (us), explaining her motivations for making it and the procedures she followed. It's partly a film about the making of a film, she says; she identifies its ingredients. Through this effort she hopes to engage us in her personal definition of the Polish struggle. The film proceeds.

Two television sets in her apartment add images to the film image. On one the Solidarity footage appears; on the other a welder, who seems to be an actor, perhaps in a TV commercial. He is talking about Jill and her political ideas. This is her lover, Mark Magill, playing *a worker*—part of his joking. "Mark made it," Jill says. The main title appears, with grease pencil marks indicating that (1) it is a film and (2) that it is an unfinished work print— a work in progress. In addition to her stated goals, what Godmilow attempts throughout is to discredit the myth of "documentary truth," and to expand the vocabulary of filmmaking.

An "Epilogue 1988," the penultimate sequence, contains a reading of letters purported to be from General Jaruzelski (head of the Polish state) to his daughter. They are literary, pensive, melancholy. It is not clear (to me) exactly what is being said by them. Godmilow concedes of *Far from Poland* that it is ideologically incorrect from *every* point of view.[7]

Far from Poland (U.S., 1984, Jill Godmilow). National Film Archive/Stills Library.

The film ends as it began—Jill talking to the camera. This is her statement, she says: what she knows and feels at this moment.

Perhaps more than the work of Marker or Godard this film resembles that of Sjöman or Makavejev. In any case, its mixture of private and public, subjective and objective, fact and fantasy, of the traditional mode of documentary with narrative and experimental suggest European analogues. Or maybe *Far from Poland* and mixed mode films like it point to the future more than to the past, suggesting a new understanding of documentary, a new role for it in relation to other forms of film expression and to actuality.

More conventional mixtures of modes have occurred in those direct-cinema films in which the filmmakers have manipulated actuality footage in order to tell "true stories." *Salesman* (1969), by Alfred and David Maysles and Charlotte Zwerin, is an example. This account of a group of Bible salesmen at work centers on Paul, whose efforts are ineffectual, awkward, and pitiable, to the point of increasing failure. Clearly the situations we see had to be set up to be filmed and the action edited (and at least partly reordered chronologically) to follow a narrative line. *Streetwise* (1985), made by Martin Bell, Mary Ellen Mark, and Cheryl McCall, is an even more skillful, convincing, and moving example of actuality—derelict kids on the streets of Seattle—bent into narrative form.

Streetwise (U.S., 1985, Martin Bell, Mary Ellen Mark, and Cheryl McCall). Museum of Modern Art/Film Stills Archive.

But traditional purposes and methods have continued as the main line for documentary. The next, final chapter will survey its practice in North America over the past two decades.

NOTES

[1] Tom Milne, trans. and ed., *Godard on Godard* (London: Martin Secker & Warburg Limited, 1972), p. 181.

[2] Fred Camper, program note for the showing of *Gadflies, Window, Trio, Rembrandt etc.*, and *Jane* (all 1976) at the Film Center, School of the Art Institute of Chicago, January 25, 1977.

[3] Fred Camper, program note for the showing of *The Domain of the Moment, Soldiers and Cosmic Objects, The Governor* (all 1977), at the Film Center, School of the Art Institute of Chicago, October 25, 1977.

[4] Fred Camper, "Bruce Baille," *The International Dictionary of Films and Filmmakers: Volume II* (Chicago: St. James Press, Inc., 1984), pp. 33–34.

[5] Much of this description comes from an unpublished study by Jerry Sider quoted by James Leahy in a program note for the Northwestern Summer Film Series (Twelfth Series, Fifth Program, 1970).

[6] In this discussion of Michelle Citron I have drawn heavily on an interview conducted by Mimi White: "Exploring *What We Take for Granted*," *Afterimage* (December 1984), pp. 7–11.

[7] Some of these observations about Jill Godmilow and her intentions in *Far from Poland* are drawn from a promotional flyer published by the distributor, Beach Street Films.

FILMS OF THE PERIOD

1967
Far from Vietnam (France, Alain Resnais, William Klein, Joris Ivens, Agnes Varda, Claude Lelouch, Jean-Luc Godard)
I Am Curious—Yellow (Sweden, Vilgot Sjöman)
Love Affair: or The Case of the Missing Switchboard Operator (Yugoslavia, Dušan Makavejev)
Quixote (U.S., Bruce Baillie)
Report (U.S., Bruce Conner)

1968
David Holzman's Diary (U.S., Jim McBride and L. M. Kit Carson)
I Am Curious—Blue (Sweden, Sjöman)
Innocence Unprotected (Yugoslavia, Makavejev)
One Plus One/Sympathy for the Devil (U.K., Godard)

1969
British Sounds/See You at Mao (U.K., Dziga Vertov Group)
Le Gai Savoir (The Joy of Learning, France, Godard)
Lotte in Italia/Struggle in Italy (France, Dziga Vertov Group)
Pravda (same as above)

1970
Vladimir and Rosa (same as above)
Wind from the East (same as above)

1971
WR: Mysteries of the Organism (Yugoslavia, Makavejev)

1972
Letter to Jane: Investigation of a Still (France, Godard and Jean-Pierre Gorin)
Tout va bien (Just Great, same as above)

1973
No Lies (U.S., Mitchell Block)

1976
Crossroads (U.S., Conner)

1978
Daughter Rite (U.S., Michelle Citron)

1983
What You Take for Granted (same as above)

1984
Far from Poland (U.S., Jill Godmilow)

SEVENTEEN
DOCUMENTARY IN NORTH AMERICA, 1967–

The documentary impulse has always been linked closely to its social and intellectual environment. In the 1920s Flaherty's films were set within the beginnings of anthropology and interest in comparative cultures. Vertov and the Soviet filmmakers attempted to meet the needs of a new state, the first communist society. The continental realists were part of the avant-garde, experimenting with artistic means for expressing concepts coming from the physical and psychological sciences.

The 1930s documentaries were connected with social and political innovations and upheavals. Totalitarian regimes used them to gain the allegiance of their peoples. In Britain and the United States they were used to try to strengthen democratic societies in the face of ailing economies at home and fascist aggression abroad.

The 1940s were the years of World War II and its aftermath. During the first half of that decade documentaries were used in unprecedented numbers by the English-speaking countries in their fight against the Axis powers. In the second half, the United States, and to some extent Britain and Canada, employed documentary in the Cold War against communism.

The 1950s, in the U.S. at least, were marked by conservatism and complacency; and, as it would subsequently appear, hidden uncertainties. It was not a significant or innovative decade for documentary except as new types of subjects and forms compatible with distribution nontheatrically and over television were explored.

In the 1960s political developments in Europe (especially a civil uprising in France) and an aesthetic shift towards postmodernism led to the radical purposes and mixtures of forms dealt with in Chapter Sixteen. In this chapter an assessment of parallel developments in the U.S. and Canada during the past two decades will be offered, beginning with social protest manifest in North American forms.

HOLLYWOOD AT THE BARRICADES

Spread across the sixties were the civil rights movement, with sit-ins, marches, and riots, and the Vietnam War resistance, with demonstrations, moratoriums, and student strikes. Along with these protest movements there arose a youth culture, as it was called. Young people in large numbers disassociated themselves from what they regarded as their parents' exclusive concern with material accumulation, lack of honesty and decency in dealing with each other, and complacency, apathy, and conformity within a society dominated by big business and the governmental and educational systems that seemed to be in collusion with it. Some of them "dropped out" of society into drugs, Eastern mysticism, and communes. Others actively attacked the political-economic structure that had dictated our involvement in what they regarded as an immoral war, and which tolerated poverty, injustice, and racial discrimination at home.

The spirit of these times was echoed in a cycle of entertainment features called the "youth films" or the "now films," which achieved significant popularity before tapering off—as did the protest movements themselves. They explored social, and some of them political, problems in one way or another. A few sounded strong notes of dissent. They also combined forms—documentary and experimental styles and subject matter along with those of conventional fiction—in ways that some of the recent films coming from abroad were doing (those of Godard and Makavejev, for example).

The trend started off indirectly in 1967 with three of the most popular releases of that year: *Bonnie and Clyde, The Graduate,* and *Cool Hand Luke.* Though *Bonnie and Clyde* was a sort of gangster film set in the rural America of the thirties, encoded within it were themes of current youthful protest: the individual against the system, and the implicit justification of violence directed against the impersonal institutions of society and the conscientious, middle-aged, and humorless people who served them. *The Graduate,* more explicit if less bold and beautiful, expressed other manifestations of contemporary youthful tension and conflict. *Cool Hand Luke* may seem a peripheral case, but it was about another resister, a passive protester who wouldn't buckle under to the demands of his society (in this case, prison).

Easy Rider (U.S., 1969, Dennis Hopper). Museum of Modern Art/Film Stills Archive.

In 1969 the youth/now cycle proper began with *Easy Rider, Medium Cool, Zabriskie Point,* and *Alice's Restaurant. Easy Rider* was the seminal film. Those two young men "in search of America" were adopted as youth-cult heroes. Like Bonnie and Clyde, Billy and Captain America were killed by the squares and the rednecks. *Easy Rider* spawned a profusion of features with related themes, some of them much more direct in their criticism of the dominant values of contemporary American society, but discussion of them belongs in another book. Here we can merely note that documentary impulses, subjects, and forms spilled over into fiction features.

CHALLENGE FOR CHANGE

During the years Hollywood was reflecting social conflict and change, documentary became increasingly militant and activist. In 1967, at the National Film Board of Canada, a project began that used documentary in a quite new way. Called Challenge for Change, it was first headed by John Kemeny. In 1968 George Stoney, an American documentarian (*All My Babies,* 1952; *Still Going Places,* 1956), was hired as its director.

The concept behind Challenge for Change was to provide citizens access to the media to express their concerns and needs and to create a dialogue with agencies of government involved in social programs. This, of course, was closer to the Grierson idea of using documentary for social improvement than to the Flaherty one of recording existing cultures—hammer rather than mirror. Grierson, after all, had been the first Film Commissioner of Canada. But, unlike Grierson, and any other prior filmmaker, Challenge for Change was proposing that rather than communicating *to* the people, or even *for* the people, it would attempt to make films *with* the people. Eventually this led to enabling the *people* to make their own films. Grierson characterized this program as "decentralizing the power of propaganda."

The first Challenge for Change project, begun in the summer of 1967, was directed by Colin Low, a crack NFB filmmaker (*Corral,* 1953; *City of Gold,* 1957; *Universe,* 1960). It addressed the problems of Fogo Island, off the coast of Newfoundland. The Fogo economy would no longer support the traditional fishing lives that its people wanted to continue. A high proportion of the inhabitants were on welfare; others were moving out. Sociologists from St. John's Memorial University along with NFB filmmakers studied and recorded the situation. Some twenty hours of footage were shot and made into twenty-eight short films.

Some of these documented and celebrated the culture of Fogo to reinforce and rejuvenate the pride of the residents. One was about Arnold, an aged folk singer; another a wedding; a third a party with music and dancing. Other films, intended to provoke discussion, showed divisions in the community that people simply hadn't been able to deal with. One film about the Improvement Committee revealed that many people thought it a strange group that met at a motel and drank beer in secret. Another dealt with differences between old fishermen and young ones. In a third the welfare system was shown to be under open attack.

Out of a second large-scale Challenge for Change project came a film entitled *You Are on Indian Land* (1969). It resulted from the closing of a bridge across the St. Lawrence River on Cornwall Island, Ontario. A treaty in 1794 had given the Mohawk Indians the right to free passage across the river. The Indian unit of Challenge for Change instigated a protest demonstration. While the mass media coverage stressed violence in this confrontation, the cinéma-vérité record shows this view as distorted—that almost everyone behaved humanely.

Screenings were held for the Mohawks, the Royal Canadian Mounted Police, the Cornwall police, the city administration, and representatives from Indian Affairs. This was the first time these people had ever sat down together. Subsequent screenings were held in the Parliament Building in Ottawa. Eventually the decision to close the bridge was rescinded.

On the Fogo Island project the NFB crew did all the production. For *You Are on Indian Land* the Indian film unit and the Cornwall Mohawks were involved in the editing as well as the shooting. In subsequent Challenge for Change work, following the introduction of portable 1/2" videotape re-

God Help the Man Who Would Part with His Land (Canada, 1970, George Stoney), a Challenge for Change production of the National Film Board which followed *You Are on Indian Land*. George Stoney.

corders around 1970, the people were taught to use the equipment and made their own tapes.

Lightweight video permitted citizens to tape and present their problems—as they saw them—to officials in a position to do something about them. The officials could then be taped responding to the tape, and their reaction in turn be viewed by the citizens. One attempt to use the video medium as a public forum as *VTR St. Jacques* (1969). It represents an extension of the documentation of social malaise and impotent complaint first evident in the French *Chronicle of a Summer* (1961) and *Le Joli Mai* (1963) into social action. Another such tape, *Up Against the System* (1969), concludes with an elderly woman outside a welfare office exclaiming to the camera: "You know what they need here? They need a revolution!"

PORTAPACKS AND PUBLIC ACCESS CABLE

When George Stoney showed some of this Canadian work to U.S. welfare officials in Washington, they asked two questions: "Does the government know you're doing this sort of thing?" and, "How long do you think you can get away with it?" Eventually Challenge for Change was allowed to wither and die, but not before it had established a precedent for the use of media by citizen organizations.

In the United States there is no tradition of government communication with citizens in peacetime that goes beyond passing out information (grudgingly sometimes) or propagandizing for a particular government department (secretly sometimes). We have no national film board concerned with two-way communication between government and citizens. But since the early 1970s, public access to cable television has opened up possibilities like those achieved by Challenge for Change before its demise.

In 1970 Stoney returned to the States to head the undergraduate film program at New York University. One of his first actions there, with colleague Red Burns, was to set up an Alternative Media Center to promote and support the use of public access cable. New York City public access channels began operation in 1971. In 1972 federal legislation reserved public access channels in all new cable installations in the hundred top markets in the country. It has seemed to Stoney, and to others, that public access channels fit within our own tradition of freedom of speech for all the people and nicely accommodate portapacks and videotape technology.

Independent documentary video production sprang up in the late 1960s and early 1970s. Frequently the tapes were conceived as alternatives to television network documentaries of the time which, it was felt, had failed to illuminate critical social issues and had served, instead, only to applaud U.S. exploits abroad and at home. Many of the alternative media operations were cooperatives bearing names such as Videofreex, Video Free America, Raindance, and Videopolis. Nearly all of these groups saw their mission as one of revolutionary scope—to inform and educate the public towards social action and social change. New York City was a center for this early activity. When it spread out into New York State it took on a community focus that has remained characteristic of access use. Here are a couple examples.

In 1971 a community video experiment began in Port Washington, New York, under the direction of Walter Dale. Operating out of the public library, classes were held for residents to show how to operate the camera and equipment that had been acquired through a grant from the New York Council on the Arts. A series of videotapes were produced which attempted a portrait of the community. These tapes were made available at the library so that people could check them out just as books were checked out. Following these initial tapes, a community electronic bulletin board was established. By 1972 nearly seventy organizations had used the project to express their views or had taken its classes.

In much the same vein, Woodstock Community Video was founded in 1971 for the purpose of opening channels for community interaction. It started with the taping of local candidates running for political office, playing back these tapes on the streets, and taping the passersby reactions to the candidates and showing that in turn. After many videotapes about local issues were made by local people with public forum screenings, the local cable company provided a studio for local origination programming in 1973.

One of the most widely seen productions to come out of this sort of activity was *Police Tapes* (1976), made by Alan and Susan Raymond, about a police station in the South Bronx. It was funded by the TV Lab of public television station WNET (Channel 13) of New York City and grants from the Ford Foundation and the National Endowment for the Arts. The tape-makers rode in patrol cars, recorded what they saw and heard, and talked with the police about their work. What resulted is a chilling view of criminal activity in the city and of public servants trying to do an impossible job.

Another noteworthy venture was *Giving Birth* (1976), produced by Global Village (an independent video group in New York City) in associa-tion with the TV Lab at WNET. It is about the issue of traditional childbirth versus some of the newer "relaxed environment"/natural childbirth tech-niques. Made by Julie Gustafson and John Reilly (another husband-wife team), the tape focuses on four couples. Like the Raymonds, Reilly and Gus-tafson spent a great amount of time getting to know their subject. They avoided a "white paper" approach, opting more for personal observation

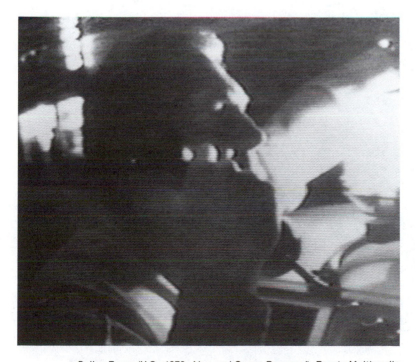

Police Tapes (U.S., 1976, Alan and Susan Raymond). Facets Multimedia.

which at the same time introduces prospective parents to choices that could be made among the various procedures.

DOCUMENTARY FILMS: GENERALIZATIONS

While videotape and public access have led documentary into new subjects, forms, and uses, American documentary not made for television seems in many ways connected to its beginnings in the 1930s. Take, for instance, the youthful, left-wing, antiwar collective named Newsreel, which was established in 1967. Like the Film and Photo League, which began in 1930, Newsreel started in New York and spread to other cities—Boston, Chicago, San Francisco, and Los Angeles. It quickly made many films. They were mostly short agit-prop pieces running from six to twenty-five minutes. To sympathetic audiences they seemed to be telling it like it is; to others they seemed merely crude and strident. Three examples will have to suffice. *Columbia Revolt* (1968) documented an occupation by students of the administration building at Columbia University. *Pig Power* (1969) showed street fighting between demonstrators and police cut to the beat of a rock-and-roll soundtrack. *The Woman's Film* (1970) was one of the first feminist documentaries to deal with working-class women and their problems.

60 Minutes, the most popular nonfiction series in the history of television, began in 1968. It is in some ways a contemporary equivalent of "The March of Time," which began in 1935. Both are documentary-like rather than documentary in the traditional sense; both apply journalistic motives

Columbia Revolt (U.S., 1968, Newsreel). Michael Renov and University of California Press.

and practices to audio-visual forms—"pictorial journalism" was Louis de Rochemont's phrase for "March of Time." *60 Minutes* was discussed in Chapter Twelve.

Federal government documentary made for general public viewing scarcely exists in the United States today, as it scarcely existed before or after Pare Lorentz's work in Washington between 1935 and 1940. (The short-lived United States Film Service was discussed in Chapter Six.) Films are made for use by the Armed Forces and occasionally shown publicly to support military policy (in Vietnam, for example); films are made and used by the Department of Agriculture; films are produced and distributed overseas by the United States Information Agency, a branch of the Department of State. It took a special resolution passed by Congress before *Years of Lightning, Day of Drums* (1968), about President John F. Kennedy (produced by the USIA five years after his assassination), could be shown in this country.

The nongovernment documentaries of the past two decades, like those of the 1930s, have tended to be large in scale and left-wing politically—to have "progressive tendencies," as it would have been put earlier. The achievements—the power of their social statements and the vitality and originality of their artistic forms—have been considerable. Finding funding for them and reaching audiences once they are made are only a little less difficult today than they were in the thirties.

Generally American documentaries have remained traditional in mode rather than becoming experiments in mixed forms like those discussed in Chapter Sixteen. Grierson's influence can still be seen even if the American films tend toward ends different from his. They are more likely to be counterculture in their orientation, intended not so much to make the social system work better as to expose its inadequacies. A much greater proportion of them are made by women than was ever true earlier.

VETERAN FILMMAKERS

Four major male figures, however, have been the sturdiest and most influential documentary makers during the past twenty years. Two are Canadian—Donald Brittain and Michael Rubbo—and two American—Emile de Antonio and Frederick Wiseman. All four entered filmmaking following other careers.

Donald Brittain worked as a journalist until he joined the National Film Board in 1954 as a writer. He has scripted most of his own films (as well as those of many of his colleagues); frequently he has collaborated on their direction. Brittain's "writing" is really his matching of words and images; the creative process for him exists centrally in editing. In this respect he makes me think of Stuart Legg's work on "The World in Action" series in the early days of the Film Board. Or, perhaps even more, of Chris Marker's. Both Brittain and Marker have an insatiable and uninhibited curiosity about people and a wry sense of humor. Brittain's approach is characteristically oblique and understated, yet he involves me with his subjects and the films they're in in a way that makes them stick firmly in my memory. This is especially true of three films made within a short time span.

Ladies and Gentlemen, Mr. Leonard Cohen (1966, with Don Owen) is an affectionate, nonadulatory portrait of the then young Canadian poet, who is allowed to participate fully in the presentation. Lest we take him too seriously, Cohen himself offers an injunction for us at the end of the film, written on a steamy glass while bathing: *caveat emptor*—let the buyer beware. Nonetheless, his talent and charm emerge in a completely engaging way.

The title *Never a Backward Step* (1967, with Arthur Hammond and John Spotton) is the heraldic motto of Lord Thomson of Fleet, who seems to have more or less purchased his title and created a mythical lineage. Canadian Roy Thomson developed a global broadcasting and newspaper empire (including Scottish Television, which aired John Grierson's long-running, popular *This Wonderful World* series). The film's view of Thomson's pomposity and ability is sly but not unkindly. Lord Thomson himself might have enjoyed it, had he found time to see it.

Memorandum (1966, with John Spotton) is an account of a reunion of Jewish survivors of Nazi concentration camps twenty years after their liberation. It centers especially on a Canadian father making the pilgrimage with his teen-age son. This subject seems scarcely open to the whimsical, irreverent approach characteristic of Brittain, yet he manages to root his observation in the mundane actual—to make very real the banality of horror. In

Never a Backward Step (Canada, 1967, Donald Brittain, Arthur Hammond, and John Spotton), Lord Thomson on the right. National Film Board.

my view, *Memorandum* is a great film on the subject of the Holocaust, comparable to Alain Resnais's *Night and Fog*. Here is a sample of its commentary.

> This is one of the more popular sights at the camp.
> The gallows where the Poles hanged the camp commandant,
> Rudolph Hess, after the war.

> His father meant him to be a priest. "I have to pray and go
> to church endlessly," he said later, "and do penance for the
> slightest misdeed."

> They worked for the SS office of Economy and Administration.
> Many were family men.
> They would go home in the evening
> and make love to their wives.

> Heinrich Himmler was proud of them. He said once—
> "To have stuck it out and remained decent fellows,
> This is a page of glory never to be written."

> ......

> And who will ever know
> who murdered by memorandum,
> who did the filing and the typing from nine o'clock to five,
> with an hour off for lunch.

And, of the visitors to the camp, and the questions it raises:

> But why should that darken the festive summer night?
> A third of them are tourists,
> a third were too young,
> and the other third is sick and tired of the whole business.[1]

Emile de Antonio came to film after careers as a philosophy professor,
a longshoreman, and an art promoter. His documentaries, all feature-
length, have received some theatrical distribution. Consistently he has advanced a left-wing point of view, frequently using compilation—"radical sca-
venging" he has called his activity—and avoiding the mainstream of cinéma-
vérité/direct cinema.

De Antonio's first success was *Point of Order* (1964), made from kinescopes of the televised 1954 Army-McCarthy Senate hearings. The title
comes from an oft repeated interruption of the proceedings by Senator
Joseph McCarthy—"Point of order, Mr. Chairman"—and the film allows the
Senator to discredit himself and his methods without voice-over commentary or manipulation of the footage other than reducing 188 hours to 97
minutes.

Emile de Antonio. Museum of Modern Art/Film Stills Archive.

Point of Order was followed by *Rush to Judgment* (1967), an investigation of the assassination of John F. Kennedy related to a book of the same title. It challenged the Warren Commission's conclusion that a "lone assassin" was responsible.

America Is Hard to See (1968) chronicles the unsuccessful 1968 presidential campaign of Senator Eugene McCarthy, who favored our withdrawal from Vietnam.

From *Point of Order* (U.S., 1964, Emile de Antonio), counsel for the Army, Joseph Welsch, in a characteristic gesture. Museum of Modern Art/Film Stills Archive.

The *Year of the Pig* (1969) is a compilation about the history of the Vietnam War. It uses a "collage" (a term de Antonio uses, as does Makavejev) of news footage, political propaganda, antiwar speeches, and other sorts of evidence and argument. It is highly critical of United States involvement.

Milhouse: A White Comedy (1971) is a witty and savage attack on Richard Milhouse Nixon made the year before he was elected president. It was compiled from newsreel and television footage and interviews with various political commentators.

Underground (1977), made with Mary Lampson and Haskell Wexler, concerns the Weatherpeople, persons of radical politics who advocated and used violence in their confrontation with the political system during and following the 1968 Democratic Convention in Chicago. Since that time they had been in hiding, to avoid arrest and arraignment.

Michael Rubbo was an Australian painter and photographer, with an education and interest in anthropology, who joined the National Film Board in 1965, after studying film at Stanford University. His best known film is *Sad Song of Yellow Skin* (1970). Another I remember especially well is *Waiting for Fidel* (1974). In an interview with Rubbo, Alan Rosenthal, also a documentary filmmaker and alumnus of Stanford, cites three distinctive aspects of Rubbo's work especially evident in these two films. First, his use of a diary form. Second, Rubbo's presence in his own films, either giving a low-key commentary (*Sad Song*) or actually participating in the action (*Waiting for Fidel*). Third is his avoidance of the expected.[2]

Sad Song was shot in Vietnam in 1969. Rather than military action, then at its peak, we see life on the streets of Saigon: the shoeshine kids ("dust of the streets"), three idealistic young American journalists trying to help them, the opium lady, who died in the tomb she lived in while the film was being shot, and a little monk in saffron robes who takes a symbolic walk each day from Saigon to Hanoi and back. In talking about his work on this and other films, Rubbo says, "these days I even make a virtue of being unprepared." He then advances a position that sounds rather like Frances Flaherty talking about her husband's nonpreconception and finding his story by living with his subjects. Rubbo: "You go out with vague ideas about what you want and then just let things happen, trusting in your good instincts. I know it sounds dangerous, but life will inevitably serve up much better stories than you could ever think up beforehand. The trick is to get involved, to get in."[3]

Waiting for Fidel (see photo p. 284) came about in a curious way. A multi-millionaire owner of radio and television stations, Geoff Stirling, had arranged an interview with the President of Cuba. He invited along his old friend Joey Smallwood, ex-premier of Newfoundland, and a Film Board crew headed by Rubbo. When Castro failed to appear, Rubbo began recording the ongoing dialectic between capitalist Stirling and socialist Smallwood about what they were seeing in communist Cuba. The making of the film itself became part of the argument. Stirling was furious about what he regarded as the waste and nonprofessionalism of shooting a non-event at a ratio of 20 to 1. Following one of these confrontations Rubbo asked his cameraman, Doug Kieffer, if he appeared in the shot. "Are you in the shot," Kieffer replied, "my God, you are all over the shot."[4]

Rubbo concluded his interview with Rosenthal by saying:

> I'm not a true believer, and am becoming less of one every day. I distrust more and more those who say they have the answers. The idealists and the utopians. I tend to want to be a weakener of strong positions where blind strength and dogmatism go together. I want to say hold on now, there's another side to that question. I want to sabotage the sloganistic response to life. [Earlier he had described himself as a "subversive persuader."] I am more skeptical than I was of societies that say they are trying to create the new man, like Cuba. I think those things appear in most of my films and will probably go on appearing in them in the future.[5]

Before becoming a filmmaker **Frederick Wiseman** was a Boston attorney and professor of criminal law. Like de Antonio, Wiseman has made only feature-length documentaries; his are made for and shown on public television at the rate of one a year. He has examined various institutions, visiting them and shooting them as he finds them, from what seems to be a politically liberal viewpoint.

Wiseman began his filmmaking as producer of *The Cool World* (1964), a fictional feature directed by Shirley Clarke. Shot in Harlem and using many nonprofessional actors, it has some semidocumentary characteristics. His first direct-cinema documentary was *Titicut Follies* (1967), which in a way came out of his legal background. It is an examination of the Bridgewater State Hospital for the criminally insane in Massachusetts. The title refers to an annual variety show performed by inmates and employees. The film offers an unflinching look at the day-to-day situation within the institution.

Waiting for Fidel (Canada, 1974, Michael Rubbo), from the left, Geoff Stirling, Joey Smallwood, and Rubbo. National Film Board.

Frederick Wiseman. Museum of Modern Art/Film Stills Archive.

Without doing more than showing the treatment the inmates receive and the attitudes and behavior of all involved, the hopelessness of the combined care and incarceration meted out becomes clear. How, we must ask, can lives be salvaged that have been so painfully reduced in their human poten- tial? The film became the subject of litigation and the Supreme Court of Massachusetts banned its showing within the state.

Since there is not space to deal with Wiseman's twenty some films, two of them will have to serve as examples of what seems to me most interesting and important about his work. *Law and Order* (1969), about the Kansas City Police Department, is the first.

After *Titicut Follies* (1967) and *High School* (1968) I had expected Wise- man to continue with what was, or might have been seen as, an exposé. Given prevalent feelings about police at the time—the height of the Viet- nam protest—it seemed quite likely that he would find brutality, corruption, incompetence, and stupidity. However, he did not find, or at least did not present, that. Some violence, insensitivity, and perhaps racial prejudice are evident in the film, but only as part of a whole that is ambiguous, no doubt reflecting Wiseman's own ambivalence about what he found. Instead, the evidence offered in *Law and Order* could have served to counter the wide- spread prejudices of the time, though this may not have been Wiseman's intention.

The attractiveness and decency of many of the men seen cannot be denied. (Though, of course, fat-bellied red-necks could have been avoided.)

Because camera and sound run for long passages without interruption, and no commentator tells us what to think about what we see and hear, what we are shown is especially persuasive. Our response to this kind of documentary comes closer to our response to drama than it does for other kinds of documentaries. We become interested in these people as persons; not only in their jobs and how they do them, but in their "characters" (in the dramatic sense). The young policeman who thinks he would be better paid in Los Angeles but doesn't want to leave his Kansas City job makes me think of the role Richard Widmark plays as a federal health officer in New Orleans in *Panic in the Streets*, mentioned in Chapter Ten.

But *Law and Order* (see photo p. 287) is not structured as drama or even as narrative, as Flaherty's films were. Though the action within each sequence seems to proceed in chronological order and has a narrative structure, the overall organization is impressionistic. That is, the parts are arranged according to considerations other than those of causality or chronology. To invoke another comparison, it is like Humphrey Jennings's *Listen to Britain* rather than his *Fires Were Started* (discussed in Chapter Seven). Jennings's impressionistic short runs twenty minutes and his semidocumentary feature sixty-five. But *Law and Order*, while fragmented and nonnarrative overall, has a coherence in the experience being presented that allows it to extend to ninety minutes.

Finally (back to Flaherty), as we came to understand Samoans through *Moana* and his family, we come to understand a bit more about cops through the members of this police force. And in both films we come to understand more about the human condition (not just its social, political, and economic aspects), which is the province of art rather than of propaganda, to close on the Flaherty/Grierson dichotomy.

The other example of Wiseman's work that strikes me as remarkable in ways similar to *Law and Order* is *Model* (1980). It is about the business of fashion modeling headquartered in New York City. The film begins with a succession of carefully composed views of Manhattan, artfully cut together like openings of the city symphonies discussed in Chapter Four. This sequence is followed by a sequence of people talking on telephones, who turn out to be part of the fashion-modeling business. Then Wiseman cuts back to the city, its traffic and rivers and bridges. Throughout, the film alternates between fashion modeling (concentrating on a single fashion-model agency) and life on the streets of New York. One intriguing sequence shows passersby watching the making of a Leggs commercial. Elderly women, construction workers, derelicts, young businessmen, and dogs regard somewhat indifferently the sexy model, the high-tech equipment, and the Hollywood mannerisms of the crew. The model business is based on glitz and illusion; real life is nitty-gritty and diverse. It seems to me that both the central subject and its context are looked at appreciatively, but that is arguable.

My own view is that *Model* is essentially a not uncritical celebration of

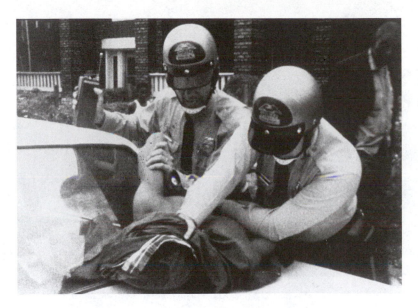

Law and Order (U.S., 1969, Frederick Wiseman). Zipporah Films, Inc.

a bizarre, fascinating, glamorous, and crazy institution in the Big Apple of our society. Other viewers regard it as an exposé of exploitative, manipulative, frivolous, and greedy people working at a profession that is the epitome of consumerism gone berserk. They hold that fashion modeling is being presented as an affront to most of the people who live in New York (and elsewhere), for whom this frenzied activity is irrelevant. A tiny fraction of the gigantic sums spent on fashion could provide better housing, a better diet, and better clothing for those we see on the streets (and for the rest of us).

There is a great deal of detail (the film runs 125 minutes) about the process of fashion modeling: interviewing and hiring (between two and five per cent of new people are accepted among those who apply to this agency), dressing, putting on makeup (sequences of extreme closeups of making-up eyes), posing, being lighted, directed, photographed, chatting and playing in between. Intercut from time to time are mannequins in department store windows. One extended sequence concerns production of an Evan-Picone hosiery commercial which involves interminable takes (up to fifty-five on one shot). The sequence concludes with the thirty-second result of all this professional skill, perfectionism, and grueling work.

This vast amount of material *can* be read in at least two ways—probably many more. But the final sequence confirms my view. It is of the fashion-buyers' show, which is like, and is shot and edited like, a musical. Beautiful young women in high-style gowns pirouette down a runway to

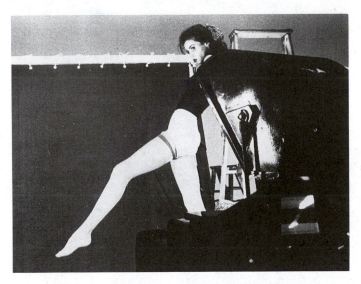

Model (U.S., 1980, Frederick Wiseman). Zipporah Films, Inc.

show tunes ("Strike Up the Band" among them). Unusual camera angles and dynamic cutting complete the choreographic effect. It ends with dancing and applause. The fact that the purpose of the film can be argued—exposé or celebration—may suggest that the many snippets we are offered form a mosaic of, or a metaphor for, aspects of our culture, which, of course, is open to as many interpretations as there are cultural observers.

A HOST OF DOCUMENTARIES

During the past two decades certain subjects and forms have received particular attention. They are grouped below under five headings: historical compilations, contemporary labor and institutional problems, biographies, performers and performances, and others. The survey is highly selective. Other films are listed in Films of the Period at the end of the chapter.

Historical Compilations

A number of feature-length documentaries have dealt with our recent past. Many of them are about labor and/or left-wing political activity; other films view other aspects of U.S. history, usually from a politically-left point of view.

Following U.S. withdrawal from Vietnam, assessments of our involvement in that struggle appeared. Like *In the Year of the Pig*, referred to in the preceding section, *Hearts and Minds* (Peter Davis, 1974) is a compiled history

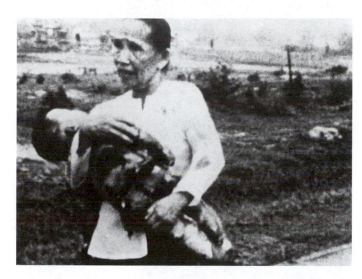

Hearts and Minds (U.S., 1974, Peter Davis). Museum of Modern Art/Film Stills Archive.

going back to the French conflict following World War II and ending with a critical appraisal of the grievous hurt the war did to Vietnamese and Americans alike. *The War at Home* (Glenn Silber and Barry A. Brown, 1979) is about the student protest movement during the Vietnam War as manifest at the University of Wisconsin in Madison.

Another cluster of historical compilations concerns labor history. *Union Maids* (James Klein, Miles Mogulescu, and Julia Reichert, 1976) is about the organizing of industrial unions in Chicago in the 1930s. It is struc-tured around the recollections of three women who had been organizers— in a laundry, the stockyards, and a factory. *With Babies and Banners* (Lorraine Gray, Lyn Goldfarb, and Anne Bohlen, 1977) is about a General Motors strike in Flint, Michigan, and the working women and wives involved. *The Wobblies* (Stewart Bird and Deborah Shaffer, 1979) offers a history of the Industrial Workers of the World (IWW), beginning with its founding con-vention in Chicago in 1905. *The Life and Times of Rosie the Riveter* (Connie Field, 1980) reexamines the experiences of female war workers in America during the 1940s, especially their struggle for equality and dignity.

There were films concerning specifically political activity. *Seeing Red* (James Klein and Julia Reichert, 1984) is a look at the individuals who made up the American Communist Party from the 1930s through the 1950s. *The Good Fight* (Noel Buckner, Mary Dore, and Sam Sills, 1984) is about the Americans who comprised the Abraham Lincoln Brigade fighting on the Republican/Loyalist side in the Spanish Civil War.

Other films argued an antinuclear war position. *The Atomic Cafe* (Jayne Loader, Kevin Rafferty, and Pierce Rafferty, 1982) is composed entirely of

A 1943 photograph by Gordon Parks used in *The Life and Times of Rosie the Riveter* (U.S., 1980, Connie Field). Museum of Modern Art/Film Stills Archive.

archive materials from the 1940s to the 1950s. It reveals (often with biting humor) what means were then being presented as protection against nuclear explosion. Other targets of the film are the Cold War and McCarthyism.

Contemporary Labor and Institutional Problems

A number of films attacked various institutions in our society from a predominantly left-wing point of view: The military, in *Interviews with My Lai Veterans* (Joseph Strick, 1971), made up entirely, as the title suggests, of on-camera interviews with former servicemen. The police, in *The Murder of Fred Hampton* (Michael Gray and Howard Alk, 1971), a scathing indictment of the shootout that caused the death of the Black Panther leader in Chicago. Our penal system, in *Attica* (Cinda Firestone, 1973), about the 1971 riot at the prison in Attica, New York, that resulted in more than forty deaths and an ensuing investigation. And the medical profession, in *The Chicago Maternity Center Story* (Kartemquin Films, 1976), about the closing of the service which was the subject of Pare Lorentz's *The Fight for Life,* on the grounds that modern medicine requires high-cost, hospital-based care.

Other films on contemporary problems concern union activity; a number of them chronicle strikes. *Harlan County, USA* (Barbara Kopple, 1976) is a notable success in this category (see photo p. 292). Its central concern is a thirteen-month-long coal miners' strike in eastern Kentucky that began

Attica (U.S., 1973, Cinda Firestone). National Film Archive/Stills Library.

when the miners decided to join the United Mine Workers of America and the owners refused to sign a union contract. *The Willmar 8* (Lee Grant, 1980) are eight women bank employees in Willmar, Minnesota, who, after enduring years of wage and sex discrimination, form a union and go on strike. They picket for a year and a half before a final victory. *The Last Pullman Car,* (Kartemquin Films, 1983) tells the story of the closing of Pullman Standard's South Chicago plant—the last factory in America to manufacture subway and railroad passenger cars. It concentrates on the efforts of the workers to save their factory and jobs.

Biographies

Documentaries about individuals first appeared following World War II when there was a widening of the subjects and forms thought proper to documentary. They increased in substantial numbers when the technology and technique of cinéma vérité/direct cinema became available. Interviews have become a major component of these films.

Some have dealt with persons whose careers had a political importance. *Angela: Portrait of a Revolutionary* (Yolanda du Luart, 1971) is about black communist Angela Davis, her political philosophy, teaching, and personality, made by one of her students while she was at UCLA. *I. F. Stone's Weekly* (Jerry Bruck, Jr., 1973) celebrates an independent journalist and irreverent gadfly who wrote and published his weekly from 1953 to 1971. "The establishment writers know a lot more than I do," he admits, "but half

Harlan County, U.S.A. (U.S., 1976, Barbara Kopple). Museum of Modern Art/Film Stills Archive.

of what they know isn't true." *The Day after Trinity: J. Robert Oppenheimer and the Atomic Bomb* (Jon Else, 1980) examines the role of the nuclear physicist in developing the first atomic bomb, the moral uncertainties he seemed to feel about this achievement, and the political suspicion he came under. *The Times of Harvey Milk* (Robert Epstein and Richard Schmiechen, 1984) is a eulogy to a San Francisco gay activist who succeeded in being elected to the City Council's board of supervisors before he was murdered, along with the mayor of San Francisco.

Another group of biographies is about those in the arts. *Gertrude Stein: When This You See, Remember Me* and *Georgia O'Keefe* (Perry Miller Adato, 1971/ 1977) are not only sensitive to the nature of each person but give a sure sense of what each was trying to create and why she had that particular urge. *Antonia: A Portrait of the Woman* (Judy Collins and Jill Godmilow, 1974) is about symphony conductor Antonia Brico and her fight to be able to use her great skill, which the film documents, in a male-dominated profession (see photo p. 294). *Never Give Up—Imogen Cunningham* (Ann Hershey, 1975) is about a photographer, another pioneer, acclaimed for her portraits and her closeups of plant forms. *The Weavers: Wasn't that a Time!* (Jim Brown, 1982) is a nostalgic recollection of this immensely popular and influential folksong group, climaxing in a reunion concert in Carnegie Hall. Along the way we learn of their blacklisting in the 1950s because of long-time left-wing activism.

Other biographical documentaries deal with uncelebrated persons

The Times of Harvey Milk (U.S., 1984, Robert Epstein and Richard Schmiechen). Museum of Modern Art/Film Stills Archive.

who interested the filmmakers for one reason or another. *Grey Gardens* (Albert and David Maysles, Ellen Hovde, and Muffie Meyer, 1975) is a cinéma-vérité portrait of a mother and daughter (Big Edie and Little Edie Bouvier) who live a reclusive existence in a crumbling East Hampton mansion on Long Island (see photo p. 294). The title of *Poto and Cabengo* (Jean-Pierre Gorin, 1980) refers to the names twin girls in San Diego have given each other in a language they invented. While solving the mystery of this created language we learn a lot about the life of these children.

Performers and Performances

A steady stream of films about rock music and musicians began with *Don't Look Back* (Donn Alan Pennebaker, 1967), which tracks Bob Dylan on

Antonia: A Portrait of the Woman (U.S., 1974, Judy Collins and Jill Godmilow). National Film Archive/Stills Library.

a concert tour of England. It deals with him offstage much more than on. It was followed by *Monterey Pop* (Pennebaker, 1968), a record of a rock festival devoted almost entirely to the performances.

In *Woodstock* (Michael Wadleigh, 1970) a third possibility is added, giving it a sociological dimension. The film devotes almost as much time to

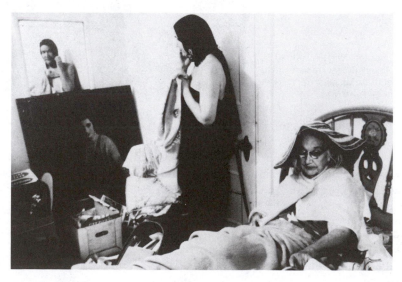

Grey Gardens (U.S., 1975, Albert and David Maysles, Ellen Hovde, and Muffie Meyer). Museum of Modern Art/Film Stills Archive.

Woodstock (U.S., 1970, Michael Wadleigh). Museum of Modern Art/Film Stills Archive.

the audience encamped on this farmland in upper New York State as it does to the performers or performances. *Gimme Shelter* (Albert and David Maysles, and Charlotte Zwerin, 1970) is mainly a record of a concert by the Rolling Stones in Altamont, California. Intercut, however, is footage of an earlier Stones' concert in Madison Square Garden, episodes of them on tour, preparations for the Altamont concert, two press conferences, and crowd scenes at Altamont. In addition is footage of Mick Jagger and another Stone looking at and commenting on what we have just seen as it is run through a Moviola for them by the Maysles.

Two subsequent rock-performance films worthy of mention are by Hollywood directors. *The Last Waltz* (Martin Scorsese, 1979) is a visual-aural recording of the farewell concert of a group called The Band. It contains many interviews cut in between the musical numbers. *Stop Making Sense* (Jonathan Demme, 1985) features the Talking Heads. It is a straightforward recording of a dazzling stage performance. There is no question of the film-makers' skill, but David Byrne, leader of the Talking Heads, is the creator essentially.

And Others

The foregoing discussion of a few types of contemporary U.S. documentary that are prevalent is not meant to imply a more limited range of subjects and forms than actually exists. Among categories omitted are the

Stop Making Sense (U.S., 1985, Jonathan Demme). Museum of Modern Art/Film Stills Archive.

diary films, like those made by Jonas Mekas (*Reminiscences of a Journey to Lithuania*), or Alfred Guzzeti (*Family Portrait Sitting*), or Ross McElwee (*Sherman's March*). Also, there are many, many feminist films, like those of Mirra Banks (*Anonymous Was a Woman*), Amalie Rothschild (*Nana, Mom and Me*), and Maxi Cohen (*Joe and Maxi*). Then there are the anthropological films, like those made by Timothy Asch (*The Axe Fight*) and David and Judith MacDougall (*To Live with Herds*). Either I have not seen enough of these films to make a trustworthy selection or, in the case of the latter category, there are so many that they warrant a separate book. Consequently, I will briefly call attention to a few significant examples that don't readily fit into any of the above categories.

Birth and Death (Arthur Barron and Gene Marner, 1968) is a cinéma-vérité observation of the weeks preceding and including the birth of a first child to a young married couple and the death from cancer of a 52-year-old bachelor. The two segments, the first longer, appear in the order they do in the title and in life. In the film "Death" complements "Birth," as it must have been intended to do by the makers. To be able to observe the end of this brave person is a moving and, in an unexpected way, fulfilling experience.

In *Soldier Girls* (Nick Broomfield and Joan Churchill, 1980) the direct-cinema technology is state-of-the-art and the technique exemplary. More important, it seems to have the same sort of aesthetic and ethical ambiguity and richness as the two Wiseman films discussed earlier in this chapter. The subjects are young female recruits in a basic training camp. The film could

Soldier Girls (U.S., 1980, Nick Broomfield and Joan Churchill). Museum of Modern Art/ Film Stills Archive.

be seen as either pro or antimilitary. The discipline and training are harsh and rigorous, but if these people are to protect us from our enemies and be able to survive, it is the sort of training they would need. The real question may be, Do we want war? In an emotional scene near the end of the film a (male) staff-sergeant instructor talks to a trainee about the effect of combat: "Your soul is gone and you don't know it." And of himself, "I can't give nothin' to anybody else anymore. There's so much missing."

When the Mountains Tremble (Peter Kinoy, Thomas Sigel, and Pamela Yates, 1985) is about guerrilla struggles in recent Guatemalan history. It uses as its central figure a Christian Indian woman. Though part of the filming is done from the government side, the major experience the film offers is seeing the conflict through the eyes of the peasants and guerrilla fighters. Most of it is direct-cinema reportage, but two other elements bring it into a mixed mode like those documentaries discussed in Chapter Sixteen. First are the dramatic reenactments near the beginning—one about an American ambassador and Guatemalan officials, another about a CIA officer. Both are said to be based on American documents. The other departure from conventional documentary is that the central woman figure is shot in limbo lighting in a darkened studio while she talks directly to us. She becomes the storyteller, describing her lost hopes for a democratic Guatemala, and the murder of her family by the security police. The events we see occurring in the country thus become an extension of her story.

Let's end this section by acknowledging the work of Les Blank. For the past two decades he has been documenting colorful individuals and ethnic subdivisions within our culture: Blacks in *The Blues According to Lightin' Hopkins* (1970) and *A Well-Spent Life* (1970); Cajuns in *Spend It All* (1971); Creoles in *Dry Wood* and *Hot Pepper* (both 1973); Chicanos in *Chulas Fronteras* and *De Mero Corazon* (both 1976); and Polish-Americans in *In Heaven There is No Beer?* (1983). He calls himself a well-meaning peeping Tom and shares with us his warm response to the food, talk, festivities, and, especially, music of these peoples. In *Always for Pleasure* (1978) the many cultures and traditions of New Orleans—a jazz funeral, St. Patrick's Day festivities, "Black Indian" dances and parades—mingle in the street celebrations culminating in Mardi Gras.

Garlic Is as Good as Ten Mothers (1981) transcends ethnicity in a loosely-constructed, culturally variegated paean to an obsession. (Blank has been known to fry garlic at the back of the hall during screenings.) The film is made up of music, performance, jokes, graphics, preparations of food, hogs eating garlic, many persons and personalities—all attesting to the virtues of the stinking rose. The pacing—the tempo and rhythm—is strikingly artful and inventive. My notes scribbled during a viewing also report that it is "idiosyncratic, lusty, sexual, physiological." A jumble of terms, I'll admit, but let them stand.

This kind of personal filmmaking seems to me to hold much promise for the future of documentary, mixing as it does art and culture, individuals and society, serious and inane. It is a shared response to life; a gift from the filmmaker to the audience.

Hot Pepper (U.S., 1973, Les Blank). Museum of Modern Art/Film Stills Archive.

THE END

This end title does not signal the end of English-language documentary film and video, of course. It means simply that this book has gotten as close to the present as a historian can before turning into a critic. Not only is the documentary idea not dead, it seems to me full of life and still growing.

At the end, as at the beginning, we need to acknowledge that documentary is, after all, a concept. Nothing in cinema or in nature suggested, let alone dictated, a documentary film. It came about because persons had information, understandings, ideas, feelings, attitudes, and programs of action they wanted to communicate to the rest of us. The picture and motion of the motion picture seemed to them an appropriate means—efficient, effective—for that communication. But the forms available—the narrative fiction film, the newsreel, the travelogue, and so on—inadequate. So they improvised new forms; forms that seemed most likely to match their intentions.

The purposes and forms of the English-language documentary over the past seven decades have been the subject of this book. Perhaps the best way, maybe the only way, to answer the question What is Documentary?, is to point to what it has been up to the present. Documentary seems by nature to be evolutionary. The documentary idea allows room for growth and change. Out of the idea new purposes and new forms will continue to come. Documentary films and tapes, and whatever new technologies and techniques appear, will continue to define documentary. They are not only the history of the documentary idea, they are its definition.

NOTES

[1]Ronald Blumer and Susan Schouten, "Donald Brittain: Green Stripe and Common Sense," *Canadian Film Reader,* eds. Seth Feldman and Joyce Nelson (Toronto: Peter Martin Associates Limited, 1977), pp. 103–12.

[2]Alan Rosenthal, "*Sad Song of Yellow Skin* and *Waiting for Fidel:* Michael Rubbo," *The Documentary Conscience: A Casebook in Film Making* (Berkeley: University of California Press, 1980), pp. 232–44.

[3]Ibid.

[4]Ibid.

[5]Ibid.

FILMS OF THE PERIOD

1967
The Anderson Platoon (Pierre Schoendorffer)
Portrait of Jason (Shirley Clarke)
Titicut Follies (Frederick Wiseman)
Warrendale (Allan King)

1968
Birth and Death (Arthur Barron and Gene Marner)
The Endless Summer (Bruce Brown)
Inside North Vietnam (Felix Greene)
Monterey Pop (D. A. Pennebaker)

1969
High School (Wiseman)
In the Year of the Pig (Emile de Antonio)
Law and Order (Wiseman)
Salesman (Albert and David Maysles, and Charlotte Zwerin)

1970
Gimme Shelter (same as above)
Hiroshima-Nagasaki, August 1945 (Erik Barnouw)
A Married Couple (King)
Sad Song of Yellow Skin (Michael Rubbo)
Woodstock (Michael Wadleigh)

1971
Angela: Portrait of a Revolutionary (Yolanda du Luart)
Gertrude Stein: When This You See, Remember Me (Perry Miller Adato)
Interviews with My Lai Veterans (Joseph Strick)
The Murder of Fred Hampton (Michael Gray and Howard Alk)

1972
Marjoe (Howard Smith and Sarah Kernochan)

1973
Attica (Cinda Firestone)
I. F. Stone's Weekly (Jerry Bruck, Jr.)

1974
Antonia: A Portrait of the Woman (Judy Collins and Jill Godmilow)
Hearts and Minds (Peter Davis)
Waiting for Fidel (Rubbo)

1975
Grey Gardens (Albert and David Maysles, Ellen Hovde, and Muffie Meyer)

1976
The Chicago Maternity Center Story (Kartemquin Films)
Harlan County, U.S.A. (Barbara Kopple)
Union Maids (James Klein, Miles Mogulescu, and Julia Reichert)

1977
Georgia O'Keefe (Adato)
Men of Bronze (William Miles)
With Babies and Banners (Lorraine Gray, Lyn Goldfarb, and Anne Bohlen)

1979
The Wobblies (Stewart Bird and Deborah Shaffer)

1980
The Day After Trinity: J. Robert Oppenheimer and the Atomic Bomb (John Else)
The Life and Times of Rosie the Riveter (Connie Field)
Model (Wiseman)
Poto and Cabengo (Jean-Pierre Gorin)
Soldier Girls (Nick Broomfield and Joan Churchill)
The Willmar 8 (Lee Grant)

1981
Garlic Is as Good as Ten Mothers (Les Blank)
Not a Love Story (Bonnie Klein)

1982
Atomic Cafe (Jayne Loader, Kevin Rafferty, and Pierce Rafferty)
The Weavers: Wasn't that a Time! (Jim Brown)

1983
The Last Pullman Car (Kartemquin Films)

1984
The Good Fight (Noel Buckner, Mary Dore, and Sam Sills)
Seeing Red (James Klein and Julia Reichert)
The Times of Harvey Milk (Robert Epstein and Richard Schmiechen)

1985
Stop Making Sense (Jonathan Demme)
Streetwise (Martin Bell, Mary Ellen Mark, and Cheryl McCall)
When the Mountains Tremble (Peter Kinoy, Thomas Sigel, and Pamela Yates)

1986
Gap–Toothed Women (Blank)
Sherman's March (Ross McElwee)

BOOKS ON THE PERIOD

ATKINS, THOMAS R., ed., *Frederick Wiseman.* New York: Monarch Press, 1976. 134 pp.
BEATTIE, ELEANOR, *A Handbook of Canadian Film.* Toronto: Peter Martin Associates Limited, 1973. 280 pp.

ELLSWORTH, LIZ, *Frederick Wiseman: A Guide to References and Resources.* Boston: G. K. Hall & Co., 1979. 212 pp.

FELDMAN, SETH and JOYCE NELSON, eds., *Canadian Film Reader.* Toronto: Peter Martin Associates Limited, 1977. 405 pp.

NICHOLS, BILL, *"Newsreel": Documentary Filmmaking on the American Left.* Salem, N.H.: Ayer Co. Publishers, Inc., 1980. 314 pp.

ROSENTHAL, ALAN, *The Documentary Conscience: A Casebook in Film Making.* Berkeley: University of California Press, 1980. 436 pp.

ROSENTHAL, ALAN, *New Challenges to Documentary.* Berkeley: University of California Press, 1987. 460 pp.

APPENDIX

DOCUMENTARY IN THE UNITED STATES
IN THE IMMEDIATE POST-WORLD WAR II YEARS

A Supplement to Chapter 11,
by George C. Stoney

Throughout this book Dr. Ellis contends that the American documentary movement was carried forward very largely by people "on the left" and I will not dispute this. But he leaves the unwary reader with the impression that, therefore, most of the documentaries seen in this country conveyed those sentiments, which is untrue. In the years after the Second World War sponsorship by industry and institutions determined the nature of the bulk of the films that circulated out of the 16mm libraries. Many of these were politically "neutral" but many, including some of them made by those of us whom Ellis rightly describes as tending toward the left politically, were far from neutral. Examples:

Almost every child in the country saw *The American Road*, produced in 1953 by M.P.O. (a large industrial film production company) to celebrate the Ford Motor Company's fiftieth anniversary. It is as fullhearted a celebration of the free enterprise system as one could make and enshrines Henry Ford as a folk hero. This film has been projected daily in the "Futurama" in Dearborn. I directed the historical re-creations. Joe Marsh, a blacklisted Hollywood writer, did the script. Alex North, the famous Hollywood composer (then blacklisted also), did the music. We all needed the money.

Almost every other documentary director active at the time has similar films to his credit. Sidney Meyers did Monsanto's *Decision for Chemistry* and lots more. Willard Van Dyke did a series for the National Rifle Association. Lee Bobker did an apology for strip mining for the Peabody Coal Company. Even Robert Flaherty's *Louisiana Story* is essentially a folksy apologia for Standard Oil's exploitation of wetlands that today we know should be protected as sources of fresh water.

My hunch is that, however justified we thought we were in making these films, by doing so we lost the respect we once had as documentary filmmakers on the part of the intellectual and artistic community. This began to be redressed when there was a new approach ("direct cinema") and a new concept ("the independent filmmaker") to inspire us and refresh our resolves. For, in truth, the disillusionments of the late 1940s and the intimidations of the McCarthy period that followed destroyed our political underpinnings.

INDEX